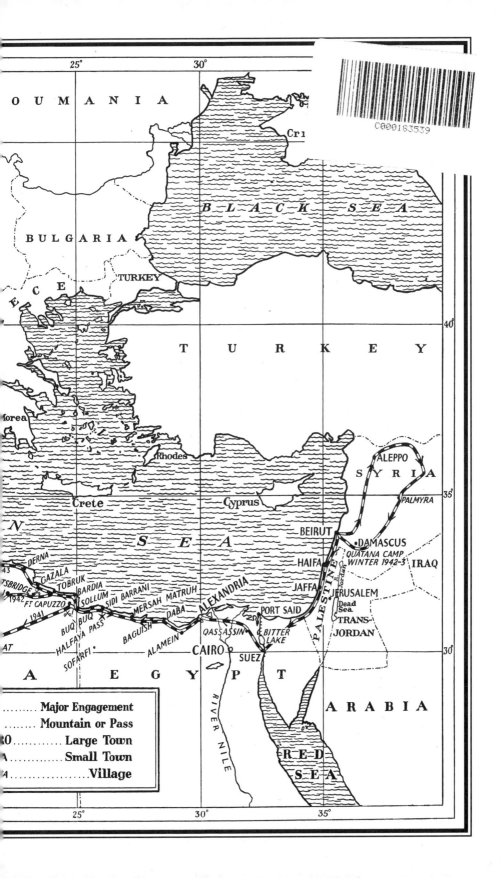

ROUMANIA

BULGARIA

GREECE

Morea

TURKEY

BLACK SEA

Cri

TURKEY

Rhodes

Crete

Cyprus

SYRIA

ALEPPO

PALMYRA

BEIRUT

•DAMASCUS
QUATANA CAMP
WINTER 1942-3

HAIFA

JAFFA

JERUSALEM

Dead
Sea

PALESTINE

TRANS-
JORDAN

IRAQ

MEDITERRANEAN SEA

DERNA

GAZALA

TOBRUK

TSBRIDGE

43

FT CAPUZZO

1942

1941

BARDIA

SOLLUM

SIDI BARRANI

MERSAH MATRUH

BUQ BUQ

HALFAYA PASS

BAGUISH

DABA

ALEXANDRIA

ALAMEIN

QASSASSIN

PORT SAID

BITTER
LAKE

CAIRO

SUEZ

SOFARFI

AT

EGYPT

RIVER NILE

ARABIA

RED
SEA

.... Major Engagement
.... Mountain or Pass
O.......... Large Town
A.............Small Town
4................Village

Something About a Soldier

SOMETHING
ABOUT
A SOLDIER

The Wartime Memoirs of
Christopher Bulteel M.C.

Airlife
England

First published in the UK in 2000
by Airlife Publishing Ltd

British Library Cataloguing-in-Publication Data
A catalogue record for this book
is available from the British Library

ISBN 1 84037 246 X

Typeset by Phoenix Typesetting, Ilkley, West Yorkshire
Printed in England by Biddles Ltd., Guildford and King's Lynn.

Airlife Publishing Ltd

101 Longden Road, Shrewsbury, SY3 9EB, England
E-mail: airlife@airlifebooks.com
Website: www.airlifebooks.com

ACKNOWLEDGEMENTS

Many thanks are due for permission to reproduce photographs and maps from *No Dishonourable Name*, the war memoirs of the 2nd and 3rd Battalions, Coldstream Guards and in particular to Mr D.C.Quilter its compiler and editor. Thanks are also owed to Christopher Bulteel's family for their help in supplying the manuscript and photographs.

The Publisher would like to thank John Previte, firstly for bringing the autobiography to our attention and secondly for his assistance in the preparation of the book and also Richard Thorpe.

Christopher Bulteel shortly after he had been commissioned.

PREFACE

These are the World War II memoirs of Captain Christopher Bulteel M.C., Coldstream Guards. They span the years 1939 to 1946. They cover, in particular, Christopher's service with the 3rd Battalion Coldstream Guards, part of the 8th Army, in North Africa and Italy.

Christopher never intended to be a soldier. He regarded himself as wholly unsuitable material for being transformed into a military fighting man. Rejected as a volunteer in 1939, on the grounds that at age 18 he was too young, he was granted an emergency commission in 1941. After 18 months of training in England he was posted to join the 3rd Battalion in Egypt. When he joined that battalion shortly after the battle of El Alamein he joined an elite. The surviving members of the battalion had fought their way out of Tobruk and were part of the famous Desert Rats. He records what it was really like to be an inexperienced and untried soldier, fighting alongside battle-hardened veterans, thrown into the fierce desert campaign against Rommel's army.

After turning the German army out of North Africa there followed the invasions of Sicily and Italy. The fighting at Salerno was bitter. Christopher escaped death by the narrowest of margins, especially in the attack for which he was awarded an M.C. Shortly after that battle he caught malaria and was invalided home, after which he saw no more active service.

Christopher's first-hand account of the fighting is exciting reading. But the memoirs are much more than that. He records how the prospect of an early and violent death first focused his thoughts on God. His spiritual quest led him to a faith which became the cornerstone of his life. So strong was his faith and commitment that for a few years, sandwiched between teaching history at Wellington College and being Headmaster of Ardingly College, he belonged to the Society of St Francis, an Anglican Order of Franciscan friars.

Reading between the lines one suspects that Christopher, despite his misgivings and modesty about his military capacities, was just as deeply and affectionately respected by his fellow soldiers as he was in the post-war years by his pupils and fellow schoolmasters.

Good travel books and autobiographies have in common the
sense of two journeys unfolding: one over land and sea,
the other inside the traveller.

Ian Robertson (in a review of *Taken on Trust* by
Terry Waite, in *The Times*, 27 Sept. 1993)

CONTENTS

PART I
PREPARATION

1

EARLY DAYS

I once led the British Army in the Second World War, against the combined armies of both Germany and Italy. This must surely be a sufficient justification for writing this memoir, for, after all, we won.

I have to confess, however, that my leadership lasted for only a few minutes. It was, in fact, the first time that I had come face to face with the enemy on the battlefield, and it was the first battlefield I had been on to. The words 'face to face' may also be a little misleading, for I saw no enemy troops and, to this day, am none too sure that there were any there. They must have been somewhere close by, though; and my active service began at that moment.

This was late in February, 1943. I should have been able to give a more precise date if the Germans had not collared my diary a few weeks later. But at least I can remember *where* it was.

Anyone who fought with the Eighth Army in Tunisia will remember Tadjera Khir, that isolated, kidney-shaped crag which wrapped itself around the desert road about ten miles to the north-west of Medenine. Back towards Tripoli, over the frontier, the road wriggled through the desert like a worn typewriter ribbon; whilst onward toward Tunis, two hundred miles away, it lost itself in the folds of the Matmata Hills, before descending once again to the flat plain, sliced by the black water of the Wadi Akarit.

It was along this road, just beyond Tadjera Khir, that I walked towards Tunis. Michael Brodrick, who was driving our fifteen-hundredweight truck, wanted to stop for a moment to write up his notes; and as there did not seem to be anyone about, he suggested that I might go for a short walk. 'But don't walk *off* the road,' he told me. 'The Germans seem to have mined all the verges. But even you can see if they've dug holes in the tarmac.'

So I walked, wondering what would happen. During those few minutes, one inhibition at least was laid to rest: I had imagined that all battlefields were going to be like those my father had described to me, with mud, wire, corpses, and the certainty of intense enemy fire. My father, who had served in the same regiment during the previous war, had horror-stories galore; and he would have been astonished himself to hear that I was strolling casually ten miles ahead of our leading troops. I too was pleasantly surprised. A little fancifully, I imagined myself continuing to walk the remaining two hundred miles to Tunis, and collecting a medal for initiative.

When I got back to Michael, I could see that he was pleased. Somehow, he had sensed my many hesitations, and was doing his best to lay them to rest – but I shall write more about him later, for he was to become one of my closest friends.

We must have driven back then, along the road, till we saw another British truck, parked in the lee of Tadjera Khir, out of sight of the Germans. We drove down its tyre-tracks, thus making certain that we would not run over a mine. The men were gunners. They were doing what every British soldier always did whenever he got out of his vehicle: brewing up tea.

'Anyone seen the war?' Michael asked.

'You'd better go and ask the FOO, Sir' the corporal in charge answered. 'He's up there on the crest, just to the left of the road. Have a cup of tea, first, though. It's a bit of a walk.'

We stopped for a while, and were handed enormous mugs of tea, while the corporal got through on the radio to the Forward Observation Officer on the hill-top. (It was wise, I saw, to give notice of our intentions.) Then we left our vehicle in the care of the gunners, and walked up the hill, with some care, finding the gunner officer, with his field glasses, looking out towards the enemy from the crest. More precisely, he was not on the actual crest, as he was at pains to point out: he had not wanted to be observed himself on the skyline; and we collected black marks for giving him away.

However, when we settled down beside him, and asked if he had seen anything, he became more chatty.

'Oh, yes,' he told us. 'Just follow the line of the road till it reaches the next outcrop, and bends right-handed out of sight. See? A small party came round the corner about ten minutes ago, to spy out the land. As they were waving their map-cases around and they were catching the sun, I thought that they deserved a small stonk. I expect I annoyed them a bit. They will have my opposite number on the hill behind them, now, I expect. If I were you, I shouldn't stay too long, now you've given my position away.'

'Is that the Mareth Line?' I asked diffidently.

'Well, not really. At least I don't think so. Not the main positions, anyway. I expect that the main line is a good deal further back. They

4

want to be sure that they can look after their front-line troops without being seen by tiresome little men like me. But my guess is that they are going to make their next big stand in this area. Are you being brought up to fight a battle, do you know?'

'I think so,' Michael answered. 'We're supposed to be the advance guard of our brigade, sent up to spy out the land.'

'There'll be some more, too, I expect.' Everybody knew everybody in this small, professional army. 'We had some Kiwis up around these parts yesterday, I hear. There's some latrine gossip about the Highlanders prospecting along the coast, and the Fiftieth Division, too. I also heard about some Indians – and another armoured division. I didn't know we even had one.'

'I suppose that Monty will try his "left hook" through the desert, once again,' Michael observed. 'But what's the going like, out there, do you know?'

'Said to be bad. I heard tell of a salt marsh, which goes inland for about a hundred miles, South from this line of hills.'

'Doesn't sound too good, then. We'll have a job to get everybody up the main road, as it is: it's mined all the way from Tripoli. And I don't see even Monty bashing straight through.'

Michael seemed to have got all he wanted; and I was not altogether sorry when he said good-bye. We walked away, more carefully this time. We had just driven off in our truck when the German shells began to land on the hilltop behind us: they *had* spotted us when we first arrived, then.

I felt very contrite. 'I say, what about that wretched gunner?' I asked. 'Ought we to go and see if he's all right?'

'For heaven's sake, leave him alone. He was expecting it, and he probably moved after we'd left. He's got his own soldiers, hasn't he? You must realize,' Michael continued kindly, 'that you simply can't have everyone running all over the place trying to be heroic. Suppose you and I get hit, too? Let's get out of here. But I don't think I want to meet that FOO for a few days. He won't be too friendly. But he will forget, in time.'

We drove slowly back to rendezvous with the rest of the party. My first day of active service was coming to its end.

2

BACK TO THE BEGINNING

I began this memoir by writing about my first taste of the battlefield. It was over half way through the war; but I was ahead of most of my contemporaries, for the invasion of North-West Europe did not take place till the following year. Until this happened, more people were killed in road accidents in England than in action, anywhere. But perhaps I ought to write a little, now, about how I came to be present in the Western Desert, leading the army into outer space, astonished to find it all so easy.

I have two different and incompatible versions of what happened on the day the war began. Perhaps a little of both are true.

The first is that I was mowing the lawn (was it Sunday?) at my parents' home in Cornwall, when someone shouted the news out of the window. As anyone else of my age would have done, I stopped work. It seemed pointless to continue with this futile exercise, if, as I expected, the rest of my life could be measured in minutes: I might as well relax, and let the poison gas kill the grass as well.

The other memory is of listening to the Prime Minister's broadcast at about 11 o'clock – which could indicate that I was indoors, not out. Within a few minutes, the air raid sirens began to warble; and I left the house hurriedly (safer in the open than with the ruins of the house on top of me) and went down the hill into the village with the vague idea of coping with casualties.

On the way, I met Mr Tamblyn, the village policeman, wearing an enormous steel helmet which I had never seen before. We were both carrying our small, square gas masks.

''Ere,' he said, 'do 'ee knaw 'ow to put on that there gas mask? You may 'ave to use un any minnut.' He was as sure as I was that our small Cornish fishing village was the first target for immediate destruction – or did we all think that it needed only a few wisps of some new concoction to destroy the whole country?

The 'all clear' sounded before we solved that question; and the villagers emerged, somewhat sheepishly, from under their beds and sofas. I remember thinking that, if the Germans had been ready to respond immediately to Mr Chamberlain's challenge, they would have found no one – in Cornwall anyway – to stop them.

My father brooded throughout the day. But after he listened to the Six O'Clock News and filled his usual tumbler, he summoned me to the drawing room.

'Now, we must all do our bit,' he told me. 'I must be too old to be recalled to the colours by now (he was over fifty) but I've just written to the Regimental Lieutenant-Colonel, to tell him that you are eighteen, and that you want to volunteer. I'm sure that the girls will be wanted, too (Diana was twenty-one, Margaret not yet seventeen, poor girl.) Di had better be a VAD, I think. That's what your mother was doing in the last show.'

I remember the actual words and phrases still! But I cannot remember my response. I was far too immature, and lacking in any form of self-confidence, to have any alternative. Everything in me – not much, I have to admit – told me that I should never make a soldier. If I had to join a service, I should probably have preferred the Royal Navy, for I was as much at home on the sea as on the land, and would rather be drowned than shot. But in those days, children – ours anyway – did not argue with their parents.

I suppose that I had been expecting it. Not only had everyone known for years that war was inevitable. In addition, my father, who had served with the Coldstream Guards during the previous war, must have thought it only fitting that I should follow in his footsteps when the time came. Though I cannot precisely remember it, I expect that he had told me so, several times already.

But, all the same, I was desperately disappointed. My stomach was churning with foreboding: I knew immediately that his decision was a mistake.

There had never been a strong military tradition in my family. As far as I know, my father had joined the Coldstream Guards by accident: in 1915, young men had to do *something*, and he enlisted in the Artists' Rifles, only to take a commission in the Coldstream when some other volunteer suggested it. (I wonder what my grandfather had had to say about it, at the time? Maybe he did not involve himself in his children's affairs.) His time in the army was the making of him. As far as anyone could, he seems to have enjoyed it: he had hardly left Cornwall in his life till then; but now, he found himself in a crack regiment, with aristocrats as his friends, consumed with regimental pride. Fortunately, he was never wounded. All around him lived and died in hell; but it was an upper-crust hell. My own school holidays had been punctuated with his endless tales of the trenches; and, even before I went to school at all, we children had been

Christopher's father,
Walter Bulteel, who was
also in the Coldstream,
in 1914.

made to march up and down the drawing-room on Sunday evenings to
his old gramophone records of the Coldstream Guards Band, playing
'Colonel Bogey', 'Old Comrades' (his favourite,) 'Youth and Vigour', and
the regimental marches of the five regiments, played in order. (But alas,
being almost totally unmusical, he failed to realize that the Coldstream,
always on the left of the line, had their march played last. I only discovered this when I joined myself.)

   This militarism had always depressed me; and, if I had had the nerve,
or the maturity, I should have declared myself a pacifist. The tales of
carnage made me sick. By this time, I had read Wilfred Owen, and
Edward Thomas, and everyone knew what had happened to *them*. Long
before this second war began, I was in a continual state of panic. At least
one of my school-teachers had told me, publicly, that he saw no point in
teaching me, not because I was unteachable but because I should never

live to make use of what I had been taught. Death, then, was inevitable – and here was my father actually offering my life away, before even bothering to tell me! Later, I was to give a name to this, the 'Abraham Syndrome': I still do not see that fathers should esteem it an honour to condemn their sons to death.

A week or two later, I was summoned to an interview with the Regimental Lieutenant-Colonel, in London.

I cannot remember how I found my way to Regimental Headquarters in Birdcage Walk. I had hardly been to London in my life, for, on the way to and from school, I had changed trains at Reading. (This Lieutenant-Colonel, by the way, must have been the one who interviewed Basil Seal in Evelyn Waugh's *Put Out More Flags*, but no two interviews could be more different.)

For me, by far the worst part of the interview was the wait in the Orderly Room, scared and uneasy, awaiting my summons to the Office. It was less than two months since I had left school; and no less likely candidate for a commission in the Coldstream Guards can ever have waited there. I was a sitting target. I had no hat, no umbrella, no shine on my shoes. I had only my school suit, of shiny dark blue serge, bought off the peg in the school shop a year before, and illumined by my old school tie, gaudy stripes of orange, yellow and pale blue on a black background. No wonder the guardsmen-clerks giggled.

The Lieutenant-Colonel, too, must have been shattered when I was led in. He did his best to be pleasant. I cannot remember what he said, but I expect that he had a set speech for all eighteen-year-olds who were being wheeled before him at that time: '. . . No vacancies at present, I'm afraid . . . No casualties . . . All three battalions are fully up to strength . . .

'I think that you should consider going on with your present career for the moment . . . Oh, Oxford. Yes, very suitable. When you go up, join the OTC, won't you, and make yourself known to the Adjutant, John Baillie, one of our officers on secondment. We'll keep in touch, then. Give my regards to your father.'

I found my way home again and, still a civilian, confronted my father, who was far from pleased. It was not until he found that most of my contemporaries had been treated as I had been that he began to believe me. Looking back on it now, I suppose that I might have gained some marks by running away to enlist at this stage, giving a false date of birth; but it never occurred to me. I doubt if my father thought of it either.

I must not give the impression that my father was a bully. If anything, the reverse was true: in his innocent way, he imagined that he was doing me a favour, using his own experience of the First World War, the people he had met in it, and the thrill it had given him to escape from his humdrum, provincial life, to enable me to follow in his footsteps. But alas, things were different. Attitudes had changed. We had moved on from jingoism to visions of doom. My generation had been told so often of the horrors of one war that they did not want to be victims of another. As the 'phoney war' went on, so our gloom grew deeper.

In early October, I went up to Oxford, as had always been intended, and lazed my way through an academic year. It was, to me, an extension of life at school. Other freshmen were either pacifists, members of the Peace Pledge Union, or prospective soldiers whom the army did not want. *Nobody* seemed to want us very much. Though they were too polite to tell us openly, the dons saw little point in tutorials, which were likely to be a waste of time for, even if we survived the next few years, we would have forgotten everything when we came back again. We agreed. There are worse places than Oxford to waste a few months, and we were still only schoolboys. We played games, ate and drank as much as we could afford, and relaxed in the evenings. We were aware that this state of affairs could not continue for ever; but the conduct of the war was the business of others.

Then, in the middle of the summer term, the Germans invaded Belgium.

Oxford in May is as lovely as anywhere in the world, and this year, the weather was perfect. We continued with our jollities while our world fell to pieces around us: a book or an essay during the morning, an afternoon on the river, a pub in the evening either before or after supper, then a night shift with the Local Defence Volunteers, guarding a few Spitfires by the Cowley factory, some apparently secret project-work in one of the university laboratories and, rather incongruously I thought, the General Post Office in St Aldate's. Sleep was not easy to come by.

The academic powers decided that, as we were doomed anyway, we might as well achieve something during the short time which remained. They manufactured a 'War Degree.'

It sounds quite an achievement to gain an Oxford degree at the age of eighteen! Alas, I cannot pretend that it was serious. We sat only a few papers, some of them probably after a night on sentry duty, and not a few slept . . . Still, it was kind of the dons, I thought; yet an indication of what they thought of our chances of return. (As it happened, I *did* return, six years later, and found that it had not been entirely worthless.) But now, I must go down. I said my farewells to my fellow-scholars, took the train to Cornwall, and immediately entered into a different world.

I shall always remember that journey. The trains were crowded with soldiers, many of them just back from Dunkirk; and everyone military and civilian, talking with their neighbours, quite unable to stop. There was a touch of panic abroad. As we sauntered through the meadows of the Thames valley, up the Kennett, down into the vale of Pewsey, down again on to the Sedgemoor flats, then on to the dirty red earth of Devon, I suddenly became aware that this lovely countryside, our priceless heritage, was under immediate threat. There was urgent action to be taken, at once.

My immature pacifist leanings disappeared without trace. I do not think that I was alone, here: a whole nation was rising to its feet. The greatest living entertainer in the world was performing on a new means of communication, the radio, to raise us out of our lethargy and call us to the defence of the realm. By the time we had crossed the Tamar I had become – to use a half-forgotten term – a patriot like everyone else.

3

INTO BATTLE

T he defence of England was entrusted to a fine body of volunteers, whom I joined immediately I returned to Cornwall. True, their only uniform was an arm-band. Their weapons also left a good deal to the imagination, for the regular army seemed to have thrown all theirs away when they swam out of Dunkirk; but what our men lacked in equipment they made up in enthusiasm. My father found himself in charge of our local contingent. He dredged up a German rifle which he had brought back from Belgium in 1918, a bayonet which, for twenty years, had been used as a poker for the nursery fire, two or three shot-guns, and a couple of pistols with no ammunition. Some farmers produced a few more shot-guns; but, to begin with, there was not enough ironmongery to provide each soldier with anything with which to defend anyone, even himself.

However the Home Guard, as it was soon named, oozed confidence and determination. Its troops shared my attitude to the regular army – it had *proved* itself useless, after all – and within a matter of weeks the Channel Coast was in our safe hands.

We were then issued with uniforms. True, they were only the 'fatigues' which the military had used to clean the latrines, but we were not fussy. Weapons began to arrive. There were some French *Mitrailleuses* and some French cavalry carbines, a 'Ross Rifle', even a couple of old Lewis guns, and – wonder of wonders – a couple of Browning machine-guns. The difficulty was that there was precious little ammunition for any of them; and no two weapons used the same. These would be brought into our house at dead of night, I remember; and as by next day they were issued to our forces, it was my duty to find out how to pull them to pieces and stick them together again. For some reason I was looked upon as an expert, and was expected to tell everyone how they worked: not unduly difficult with rifles, but puzzling with automatic weapons I had never seen before.

Later came an issue of rifles, sufficient for all, and all – at last – using the same ammunition. The trouble, once again, was that it was desperately short. At least, we could *carry* weapons, though. It helped morale.

One afternoon, my father decided that we ought to find out if – and, if so, how – they worked. From our tiny stock of ammunition (the name of the rifle escapes me for the moment, though I remember well enough that the cartridges it fired were almost unknown to science; and it was an agonizing decision for him to tell us to use any of them for practice rather than for mowing down the enemy) we were issued with five rounds each. I had spent the morning alone with a paintpot, daubing the outline of a German soldier on a rock beside a local beach, under the cliff, well out of harm's way.

So we paraded in the village, were issued with our ration of ammunition, and marched over to Crinnis beach. The obvious place to put our cartridges was in the magazine; and the obvious way to carry the rifle was in its sling over our shoulders. To 'march off' meant to stroll next to a congenial companion, smoking and gossiping; and before long we were all strung out, till eventually the road dipped down on to the beach. My father, I noted, had stayed at home.

It was on this cliff path that the enemy 'buzzed' us. Little did the pilot of the aeroplane know that he had stirred up a hornets' nest! To a man, we all pushed forward the safety-catches of our new rifles, and let fly, 'allowing off' for flight as though the plane were a pheasant. Even for us on the ground, it was quite dangerous for a few moments, till we had run ourselves out of ammunition without, alas, bringing down the machine. (Come to think of it, this may well have been the only time in the war that I fired in anger.) At least, we seemed to chase him off. *Much* better than practice, we thought. The rifles had all behaved splendidly. The only problem was what to do next. So we marched home, very pleased.

'How did your practice go?' My father asked, later.

'It all went all right, I think.' I was only a private: it was the privilege of someone else to tell him of our encounter with the enemy. A few minutes later, he remarked: 'An extraordinary message has just come in from the RAF. They are claiming that one of their machines was flying over the coast when it came under fire. The pilot was hit in the leg. They are asking if the Germans have landed.'

First blood! Everyone (except my father) was delighted.

I learned a great deal from this sojourn in the front line. German aeroplanes flew over us, and I learned (later) to identify them. (My mother found it too difficult; but she claimed that one of her chickens knew. When a German aeroplane flew over, it would run into its coop and hide; but by the time my mother reached it, the enemy airman would have been landing back in France.) I learned about weapons; and about explosives, for we once tried, without success, to blow up the cliff paths. I even saw an enemy ship.

13

I was doing a spell of sentry-go on the cliff path at Duporth one night, gossiping with a clay-worker named Rowe, when the silhouette of a German E-boat crossed the path of the moon.

'Ere, what shall us do, then?' He demanded. (We had no telephone.) 'Should us warn them sodjers?'

German E-boats had been seen before. I did not think that they were really leading an invasion.

'I think I'd better go and tell my father,' I said after a pause. I did not think that he would want to hear bad news from me in the small hours of the morning. However, he was more concerned than I expected. He telephoned his superiors, and even considered ringing the church bell, to warn the village of invasion. (To him, this was the only reason for having a church at all.) But sleep won.

The lovely summer turned to autumn. A German aeroplane dropped a bomb on the village, and my mother gained much credit for binding up the wounds of a few soldiers who had been doing PT, half-naked, on the road outside, while our living-in maid was having hysterics in the kitchen. We nearly shot the local coastguard. He may have been able to guard the coast, but he was stone deaf (everyone knew this.) So when my father's office clerk, in Home Guard uniform, shouted 'Halt, who goes there?' and brandished his rifle and bayonet at him, he continued to walk on into it, despite everyone's appeals. He simply could not believe that we were serious.

After defending the Channel Coast of England, however uselessly, against a real enemy, for about four months, I now had to join the full-time army. There was only myself now to defend.

I found, immediately, that my earliest reactions had been absolutely right: this life was not for me at all. In fact it was not war, but theatrical play-acting, which I completely failed even to understand. I no longer had my home to defend against a deadly enemy (who, fortunately, had had more vital targets to attack than our Cornish village.) Instead, I found myself in a lunatic world, with everybody shouting, stamping their feet and carrying out meaningless antics on a parade-ground where, I considered, the actual business of fighting a war was quite unheard of. Heaven knows, I was not *looking* for battle: nobody could be more frightened than I. But it seemed that I must adapt myself to an environment which I knew immediately was entirely foreign to me, and probably bogus to boot.

I knew the way to Sandhurst, more or less: it was only four miles from my old school, Wellington College, where I had spent an indifferent adolescence, only relieved by the consoling thought, often expressed, that no matter how awful it was, it was at least better than the two other prominent local institutions, the Broadmoor Criminal Lunatic Asylum and the Royal Military College at Sandhurst. We had dubbed the latter 'Hell over the Hill'. Now I was roasting in it.

Mercifully, I was given a room of my own. On the first morning, though, we were all summoned to an opening session in a lecture room. Here, I found that I was the only cadet not in uniform.

At Oxford, I had joined the University OTC. It had met once a week; and together we had languidly discussed military matters, emerging on to Christ Church Meadow from time to time for a 'TEWT' or tactical exercise without troops.

Nobody had taken them seriously. However, like the degrees which the academics showered upon us when we left, the officers (most of them dons in disguise) had distributed yet another document, named 'Certificate B', which, we were told, would save us from the fatigue of enlisting in the army through the ranks.

This had been a mistake, as I found out that morning. This piece of paper was given only to ex-undergraduates of Oxford and Cambridge; and, as I could see, I was the only one in that Sandhurst intake. I had arrived in my only tweed jacket, flannel trousers, perhaps a less flamboyant tie, but a civilian shirt and brown leather shoes. Everyone else was in uniform. Our 'squad', destined for the Brigade of Guards (twelve of them for the Coldstream) had been called up two months previously, and had already done their 'square-bashing' at the Guards Depot at Caterham. They were old hands, now. Not only had they arrived in uniform, with boots which they had been buffing up themselves for weeks, and tunics which the regimental tailor had been bribed to fit for them; but, more important, they had been shouted at by every old soldier, drilled to exhaustion, and taught all the ins and outs of barrack-room life. Their foul language was their especial pride.

For them, it was quite natural to be ordered out on to the parade ground immediately after the introductory session; but what about me? My case was a matter of some doubt even for the immaculate Scots Guards captain who had charge of us. It was even more of a surprise for the Scots Guards sergeant who was to be our drill instructor.

'Sergeant, I think this cadet has only joined the army this morning. He won't know your words of command. I shall be checking with the Quartermaster's department about a uniform during the morning.'

'Sir!'

'Cadet Bulteel, *do* you know the words of command? Have you ever done any drill?'

'Well, yes, Sir. A bit.'

15

'Well, do the best you can.'

So it all began: agony.

After drill came weapon training: a lecture from a sergeant in the Coldstream, without exception the dullest I had ever heard. Oddly, I found that I knew a little more about Bren guns than the others – even the instructor – for at Caterham no one had been allowed to look at them. The idea of *using* them had scarcely registered. I had been *living* with them, for months.

I was taken to the quartermaster's store and issued with my uniform, and boots; and foresaw trouble here. Would my elderly 'scout' be willing to buff them up for me? If not, then I should have to ask my fellow-cadets what to do. My uniform did not fit. I was absurdly conscious of my own physical deficiencies for, with the best will in the world, I should never look like a soldier, with my frizzy hair, stooped shoulders and pigeon toes. (Alas, I was dead right about this: I never did.) When I got to my room at the end of that first, dreadful day, I threw myself on to the bed and wept my way to sleep.

I was desperately lonely, of course. The other cadets knew each other well, for they had all been at Caterham together. Also, I soon discovered, most of them had been at school together for four years before that. Perhaps I was suffering from some sense of inferiority here, but I was conscious that not having been to Eton put me almost outside their experience. Looking back, I can see their difficulty. They were young, too, only nineteen, and despite their surface sophistication they had not had to deal, as yet, with an alien human animal. The easy solution was to carry on with the friendships they had already formed, and leave this odd stranger to come towards them, if he could. It was not that they disliked me, or tried actively to be rude. But they did not want to give their friends a chance to accuse them of slumming.

Less than half of my intake, or 'company', were embryo Guards officers, however. The rest had come from regiments of the line, and hoped to go back to them as officers at the end of the four-month course. (I do not think that any 'specialists' came our way – gunners, sappers or cavalry, for example: we were infantrymen only.) But our officers, and nearly all our non-commissioned officers, for that matter, were guardsmen. They gave the impression that anyone who was not a guardsman was hardly a soldier at all. Some of our sergeant-instructors were magnificent men; and our Company Sergeant-Major, Lord, a Grenadier, had a turn-out and a swagger which I still recall. I think I made a tactical mistake in getting to know one or two cadets who were not guardsmen, for this was to 'break ranks'. But I was lonely; and I did not realize that a member of the Brigade, officer, NCO, or even cadet, was a member of an exclusive club, segregated from the ordinary world, quite convinced of his own superiority, reluctant even to speak with lesser breeds.

I was unhappy about this. I never felt superior to anybody, and it was all too clear that my instructors considered that I was falling below the standard expected of a prospective Guards officer. If I had had any option, I would rather have been one of the shoal than an under-performing fish in a hyper-exclusive pond.

The ultimate threat was RTU. Any cadet who was considered unworthy could be 'returned to unit' and relegated to the ranks; and I must have come very close to this. The irony, though, was that I had no unit to return to, as I had not come from one in the first place. Anyone could see that I should look even more ridiculous as a guardsman than as an officer. Better to go on, then: when eventually I became an officer I should at least have a servant to look after me, to see that, when I went on parade, my uniform did not look like a horse's nosebag. I myself was too miserable to care.

I remember working all this out, during one of our silly Sunday Church parades. Nobody seemed to want me, my fellow-cadets, my regiment, the army. If there was a God out there, in the distance, he must have been laughing like anything, I thought, watching this untidy mannikin making such a mess of what was left of his life.

Though I was still the sloppiest cadet in the squad, as everyone took pleasure in telling me, I discovered for the first time that I had one un-suspected military skill.

Occasionally, of an evening, we had to listen to each others' 'lecturettes' on various military subjects; and I dreaded my turn in front of my suave fellow-cadets. When it came, it must have been on the Bren Gun, one of the weapons we were supposed to know about, as it was to be carried by infantry platoons throughout the war.

I could never remember the technical terms traded around by the sergeant-instructors; and I found myself improvising as I went along. But I did remember the 'barrel nut retainer plunger'. Its specific function does not matter; but I was able to compare it, and indeed its function, with the sexual machinery of the male animal. The phrase 'Bren gunners do it with a barrel nut retainer plunger' may well have been the first ever coined of that genre. This, and my reminiscences of 'weapon training' with the Home Guard, caused the rest of the squad to double up with laughter, as I went beyond the allotted time. It labelled me as the squad comedian – the first and last time, alas, that I could ever claim that title. But it helped me to gain my commission, I am sure.

This was assured when I was told to order my officer's uniform. Nothing is made easy in the Brigade of Guards, of course; and our choice was restricted to about a dozen Savile Row tailors, who actually had to bring our half-cut uniforms down to be fitted at Sandhurst, for the approval of our squad officer. As I had never been to a tailor in my life, I teamed up with a fellow-cadet, Tom Jackson, and while the uniforms took shape, I braved the London Blitz to be fitted for my caps, shoes and boots by exclusive Mayfair specialists. The costs were astronomical – I must return to this, later – but unavoidable; if I had been denied my commission at this stage, I felt that I could sue! By such mischances, subterfuges, and inevitabilities I was sucked in towards my commission, which I took away with me to Cornwall at the end of the course.

4

TRAINING

I firmly believed that this leave would be my last. I could walk the cliff paths alone, sentimentally, bidding farewell to my favourite haunts, apprehensive about the horrors which awaited me, vaguely wondering if there were another life to come but coming, equally vaguely, to the conclusion that there was nothing to hope for. I was being sold down the river.

My father left me to myself. He had done his bit. He had brought his son and heir to the altar, and could leave the actual sacrifice to others to administer. (He was still beset with his own memories of 1915, when he and all his generation had marched cheerfully from their tents and billets to the holocaust of Loos.) Now, it was my mother, who wanted to show me off in my new uniform to her friends. No one asked how I had paid for it.

I felt a fraud. Did I have to go through this only to abet my mother's snobbery? No one wanted soldiers, at this time. The Royal Air Force had had its hour of glory, and now it was the Royal Navy which was in the news. It deserved it. Impossibly stretched, and suffering grievous losses, it could still defeat the Italians in their own sea. In the Atlantic, though, the toll of both warships and merchantmen was enormous. We used to tell each other that if the Germans went on like this, we should soon be able to build a road over the wrecks across the Atlantic.

But the army was doing very little indeed. True, there had been some successes in the Western Desert, against the Italians; but our advances had been countered when the German *Afrika Korps* came across the Mediterranean; and we had also tried – disastrously – to rescue Greece, then Crete, from invasion.

I could not see that my arrival, as a newly-commissioned officer, was likely to alter the status of the army very much. The war was eighteen months old. We had been marching backwards for nearly a year without even trying. New officers and men were coming in, now; but – to my mind anyway – we were still being trained for peacetime rather than war.

My arrival at Pirbright, to join the Training Battalion, may have caused a stir but, alas, not a stir of excitement. I could look scruffy even in my new uniform, it appeared. The adjutant, Bill Gore-Langton, after the usual introductory 'Get your hair cut!' had us on the parade ground in no time. I came to dread the daily 'Adjutant's Parade'. He would look superb, in his knee-high boots and breeches, his Sam Browne belt (which shone like a mirror,) his trim military moustache, his back like a board. I could never hope to be like this.

As he called the men to attention, the young officers clustered behind him, ash-plant sticks under their left shoulders, service dress beautifully cut, plus fours, puttees and brilliant brown boots. The men were wearing the new battle-dress, belts and gaiters blancoed to the colour of green mud, rifles which made a great rattle when they bashed them to the ground (but less effective, I imagine, when fired in anger.) They would drill for an hour each morning.

So would the young officers. All battalions had two 'drill-sergeants', just lower in rank than the Regimental Sergeant-Major, and one would march us round the corner to drill us into a muck-sweat with rapid marches, 'Lef-ri-lef-ri-lef-ri-lef-ri-lef!' left turns, right turns, about turns, slow marches, double marches, till our feet were bruised with stamping and my new uniform was fraying at the armpits. My mind, too, was in a whirl.

Things went badly from the beginning. It was not only that I had a stoop. Also, I had outsize calves; and there was no way to wrap my puttees safely round them. Others were able to secure them till their legs looked like bars of barley-sugar; but with me, one spiral would sink to the spiral below, till a sliver of pink calf would appear. More than once, the whole puttee would collapse like a cow-pat on to the ground. Why *me*? It was utter humiliation.

More drill; weapon training; PT; lectures – we had them day and night, and they were all deadly. Every now and then, there would be firing on the range, throwing hand-grenades from a pit, route marches along the local roads: then back, to inspect feet, barrack-rooms, meals, latrines, defaulters. War was very far away.

I was given a soldier-servant (not a 'batman' – something to do with the tradition that the Household troops never went to India, I believe) responsible for getting me into my uniform and keeping me tidy. I became almost smart. My leather-work was soon gleaming, my tunic fitted like a glove, I had a 'British Warm' which really was, and there were 'Blue Patrols' to wear in the Mess of an evening. (I believe that the blue trousers, with their broad red stripe, were the lower half of the full dress uniform, with its scarlet tunic, and its buttons set in pairs – I did not have to buy this latter, one of the economies of war, I suppose – and what was once a 'casual' tunic for an officer to slip into when he left his scarlet tunic and the bearskin with his servant, for an evening's relaxation in the Mess.)

The cost of buying this uniform had made me more miserable than ever. The official grant was £30, but I had spent over £200, cash which I did not possess. I had no private means, and my father knew nothing of my difficulties. (In his day, when new officers had been sent almost straight out to the Front to be killed, they did not need money unless they survived long enough to go on leave.)

But Guards officers in peace-time were expected to pay to look beautiful; and the practice still stuck. I did not ask my contemporaries about their personal allowances – it would have been undignified even to mention money – but they were not short. Some had cars of their own – I had not even learned to drive – and, every weekend, if they were not on duty, they were expected to go home, or go to London, where they were always welcome in the social merry-go-round which still continued despite the Blitz. Once or twice, they asked me to join them at a local restaurant during the week, and, once or twice, I thought that I ought to join them. My overdraft mounted. On most weekends I offered to remain as a 'duty officer' because I had nowhere to go and no money to spend. But the others grew increasingly suspicious of this.

The Officers' Mess at Pirbright was famous. It was said that some of the best chefs in London had been enticed to put on uniform to come and work in the kitchens; and the Mess Sergeant, Callow, was a genius. At this worst time of the war, with whole convoys being sunk together and rationing getting really serious, we fed like kings.

There was not only food. It was the easiest thing in the world to order a drink: all an officer need do was press a bell, and an obsequious guardsman would be at his elbow in no time. It was a relief to find that we were not allowed to stand drinks to our brother-officers; but if I were talking with a friend, and *he* ordered a drink, it was difficult for me not to order one, too. The basic mess bill was three-and-sixpence a day, and there were a few compulsory extras – guests, and newspapers come to mind – but my drinks bill frightened me when the totals appeared in my pigeon-hole at the end of the month. With my pay at eleven shillings a day, there was never a chance that I could make ends meet. It was not surprising that I felt ill at ease in the Mess. It haunts me still.

For some reason, Guards officers did not take off their Sam Brownes when they came in; and quite a few of them would eat their meals with their caps on. Perhaps, in the dim past, one of our kings had told them that they must always be ready for an emergency? Frankly, not many of them looked ready to go into battle in a hurry. It fascinated me to watch a couple of majors, sitting on the fender and warming their bottoms, their gin being replenished every five minutes, before they went in to a gargantuan luncheon. After it, they would need an hour or two to sleep it off.

After a couple of months, I was moved on to the Holding Battalion, and was condemned to a military life in London – this because the next batch of newly-commissioned officers was due in from Sandhurst, and there were too many useless mouths at Pirbright already. London was incomparably worse.

My pay was the same, but the basic mess bill increased to four shillings and sixpence a day. Dinner each night was formal; and after dinner the port circulated. Very good it was too – better than the food – but it was hard not to refill my glass when the decanter came round a second time; and my monthly mess bill became a nightmare. What was I to do? Whilst I was there, my godfather, 'Uncle Bertie' died, and I heard that he had left me £1,000. So, with a sigh of relief, I wrote to my father, who was not only an executor but also a substantial beneficiary. He wrote back, to tell me that I could not touch this money till I had reached the age of twenty-one.

I had to confess my sins to him, then, for my overdraft was well over two hundred pounds by this time. My father went to see my bank manager in St Austell; and it was agreed between them that it should be 'frozen' at that figure. My father sent me a cheque for £10.

So I had a year to wait, then, for my twenty-first birthday. I could not beg again. With nowhere to turn, this was, for me, the lowest point in the war: I was even hoping that I should be killed by a bomb. (There still seemed to be a chance of having my problems solved for me like this, for the Blitz went on around us till May. It was difficult to find a good night's sleep. We were growing a little careless, I recall, and our nocturnal activities, such as they were, did not come to a stop. It might be wise to shelter in a doorway if it seemed that the end bomb of a 'stick' might land somewhere near. It was harder, though, to anticipate the fall of all the ironmongery which we ourselves were throwing up into the night sky: it had to come down again, somewhere.)

I would take the odd evening off, chiefly to avoid the Mess and the interminable, costly dinners. This meant walking to the West End from the north-east corner of Regent's Park (we were not allowed into buses, or the Underground, and I could not afford a taxi.) My private refuge was the Berkeley Buttery, where I might have a lonely whisky. Then I would walk back again, ignoring the whispers of invitation from the tarts in Bond Street, across Oxford Circus, up Great Portland Street and Albany Street; and so to bed.

Michael Mitchell had come to the Holding Battalion with me, and found it as dreary as I did. We discussed mutual problems whilst on a stroll through the Park, near the Zoo.

'The trouble about the Holding Battalion,' Michael said, 'is that this is exactly what it does. It's just a dump for useless old throw-outs from the service battalions.' He mentioned some names. I had to agree that it would be a disaster if they were ever to see active service: they could only do ceremonial duties (I must describe these, next) then limp back to their port and their comforts before they pottered back home to recuperate over the weekend.

Do you think that we've been sent here to join them on the central reject pile?'

'No. They've thought up something nastier for us,' Michael said. 'We've just been dumped on one side, till the fighting begins. But I hope they don't forget about us. I don't want to go on guard again with Edgar (one of the fat old blimps we had been talking about.) Did you hear what happened? Just outside Buckingham Palace, as we were marching off, some facetious woman broke through the police barrier and gave him a bun. She said he looked hungry!'

'Are we really fighting for old dimwits like that?' I asked: 'Or – worse still in a way – do *they* think they are fighting for *us*? There isn't a chance that they will ever fight at all.'

'I feel rather wasted, here,' Michael confessed. 'On the other hand, it's fun to be stationed in London, don't you think? At least, we can all have a good time.'

'It's OK for you.' All my distress suddenly erupted, against my better judgement. 'My trouble is that I'm broke. I'm supposed to be living on my pay, but you know as well as I do that it's absolutely impossible.' Then I wished that I had kept quiet.

Michael, bless his heart, was horrified. 'Let's get out of this place,' he cried, 'tonight! I'll stand you a decent dinner somewhere; and we can both have a private, confidential bitch about these terrible old men.' So we did. I wondered if we were breaking some unwritten code of conduct; but, that evening, we both let our hair down and drowned our sorrows in Michael's wine. The only trouble was that, as the evening wore on, Michael began to enjoy himself. By midnight, he was seeking further excitement.

'Let's go on from here,' he said. 'The night is young. What about a spot of dancing?' He had entirely forgotten my own predicament by this time, though when we went on to the Cabaret Club he paid my entrance fee and ordered another bottle. Within minutes, a couple of girls came up, and Michael set them down boisterously. Here were our partners, then.

We shared a drink, and I think I had a dance; but then I panicked. I made the usual excuse to leave the table; but I was outside the front door in a flash, and stumping my solitary way back through the Blitz to Barracks, leaving Michael to cope with the girls himself. Too bad! But he had taken the initiative. He could cope.

Michael *knew* that I was broke, I thought miserably to myself. He should not have presented me with this. I had never been to a nightclub before, and never wanted to go to one again. I did not 'know the drill,' as we used to tell each other about all new situations. Michael did. (But I wonder how he *did* cope? After a time, he must either have paid one of them off, said goodbye to both, or gone to bed with both at once . . .) But in those days, of course, not every nightclub was a brothel, nor every hostess a prostitute; so I may well have misjudged this situation altogether.

Today, boys of twenty years old would probably have their own store of sexual experience, but it was not as common then, I think. Though there were prostitutes in every doorway along the West End, it was not every young officer who picked them up. Either sex was a rarer indulgence, or we were less 'mature'. Also, I should say at a guess that a respectable girl would normally spurn any overtly sexual advance. But I may be wrong about this.

My rich brother-officers may have been the exception, for they were a good 'catch'; or they could pay for their prostitutes, too, if they wanted them. I would hear boastful talk in the Mess about other nightclubs, and of the girls that were 'picked up' there: the 'Slip Inn' seemed to be almost the monopoly of Guards officers, who would swap the girls' Christian names with one another. However, I gathered that it was 'safe' to take their own girlfriends to the 'Suivi', and get them to join in the house song:

'Susie, Susie,
Sitting in the shoe-shine shop.
All day long she sits and shines.
All day long she shines and sits,
Susie, Susie,
Sitting in the shoe-shine shop.
She sits and shines, and shines and sits,
Sits and shines, and shines and sits,
Susie, Susie,
Sitting in the shoe-shine shop.'

If this was as dirty as they could get, I used to think even at the time, it didn't sound too dreadful! But I couldn't think of going, myself. I had no girlfriend, and no money.

The justification for our existence in London was to provide the Guard at Buckingham Palace and St James'. I was roped in twice, and found it a formidable experience: it had all the ingredients I feared and hated.

First of all, there was the preliminary drill, of course, every day. My puttees kept falling off. My legs hurt. My spirit rebelled. But when it came to the day, we paraded in battle-dress, after all. The Regimental Sergeant-Major, 'Tibby' Britten, weighed twenty stone and had a voice which could be heard, over the traffic, from the other side of Regent's Park – more often than not addressed to me, for my drill was terrible. One of the drill-sergeants, whose name I prefer not to recall, insulted me before the men, and seemed to bear me some particular grudge.

We marched out of barracks, shepherded by a mounted policeman, and all the traffic – not much, incidentally – was brought to a halt around us. We would detour round the ruins of the previous night's bombing, roughly along Albany Street, across the Euston Road, along Great Portland Street towards Oxford Circus, then through Mayfair, across Piccadilly and out through Marlborough Gate into the Mall. We halted on the barrack-square at Wellington Barracks, tidied ourselves up and waited for the band to march us into the Palace forecourt. Then, things grew really serious.

I forget the movements now, but there were beady eyes amongst the crowd who knew them all, and did not hesitate to inform the newspapers of any mistakes. (It was said that the King, too, watched from time to time.) The outgoing guard were drawn up, awaiting us, and we faced each other for about half an hour.

Keys of the two palaces were exchanged. (In fact there were none, and the outgoing captain had to find something else – rumour had it that one of them handed over a live mouse! But anything would do.) I suppose that laggard sentries had to be rounded up on the perimeter, and fresh ones detached from the new guard to replace them. But the time came to march off: the outgoing guard over to Wellington Barracks, behind the band, and the new guard to their two guardrooms. Does the same system still prevail, I wonder? It kept – and still keeps – the spectators happy; but any suggestion that the Guard actually *guards* anything is false: the gates are guarded by policemen.

We would spend our time – forty-eight hours at a stretch, during the war – in the Officers' Mess in St James'. The Captain of the Guard would not vacate it much, leaving the 'rounds' of St James' to the Ensign, and of Buckingham Palace to the Subaltern. There was nothing much else to do save drink, entertain visitors and sleep; but the entertaining was a burden.

It was understood that the three officers shared the expenses of entertainment equally between them, but it was generally the Captain's friends who were invited. On one evening our Captain invited a duke and duchess, for instance, and we all paid for their drinking. But, after dinner, someone suggested poker. What on earth was I to do? I was told how to play; but not how I was going to pay for my losses. I could only go broke as soon as I reasonably could; but even that was not cheap, to me.

(However, I was spared the rule of one Captain, who sent out into Jermyn Street for a prostitute, and made his junior officers mount her on the dining-room table.)

So I endured my first six months as an officer in the Coldstream Guards. And, all the time, the bombs landed, the ships sank, and the German army spread across Russia like ink over blotting-paper. My over-draft hung over me. Was this *really* war? I was almost looking forward to the inevitable, hideous reality of death.

5

THE SIXTH BATTALION

It could not go on like this. My life was fast becoming impossible, not only because I knew, clearly, that I was in the wrong place and in the wrong social class (these padded aristocrats were altogether too exalted for me) but also that there was no chance of getting myself out of debt.

In the Mess, officers would play picquet with one another, gaining or losing five hundred pounds an evening, nearly three times my gross annual pay. They kept cars, owned racehorses, went to their country homes at week-ends, helped themselves to women (I guessed) and were familiar with all the luxuries of life. They had their own racecourse at Hawthorn Hill, their own yacht club on the Hamble (both closed down for the duration, but not for lack of money) and their own round of parties. This was a world in which I had no place. I had joined up, I thought, to fight in a war. But there was no war for soldiers, as yet, and there never would be for these high-living drones. Mercifully, not all of them were like this.

During the summer of 1941, though, the Germans invaded Russia. Ten million men were now fighting one another; and the people of Britain began to appreciate that the country could not continue to depend exclusively on its navy and air force. A role for the army must be found. Even the civilians were doing more useful work, suffering nightly bombings and living on food which was strictly rationed.

The High Command – the Brigade of Guards, anyway – had to come to terms with this crisis of confidence. (Preparations must have been going on for quite a time – otherwise, why would a dozen new officers have been admitted to the Regiment every two months? – but the reorganization had passed me by. So far, I had only seen the relics of the peace-time, toy-time army, now redundant, poisoned with vintage port in the Holding Battalion.)

But for us young officers, commissioned for the 'duration of the emergency' it was the formation of the Fifth and Sixth Battalions at the end of this miserable summer that broke the log-jam.

Three Coldstream battalions had already been fighting, and the Fourth Battalion had recently been formed. Probably, the rest of us had been 'stock-piled,' ready to join the Fifth and Sixth when the time came. I wonder why we were not told? ('Be like Dad. Keep Mum!' ran the advertisement, perhaps in poor taste, pasted up on every billboard. All the same, a hint might have done something for our morale.)

The relief of getting out of the Holding Battalion was almost palpable; even though our new abode was to be in a London suburb. The headquarters of the Sixth Battalion, which I was to join, was in one of the school houses at Harrow-on-the-Hill; and I found my way on to a building estate at Eastcote, about three miles away, where I was given a platoon of my own, at last, in No. 2 Company, commanded by Cuthbert Fitzherbert.

From that moment, my life changed. My terror of war did not go away, of course, nor even my conviction that I should never be a soldier. But at last I found in Cuthbert a leader to respect, one who seemed interested in me as a person; and I found in my new platoon a field where I could, for the first time, deal in human beings.

Cuthbert was forty, a member of the old squirearchy of the North Midlands, a Roman Catholic, married to a delightful wife whom I later came to love and admire. They had five children. Cuthbert had served in the Coldstream at the end of the previous war, but had been badly wounded on his first day in action; and, between the wars, had worked himself up into the higher reaches of Barclays Bank. He was no regular soldier, then. But he was adaptable and experienced enough to become the best officer under whom I ever served.

It was a revelation to find in him an older man with whom I could talk. I doubt if, till then, I had ever spoken freely to an officer senior to myself, for most of them were regulars, heavily moustachioed, unnaturally smart, generally stupid, and of course incredibly rich, part of another world. I could ask Cuthbert what I really wanted to know.

'Cuthbert,' I asked one evening, after a fortifying drink, 'what's it really like to be in action?'

'I don't think that I'm the person to tell you,' Cuthbert answered. 'You see, I only had one day, and not much of that, for I got hit quite soon. But let me tell you one secret. I was drunk.' *Not* a very helpful answer to my enquiry! But at least it was frank.

His interest and care extended over all No. 2 Company. I was not the only beneficiary.

There was Eddie Dawson, his second-in-command, another married man, perhaps a little younger. Why *he* had joined the Coldstream I did not discover, but he had never, surely, been a regular soldier: he owned a laundry in Byfleet, and was still trying, none too successfully, to run it and to be a soldier as well. Eddie had a warm and easy personality. I suspect, looking back on it all now, that Cuthbert considered that he lacked his own overmastering dedication. To me, though, it was a relief to share his laid-back view of regimental soldiering, and his care over how he spent his money – but a little irritating, also, for he would retreat home to Byfleet whenever he was given a chance.

Then there were the two other platoon commanders, Tom Jackson and John Chaworth-Musters, both of my own age, more or less. Tom had been in the same squad with me at Sandhurst, but had done better than I had (of course!) and was therefore senior; whilst John was of an earlier intake. I was the junior officer, then. I did not care. After a while, Cuthbert made it clear to me that I was doing best; and soon my platoon was the one entrusted with the most demanding tasks, as we settled down to intensive training.

I had never spoken to 'other ranks' till then. It was as though officers looked upon themselves as a superior species, and had no common language – except orders, shouted on the parade-ground or passed on, generally as punishments, through their company sergeant-majors. (I am exaggerating this, of course; but, all the same, I found it disturbing to discover, later in the war, that guardsmen seldom seemed even to know the names of their officers.)

But now, I had men of my own. True, it was my job to order them around; and I doubt if I did it very well. But at least I could discover their names, and look upon them as people, not machines. It was a heady discovery. After fifty years I remember them well.

The man who, in practice, ran the platoon was the Platoon Sergeant, 'Honest John' Harness, a Yorkshireman or Geordie, who had done his stint as a regular, and had then gone on into the Police. To me, he seemed utterly confident, widely experienced, supremely wise, a bulky, tough, noisy, deliberate leader who did not need an officer to tell him what to do. Slowly and tactfully, though, he showed me what my responsibilities were, and I learned almost as much from him as I did from Cuthbert.

The three sections were commanded by Lance-Sergeant Otter, a rather morose, ugly old sweat, given to grumbling (lance-sergeants in the Coldstream were the equivalent of full corporals,) Lance-Sergeant Brock, a younger, handsome, dashing regular, and Corporal Crewe, a smaller, rather precise, trim, well-spoken man who had run a fish-and-chip shop in peacetime.

Each section must have had ten to twelve men, guardsmen, of a minimum height of five feet ten inches, mostly from the north (the main regimental recruiting ground) with their strange accents, but tough and reliable. There were additional corporals: Neville, who had a foul mouth and an endless repertoire of filthy songs, Lacey (later promoted to sergeant) who had been a coal-miner and whose face was still marked with black flecks; and there must have been another, second in command of the third section. But no name springs to mind. (Odd: I thought that I should remember them all.)

I must mention the two platoon comedians, Willie Turner and Larry McCormack. They were both Yorkshiremen. McCormack was the 'straight' one, I suppose, and was thin and sallow, not unlike Stan Laurel in a way. Willie Turner was fatter, irrepressible, always talking, always cheerful, informing Larry that his home town, Leeds, was a far better place than Larry's, which was Rotherham. At the worst moment in a long route march, for instance, the two of them would break ranks and dance in front of the platoon, Larry stiff, Willie waddling, cheering us on. I hoped that Cuthbert would not come looking for us at those moments! It may have been bad for morale, but it did not *seem* so to me; and, if their antics were a threat to my authority as an officer then, I thought, that was just too bad.

Cuthbert told me to select my own soldier-servant from among them; and after a great deal of thought I asked one of the platoon, Willie Mitchell, if he would be prepared to look after me. He was a quiet lad, who came from Nelson in Lancashire, where he had worked in a cotton mill. I was not sure that he would take kindly to the officers' way of living, for he seemed to lack sophistication, and spoke with an accent so broad that, at times, no one else could understand it at all. How wrong I was! He soon learned the life of an orderly in the Mess, served at our meals and got to know the idiosyncrasies of the other officers; yet he found it equally easy to keep his natural place in the platoon, and never allowed his double life to worry him. (We stayed together till I was carried, feet first, from the battlefield; and when the war ended we remained in close touch.) I should have been lost without him. When he grinned, it was from ear to ear; and with his protuberant ears extending horizontally from where the grin ended, it looked like a slice of water melon on a plate.

Was it Willie who once said, sententiously, about the other regiments in the Brigade of Guards? – 'Ee, boot when it cooms to t'push, they all pull together.' He had gems like this.

My greatest joy was that we were at Eastcote, three miles away from Battalion Headquarters, and that we could run our own lives. The other companies were billeted separately, ostensibly on the circumference of the Polish fighter aerodrome at Northolt: not that the Poles seemed to need much protection. I might occasionally be sent to Battalion HQ with a message; and occasionally the Commanding Officer, Colonel Bunty

Stewart-Brown, would come to see us. I found him charming. The Adjutant, Rupert Hart-Davis, was not a regular at all, but a successful publisher, one of the best-read officers in the army. How different it all was to the militaristic nonsense of the Holding Battalion! I suppose that there was a Regimental Sergeant-Major and a couple of drill-sergeants, but I seldom tangled with them, and, for the life of me, cannot even remember their names. And was there a Chaplain? If so, he never came our way.

So we continued with our drill, but on our own. I do not remember the officers being drilled by a sergeant-major.

Then there was the inevitable PT. It seemed only right that the officers should do their exercises with the men, even to call out the exercises to be done. All too often, there was a race, or a scrum, or a childish game. These took place amid hoots of laughter.

The next task was to make ourselves familiar with our own weapons; for as autumn drifted into winter, so we were equipped up to our 'G.1098' scale, the weapons which a platoon would take into battle: three Bren guns, one for each section, a two-inch mortar for each platoon, and an anti-tank rifle, the least popular weapon, as it was twice as heavy as anything else; and, of course, a rifle and bayonet for everyone else. (These were the old SMLE rifles, with the long bayonets, relics of the previous war. We did not get our new rifles and bayonets till we went overseas.)

Then we learned how to fight in war. 'Section in the attack' was a fairly easy but not a very convincing exercise, but everyone had to know how best to make use of the Bren gun. Then we would manoeuvre as a platoon; then as a company.

Within a couple of months, we had to exercise in open country, for the quiet streets of our building estate were also occupied by civilians; so, day after day, three-ton trucks would take us off to some pre-chosen battle area.

Cuthbert had plenty to do. After watching us at our exercises, he would then reconnoitre sites for the next day, arrange transport for it, invent a situation for us to solve, and pacify the farmers and householders whose lives we were about to disrupt. There was a war on, he would tell them. His troops would do their best not to break anything, but they would not cause any intentional harm. His regular 'charm offensive' always paid dividends, and we became accepted in the neighbourhood as an inevitable nuisance.

By winter, we were ready for battalion exercises, and needed yet more open space, out towards the Chilterns. We learned to get out of our trucks at the 'assembly area', march to the 'start line', find our way, mostly by maps, to where we imagined the enemy would be, then charge hopefully at a non-existent enemy line. Then we would collect ourselves together, and be told what we had done right and wrong, before the trucks miraculously found us again and took us back to our billets in the gathering dark. I enjoyed it all. A bath, a sleepy supper together in the Mess, and a drink or two, and I would log out on my camp bed to sleep dreamlessly.

We met the other officers of the Battalion from time to time, either on these exercises or on 'courses' of one kind and another. I first met Peter Wyld when we were learning how to drive motor-bikes. One of my earliest memories of him is of driving past him down the A5, somewhere along the stretch between Markyate and Woburn, Peter standing hopelessly beside a machine which, as far as I remember, was spread in pieces across the road.

By the spring of 1942 we became conscious that our battalion was one of a brigade, commanded by a Grenadier, Julian Jefferson. The first full brigade exercise, as far as I remember, was a three-day affair across the Sussex Weald. Early one morning, we were decanted on the Dorking bypass – and I suppose that somebody will remember what, if anything, we achieved.

I had my own reservations about this: to me, the whole exercise was completely incomprehensible. This was – still is, probably – one of the commoner ingredients of a large army scheme. I wonder if Cuthbert was able to discover what it was all about? In a way, I can see now that it was of value, for it enabled company and battalion commanders to control (or fail to control) the march of events in what is euphemistically called a 'developing situation' or, more properly, an ongoing shambles; but it was hard on the troops, if good for their vocabularies.

I remember it chiefly because, when we ground to a halt in a farmyard near Edenbridge, I was told to pilot the convoy back to Harrow.

We had become the 'marker platoon' for convoy duties. This meant having the use of two trucks, not one: the first would lead the convoy, with everybody in it, and I would drop one off whenever a 'policeman' was needed to signal a choice of roads, whilst the second truck would be at the tail of the convoy to pick him up. In those days, when there was little traffic on the roads anyway, it was not very difficult, and it gave the men something useful to do.

But to pilot nearly a thousand vehicles across London, from south-east to north-west, was another story. I was given the whole Company, over a hundred men; but as I had no idea myself about where I was going and had only the map to help me, it was a problem to know which turns needed a man to point the way – I might easily use them all up before we reached the Thames. All was well, though. With a little pushing and pulling, we brought the convoy through, and I returned to my billets exhausted but proud. It was a blow to my self-esteem to be at the receiving end of a 'rocket' from the Brigadier. He passed a message down the line that my men had looked 'scruffy'. It was true, of course: they had been in the open for three days, had had no chance of a shave that morning, and their boots were muddy. But this was the army, I mused: I had to console myself with the knowledge that we had all done our best.

It must have been at about this time that everything suddenly went into a higher gear. Perhaps we began to realize that if we went on at this pace we would lose the war altogether.

In December, 1941, Japan had entered the war. In a few minutes, half the American fleet was destroyed at Pearl Harbour; and, within days, the Japanese army set about to destroy the British presence in the Far East. We had no sooner absorbed one crippling blow before another struck; and on our wireless sets in North-West London we found the defeats almost impossible to comprehend. Hong Kong, then Malaysia, then Singapore, then Burma, all were lost in a twinkling. Our two most prestigious capital ships were sunk, our island dependencies of the Western Pacific fell without a struggle; and before we dared even to think about it all, the Japs were halfway across New Guinea and nearing the vulnerable coasts of Northern Australia. They were on the Indian border, too; and yet a third of our 'dominions', New Zealand, was at risk.

The Americans, our allies and partners now, staggered under this flow of disasters. Distance seemed to matter little to these new enemies: conceiveably, they might next do their island-hopping trick along the line of the Aleutians till they reached the mainland of Alaska. Thence, they could turn down the coast of the Eastern Pacific, through British Columbia, and attack the very homeland, the states of Washington, Oregon, and even California itself.

Nor, during the early summer of 1942, was this all. The German army was penetrating into Russia, and was within miles of Moscow. Its southern armies spread inexorably across the steppes till they reached the Volga, and could almost see the mountains of the Caucasus. Losses of shipping, now both in the Atlantic and the Russian convoys, were higher than ever. Even our little military effort in the Western Desert was coming to grief. We had captured a good deal of ground there at the end of 1941, but the final humiliation was to lose it all the following summer; and after the fall of Tobruk in June, the *Afrika Korps* was to race forward in an attempt to grab Egypt from us. Only the English Channel gave us protection, albeit limited, now. We seemed almost to have lost the rest of the world.

But in the High Command, and amongst those whose business it was to know these things, there were stirrings. There were plans to help the Russians, who were suffering the worst of the punishment; there were plans to stem the Japanese advances; there were even plans for a counter-attack in the Western Desert. During that spring and summer, the greatest industrial nation in the world went on to a war footing, and before long a vast stream of armaments was to run out of ten thousand factories. But it could not be used till there were men with the experience and will to use them. First, the British army, so long inert, must acquire a new dynamic.

This was the intention of 'battle-drill'. That intrepid but rather bogus officer, Bulteel, went on one of the early courses.

It is difficult to describe these, except to admit that they were beastly – but that, in a way, was the intention. In early May, I joined a group of young officers at a large house on the southern edge of Chobham Common (it can almost be seen from the M3) and, for a fortnight, did not draw breath. We learned to be 'aggressive'. Looking back, it seems a little childish, and I am ashamed as I remember some of the tasks we had to perform. We were ordered to snarl to one another: 'Remember Hong Kong!' *What* we were supposed to remember about Hong Kong, we did not know, for no one had been there, but the warning was supposed to make us hate Japs. Perhaps it did. But the officers there from the Brigade of Guards would lisp out these imprecations as a joke.

Smoking and drinking were forbidden, and we moved everywhere at the double. Out on the field firing ranges, they threw live rounds at us. There were casualties. Bayonet practice, charging at sacks painted to resemble Japanese soldiers, and shouting defiance as we did so, was 'marked' by our instructors on the hate we showed. At Hascombe, in a deep valley, marksmen fired live rounds to miss us, but closely; and machine guns fired on 'fixed lines' before us and behind. There were no stragglers.

I returned to the Battalion, fit and leaner, and was told to introduce 'battle drill' to the Battalion. We all moved to Ilfracombe, of all places; and lived under canvas in the fields above.

At least, I was near familiar country! It was good to be out of the London area – and in the summer, too – but I felt a little uneasy at the desecration of those wonderful beaches, cliffs and moors. However, there was a war on, I thought to myself. I was getting tougher, partly as a consequence of my battle-drill training.

Actually, very few of the decisions were mine to make. I have no idea who dreamed up the exercise of marching companies of men across the beach at Woollacombe, machine-guns in the sand-dunes firing streams of bullets just in front of them and just behind; but this was a battle-drill ploy; and it was natural that I should collect some of the blame.

I was also blamed for a long, over-eventful day on Exmoor, not far from the Doone Valley. The Gunners had been brought in, here, and we were ordered to advance under a barrage from their own twenty-five pounders, landing their shells just ahead and then 'lifting' their sights at stated intervals. It was not pleasant to entrust our lives to the whims of fellow-soldiers we could not even see; but, as far as I know, we all survived the experience.

We emerged from the barrage, a little breathless, only to be suddenly told that we were to march through an area which had been drenched in mustard gas.

There it was, just in front of us, with a band of white tape at the start-line and at the finish. (Thank goodness, the barrage had now ended. It had already frightened us quite enough.) So into the 'Valley of Death' we marched, careful not to touch the heather with our hands. To be honest, it was like marching, anywhere; but it was a relief to cross the finishing-line, all the same. The important task now was to strip our nether garments before the mustard worked through to the skin.

'Goodbye to me boots!' Willie Turner cried. 'They'll niver see Leeds Town 'All again!'

'Ee, an' I niver see thee take down tha trousies so fast!' responded Larry McCormack, tearing off his own as though his life depended on it (which, in a way, it did.)

'Twill take moonths t' boof oop me nixt pair o' boots, too.' Willie Turner was more interested in boots than trousers.

'Well, what about *my* boots?' I put in my own grouse. 'I paid ten quid for those.'

'What doost *tha* think, then, Willie?' Larry McCormack asked Willie Mitchell. 'Tha moost have sweated blood over t'years, boofing 'is boots. Now you'll niver 'ave to do it again.'

Willie grinned. 'Ee, but I'll 'ave to start on a new pair, that's all,' was all he could think of. He was queuing up for new boots and trousers, himself, rather embarrassed at being naked from the thighs downward. What a waste! We left behind us a great pile of our clothing, never to be seen again; and the only benefit we could derive from the experience was the knowledge that we could get our clothes off before the mustard could penetrate.

Off we ran (at the double, of course) to the next encounter, probably just as unpleasant.

When we returned from Exmoor, we were shunted into a new company billet.

We were now in Nissen huts on Down Barns Ridge, looking down on to the runway at Northolt from the south, just across the Western Avenue. As we marched along the dual carriageway, the Polish pilots would 'buzz' us in their Spitfires, lifting a wing every two hundred yards to clear the steel posts which had been set in the central reservation just to prevent this low-level 'strafing'. We would fall flat on our faces. One pilot, I remember, actually bounced off the road, breaking the propellor of his aeroplane and knocking off a piece of metal which, I was told later, was the cover of his air intake. Fortunately, he had enough speed to zoom upwards, turn sharply, and land on the runway which ran beside us.

There was an air of expectancy abroad, late that summer. It seemed just possible that our army was about to *do* something, at last; and that, on a more world-wide scale, the tide was on the turn. Even amongst the officers of No. 2 Company, uncomfortable in their Nissen huts on Down Barns Ridge, amongst the spent cartridges of what had been, in peace-time, the largest 'school' in the country for shotgun practice, we were all conscious that we were ready to move.

Eddie Dawson had moved on. He was succeeded as second-in-command by a series of regular officers, none of whom seemed acceptable to Cuthbert. There was the one who insisted on bringing his own bed – only to find that it was too large to get in through the door. There was another, who found his steel helmet too heavy and un-comfortable, and so had a replacement made by his hatter. On a fine day, it deceived even Cuthbert: on the right side was a painted red 'flash' which we favoured (the Coldstream bearskin has a red tuft of horsehair on the right) and the rest was properly painted steel-grey. But alas, it was not steel, but papier mache. When it began to rain, heavily, the helmet wrapped itself around this officer's head; and the paint which ran off it down his cheeks took a considerable time to scrub off. So yet another regular officer had to be moved on to a less demanding post outside the Battalion: we said to one another, unkindly and not always accurately, that regular officers could not lead troops in battle: this was why they (but who were 'they'?) had brought in us amateurs.

Then both John Chaworth-Musters and Tom Jackson were posted to the Second Battalion (both, alas, to be killed later, in North Africa.) Then came the real bombshell.

The Sixth Battalion, we heard, was to continue, but not as a fighting unit. It would act as a 'reinforcement' battalion, periodically providing 'drafts' when other battalions had casualties. Cuthbert, alas, was adjudged too old for service in the field. It broke his heart that he was not to lead No. 2 Company into battle. However, by some means, he was able to ensure that the Company remained intact – he must have gone right through to the High Command to achieve this – and that the best-trained company in the Coldstream would at least retain its identity.

Cuthbert took me out of the Mess one evening, and told me the news. He was in deep distress. I remember it all distinctly – though I still wonder if I had the tact and courtesy to comfort him as he needed. It was an emotional moment; for he then went on to tell me that the authorities had agreed, not only that the Company would be sent out as a single unit to reinforce the Third Battalion in the Middle East, but that I should be in charge of the draft.

'Though I say so myself,' said Cuthbert, 'this will be the best reinforcement the Third Battalion is ever likely to get. If you can only manage to keep them all together when you arrive, then I shall look upon this transfer as my major contribution to the war.'

'What about the other officers?'

'No, I don't think they will be able to go, at least at the same time. But I have no doubt,' Cuthbert continued hurriedly, 'that they will follow soon. All the fighting is in the Western Desert (none of us yet knew of any other invasion plans, of course) and this will mean a steady stream of reinforcements.'

'Well, Cuthbert, thank you. I don't have to tell you how proud I am. But I shall do my best to keep them as *your* company, and to carry on the good work. You began it, you know.' (Yes, we really spoke like that, in those days! Cuthbert was entrusting me with the sacred flame of his efforts and achievements, and I had to let him know that I was aware of the honour.)

I departed into the night to debate with my bosom awhile. Here, then, was the death sentence which I had been anticipating for years. Although I was as certain of this as anyone could be, yet curiously I was not despondent. On the contrary, I was suddenly and, alas, temporarily, overcome with exhilaration; and I danced for joy in the darkness. There were more important issues than death, I suddenly realized. I was to go with Cuthbert's men into Armageddon; and Cuthbert, whom I had come to admire this side of idolatry, but who could not go himself, had actually chosen *me* to lead them.

6

TROOPING

We were just out of Avonmouth. 'Look, there's Brean Down,' I cried out to Peter Wyld, overcome with excitement. 'And there's Steep Holm, just ahead; and Flat Holm over to starboard.' My old prep school was just round the corner of Brean Down. We used to go for walks along the golf course, and play in the sand-dunes. I used to watch the ships in the distance, going up and down the Bristol Channel.

'Is the sea always as filthy as this?'

'Yes. Afraid so. It doesn't get blue till we're beyond Exmoor.'

It was like chocolate. We used to tell each other at school that it was because of the sewage which came down the Severn from the Midlands; but within a few days, I thought, we may all be quite looking forward to the next stretch of stinking mud.

It had all come true, then. Number 2 Company of the Sixth Battalion was now on its way to reinforce the Third. It was said to be in Syria, and down to less than two hundred men (about six hundred would have been the norm.) The only way to get there was by ship – air trooping was out of the question in those days – and the only way a ship could get to the Middle East was round the Cape of Good Hope, for the Mediterranean was a no-go area. We knew that we were in for a long and tedious journey; dangerous, too.

No one was willing to tell us our likely route. We began by going the wrong way: up the Irish Sea to rendezvous with the rest of the convoy off the Mull of Kintyre. (In fact, I do not believe anyone used to sail around the South of Ireland, for it was said to be one uninterrupted minefield.)

Our ship, the *Arawa*, was a single-funnel general-duties ship of the Shaw Savill Line, of about 15,000 tons, with considerable 'upper works' for passengers.

We had embarked at Avonmouth, after a confusing journey by troop train across Southern England, along railway lines which now no longer exist. But now we were at sea. Nobody could stop us. I very much doubted if I should ever set foot on English soil again. It was Wednesday, 28 October 1942.

I must have been a nuisance to Peter all that day, for I insisted on proclaiming my maritime knowledge all the way up the Irish Sea. There was Lundy Island to port, then the island of Skokholm to starboard, followed by the distant tangle of Welsh mountains; and the line of the Irish coast over to port. I pontificated on the ships, Peter on the sea-birds, in the October sunshine. I could hardly bear to go below.

On the following day, the convoy formed off the Mull of Kintyre. There was the *Empress of Scotland*, a traditional three-funnel liner, the *Stirling Castle* and *Athlone Castle*, very modern-looking to us; and our sister-ship, the *Largs Bay* and others; all escorted by half a dozen destroyers – which, I suppose, proved that we were an important convoy, loaded to the gunwales with troops destined for India and the Western Desert. We were also a 'fast' convoy, able (we hoped) to outpace the U-boat packs.

We ran into heavy weather as soon as we cleared Northern Ireland, and all the men were seasick. I could scarcely force myself to visit them, deep in the belly of the ship, probably below the water-line, hideously uncomfortable at the best of times but now, for a few days, like the wounded at Scutari.

The officers fared better. I was sharing a cabin with Peter Wyld, while Michael Mitchell shared another with Ian Dickinson, whom I had not met before. The most senior officer of the draft, however, was Alan Davidson. I did not know him, either; and looked askance at him, for I had been enjoined by Cuthbert to look upon the whole draft as my own. Alan must have recognized this, for he found himself a niche elsewhere amongst the troops, and I was left almost completely in charge.

Neither Peter nor I were actually sick, though we may both have come close to it. I kept eating. The Goanese stewards treated us as they had treated their pampered passengers in peacetime, and the saloon became an officers' mess. 'Oranges, grapefruit, kidneys; soup, fish and meat in one meal!' I wrote in my diary after the first breakfast – or could it have been lunch? I added that the price of drinks was also much to my liking: 'Fourpence for a pink gin, sixpence for whisky, eightpence for sherry and port!' I continued. A packet of twenty cigarettes ('not very good ones') cost eightpence – this must have been in addition to the cylindrical tins of fifty Players, issued free every week. The surest preventative against seasickness, I noted, was a stiff brandy and ginger ale.

The men finally staggered back on deck, to look apprehensively at the mountainous seas around them. They began again to eat what they had lost; and, before the storm ended, we were back on drill parades each morning. It was amusing to watch the lines of men standing to attention, until the deck beneath them made it impossible – but guardsmen must be able to stand to attention even when held upside down! So we proved ourselves in the North Atlantic, that autumn. We even began to enjoy it.

We left the storms behind us eventually, and before long we were edging into the North-East Trades. I had never till that moment been out of England, though I had read myself into a stupor about sailing the sea. This experience was the revelation of all that I had dreamed.

I found Peter an entertaining companion from the beginning, for he had a worldly wisdom which I lacked, and a heavenly vision too, in which, alas, I was sadly deficient. Also, it seemed that he was interested in me, as a person. Where Cuthbert had, in his time, treated me as a favourite disciple, to whom he could impart his dream of an invincible army, Peter seemed really to want to know 'what made me tick' (that phrase was already familiar to us.) Of course, I did not know. No one had ever asked me before, so I had not tried to ask myself. Now, I was forced to articulate my vague imaginings into coherent sequence. That was not easy, either.

I probably told him first about the draft, and what the men meant to me. He was not as impressed as I had hoped.

'Of course, I can see that they mean a lot to you, at present,' he observed, 'but I don't think you should be looking on their welfare as a sacred trust, exactly. What happens when some of them get killed?' (I have to paraphrase a good deal of this, for it was not all said in one early session.) 'Although you think it is vital that they should all go into battle together, you must see that this is incredibly unlikely. You won't have any say in the matter. Can you imagine our new commanding officer, whoever he is, doing what Cuthbert wants, just because you say so?'

'I hadn't thought of that,' I replied, crestfallen.

'Don't you see, Chris, that it would actually be a *mistake*?' Peter pressed his point home. 'Let's assume for a minute that some members of the Third Battalion have seen fighting before, some of them a little and some a lot. Then let's assume that there's a lot which an old sweat can teach a new boy. I wouldn't know what, not having had any battle experience myself; but it stands to reason that there is a good deal yet to be learned from those who have actually done some fighting: how to dodge shells, how to avoid danger when there is no particular point in sticking your neck out at that moment, even how to open a tin of bully without a tin-opener, or how not to get sunstroke. Of course, we are all going to get scattered around the Battalion. Men have been killed and wounded, that's why they have sent for us to fill the gaps. Then, some of *our* soldiers are going to get killed in their turn. Cuthbert must have realized that.'

40

Peter was right, of course. This is exactly what happened when the time came. The fellowship was doomed, because it was what it was, a body of soldiers preparing for battle. Only the memory would remain, and then only among the survivors. There was no room for sentimentality on a troopship, itself liable to be sunk at any moment and to take the whole draft to the bottom of the sea. But it still depressed me. I seemed already to be letting Cuthbert down.

Leaning over the rail and looking over the sea, brilliant white and brilliant blue, we talked about our time together in the Sixth Battalion, and I of my months in the Holding Battalion before that.

'I only just got away in time,' I confessed to Peter. 'There are dozens of my creditors shaking their fists on the quay at Avonmouth.' (This, I admit, was not true: I had paid off my debts on my twenty-first birthday the previous summer – but I had still been living beyond my means, till we sailed.) Peter wanted to hear all about it.

'Well, you should be rid of those problems from now on,' he assured me. 'But, all the same, it seems an odd reason for wanting to fight Germans. Is it the only one?'

'I'm not sure that I want to fight Germans at all.'

'I used to think that, too. It's monstrous that we should have to kill people, I know. But we have to think what will happen if everyone refuses.'

'And we have to think what will happen to *us*. We will probably get ourselves killed, sooner or later.'

'Possibly; not probably. So what?'

'Well, tell me how we are going to win.' (We had not yet heard the news of El Alamein; and the great world battles of Midway and Stalingrad were still a closed book to us.) 'I refuse to believe that we will lose, of course; but it will be years, surely, before we can win? If the last war is anything to go by, then our own chances of survival must be pretty remote.'

'Too bad. Come inside, and let's have a drink to celebrate.'

The sun went down like a great red balloon over the ocean, as, in the convoy, ten thousand soldiers went inside, all privately wondering if a torpedo would get them that night.

The weather grew warmer than ever, and the sea bluer than I had ever seen it. Travelling before the trade winds, we scarcely felt them, and the broken water beside us sparkled in the sun. As yet, no one had bothered to tell us our next port. But, after a fortnight or more, the rumour trickled through that we would be stopping off at Bahia, in Brazil. I was given the impression that, to some extent anyway, we were trying to dodge known locations of U-boat wolf-packs; and there were certainly days when our escorts left us to fend for ourselves whilst the distant mutter of explosions indicated that danger was not far away. One dark night, leaning against the rail alone, I became suddenly aware of some monstrous presence beside me: the *Stirling Castle* (but I am guessing) had run a few degrees off course and was slicing across into us. Fortunately, the sailors became aware of it, too; and, just as slowly, the vessels drew apart. I knew nothing of radar, then. It must have been *invented*, surely? Perhaps the radar operator, on one ship or the other, had read the 'blips' wrong, or had failed to notice.

Then someone passed on the news that we had crossed the Equator: another thrill for me, of course. I felt certain that I had seen the sea discoloured, and had pontificated to Peter that we were off the mouth of the Amazon. Flying fish flipped beside us. Dolphins jumped. The weather grew very hot indeed, and we had been in our tropical kit for some time, khaki drill shorts and shirts, but still the long, thick stockings which enabled us to keep to our boots and do our daily drill. The solar topi had been discarded as an item of headgear by this time, though we had brought ours with us. I grew worried about sunburn, and warned the men not to strip.

We must have been running along the eastern shore of Brazil by this time, and though Bahia was now confirmed as our next port, it seemed to take a long time coming: a pity, perhaps, that there was so little communication between the ship's officers and their passengers, for it was the duty of the army officers to keep their soldiers interested, and we were all bored with endless instruction on the Bren gun, PT on the boat deck, daily boat drill, kit inspections, and occasional lectures from anyone who had anything useful or interesting to talk about.

Then suddenly, one Sunday morning in the middle of November, we were in Bahia, the first foreign land I had ever seen.

I was wild with excitement. The church bells were ringing in the distance, the first I had heard since 1939. The trams were crawling along the distant esplanade; the heat was intense; the little boats were carrying their cargoes of bananas; the green jungle was in the distance. We all longed to go ashore.

But nothing happened. No one even suggested shore leave, and we sweltered on, longing, miserable, cooped up in the prison-hulk with only dreams of freedom. One afternoon, it was suggested that we might try out the ship's lifeboats; and so they were slung out and lowered into the harbour. (I disgraced myself, here. It was not difficult to persuade a bored sailor to hoist a mast and sail, once we were clear of the ship; but what no one realized – sailor or landsman – was that both wind and tide would carry us out to sea. This lifeboat had not the sailing qualities to which I had been accustomed in my own dinghy; and I must have lost a good deal of face when a rescue launch towed us back up the harbour, to encounter the contemptuous stares of the ship's crew when we eventually hooked on. Well, it was an experience!) But no one at all was allowed to land at Bahia. I have still not set foot on the continent of South America.

Now, it was out into the South Atlantic, much wider and lonelier but, presumably, a good deal safer. I think that we were becoming a little bored with it all, by this time: we seemed a long way away from the action, even from the land. News of the Battle of El Alamein must have come in, and rumours even more exciting than this: that a joint Anglo-American force had landed in the north-west of Africa, and was racing to join up with the Eighth Army, already advancing towards them. It seemed as though our long journey round the Cape of Good Hope could reach its destination too late.

We were wrong about this, of course. Odd though, that we should actually *want* to be a part of this pincer movement! But of course it was easy to be brave at this distance.

It was down in the middle of the South Atlantic, on the way to the Cape of Good Hope, that I reluctantly decided that I ought to take my religious inclinations a little more seriously.

It must have been Peter who persuaded me. However, I do remember that I had decided before we set off, that I should have to tackle the problem, or God might easily 'write me off' and let me get shot. But it all seemed so difficult. The saints, I am sure, are able to put a date to their conversions. But I never thought to join that fellowship of the elect. The only consideration that mattered was how best to save my skin.

The following passage is telescoped, and quite possibly bogus. But let me put it down as a conversation with Peter: we certainly talked a good deal, leaning over the taffrail during those colder, dark nights, trying (unsuccessfully) to identify the Southern Cross, as it swam into our ken.

'Now tell me,' I said, 'what it's all about. Why do you talk about religion as though it were important to you? Why do you read your bible? Why do you go to Church?'

'I was just brought up that way,' Peter said. 'My family is a churchgoing one, I suppose; and I learned a good deal at school. I'd like to learn a good deal more. Wouldn't you?'

'My father,' I said, 'only goes to church on Armistice Day. I can't think why. Last year, my sister says that he actually began to sing a hymn. He was enjoying it all so much that he didn't notice that the man next to him had fainted.'

'But surely you were baptised?'

'I must have been. I had a couple of godfathers, anyway.'

43

'Didn't your mother take you to Church, even sometimes?'

'No. We weren't allowed out of the garden when the villagers were going to Church and Chapel. We were just told to keep quiet.'

'Weren't you Confirmed, at school?'

'Oh, yes, rather. All my year had to go through it, before we reached the School Certificate.'

'I don't see what the School Certificate had to do with it.'

'Neither do I. Don't muddle me. It was just one of the things we had to do when we were at school. They brought in a retired bishop to do a hundred of us at once.'

'It doesn't sound very religious.'

'It wasn't.'

'Well,' Peter said. 'What are you going to do about it now?'

'You tell *me*. I haven't a clue. I can't imagine that God wants me to join the club, just because I'm scared of getting killed.'

'Idiot. Do you really think God is like that? I think that the best thing for you to do is to come to Church Parade with me next Sunday. Or perhaps it would be better to get up early and come to Communion. I'm going. I'll wake you up anyway, whether you come or not. No, I'm *not* going to try and persuade you, because I know that you will just be obstinate. If God has anything for you, he will tell you. I have no intention of getting in his way.'

So I did go to Communion, from time to time. Peter kept quiet, unless I asked him specific questions (though I suspect that he prayed for me.) The ship's chaplain was not forthcoming, either. Does everyone come to Christianity like this? We returned to our vain search for the Southern Cross. It was much more interesting.

What we did see, one afternoon, was Table Mountain. It appeared out of the haze, about fifty miles to the north-east. The convoy stopped, rather unwisely, I thought, for I guessed that there could be a wolf-pack of U-boats waiting to greet us here. There was – or rather, there had been. We had stopped to pick up survivors from the convoy ahead of us.

We did not call at Cape Town, but at Durban. These two ports shared the dubious privilege of coping with the convoys of randy troopers, but so far they were not exasperated with the constant disturbance; and we came to rest on Friday, 4 December, after a voyage of about six weeks, to spend nearly a week ashore.

For about the first time in the war, we were in no danger from the enemy. I wonder if the others felt this relief as strongly as I did? Durban was the length of an enormous continent away from German soldiers, and its people saw the progress of the war only through the eyes of others: the trickle of wounded returning to Britain, the few survivors of German submarine sinkings (a trooper, the *Llandaff Castle*, had just been sunk in the Mozambique Channel, through which we were soon to sail ourselves) and their own wounded heroes coming home to convalesce. Many South Africans, alas, had been captured when Tobruk fell a few months earlier, and the white population had discovered, to that extent, the harsh realities of war. They could not have been more generous to us, on our way to the battlefield: no one who passed through Durban, on the way to Egypt and India, will forget the welcome.

It was best not to enquire too primly about the adventures of the troops, as they scrambled ashore after two celibate months. (It was often said that, after sixty days at sea, men were morally, if not legally, entitled to have sex with one another; and I remember one complaint was brought before me by an outraged guardsman who had been 'propositioned' by another. I was immensely shocked, myself, and at a loss what to do about it.) Now, we could go ashore, and meet the opposite sex. We did.

But not on our first morning, I marched the draft along the sea front, for a swim in the Indian Ocean. This loosened us all up. (Only when I swam out myself did I remember sharks; and I had a moment of utter panic when I found myself followed by a large black shape below and behind me. I was sprinting from my own shadow! This, I thought sourly to myself, only indicated my own state of mind, for I could not lay my fears, even in Durban.)

On this first, innocent day, Peter and I found a hotel in which we had lunch – a pleasant, fresh meal for a change – but did not venture much further. The other officers came back with lurid tales of local hospitality; so, next day, we thought that we might sample it. It was true. Girls sat in their cars along the wharf, asking if we would like a lift. 'Tarts!' we told each other, righteously (and perhaps they were.) But then a young man called to us from his car. Were we waiting for anyone?

His name was Raymond Briggs. We were soon told that his parents were waiting to see us, and – still a little suspiciously, for this was our first foreign landfall – we went along. Lunch was ready: Mrs Briggs had spent all morning on it, and had dispatched Raymond to collect a couple of officers: it was as random as that. Mister Briggs poured out beer; but when the meal began – roast beef, Yorkshire pudding, and a mound of fresh vegetables – we were plied with the local red wine and asked about conditions in the 'Old Country'. We were heroes, it seemed. Like everyone in South Africa, the Briggs family could not have enough news about the Blitz, about the defiance of Churchill after Dunkirk, about the privations of the people, and our opinion about the 'turn of the tide'. What did we think?

As we loosened up, we began to ask them about conditions in South

Africa, about which we were woefully ignorant. (It was a 'dominion' now, fiercely loyal – even the Afrikaans-speaking ex-Boers were friendly, it seemed. It is sad to record the change.) Mister Briggs proposed a ride in the car during the afternoon.

It was magic. On that sunny summer afternoon, there was no country to equal Natal, where everyone seemed contented. I saw no signs of racial tension, and the natives (we were allowed to call them that, in those days) seemed as pleased to see us as the whites. Mister Briggs muttered darkly, it is true, that nothing was as peaceful as it seemed: there were old Boers who still remembered their war with Britain forty years before, and there were legends of bitter wars against the Zulus, long before that. But no one could think bitterly on a day like this.

Flowering shrubs – jacaranda, flamboyant, bougainvillia – blossomed in the trim, green gardens, and there were fruit trees everywhere. Peter went crazy about the birds: I remember him pointing out a roller, but that was only one of hundreds. Then, as we went higher, the trees and shrubs gave way to what I imagined was *veldt* – rolling, grass-covered downs over which the cattle roamed and where the feeder-streams of the Umgeni River bit deep into the rounded hills. The air was like champagne.

We stopped for tea at 'Rob Roy', looking down on to the Valley of a Thousand Hills; and, far out to the west, at the line of the Berg beyond Pietermaritzburg, fifty – a hundred and fifty – miles away. One of the memories I have brought back from Africa is the sense of vast distance. Whereas, in England and the British Isles, the view is limited by haze, and a view of twenty miles only comes on fine days when showers threaten, there is no limit in Africa but the curvature of the earth.

My diary reads:

> 'We looked down 600 feet into the valley. It was short grass, and green. Through the middle wound a yellow track. All was deserted. Scattered like tiny dots were the huts of the Zulus who use the reserve . . . There were trees about two miles away, in a hollow, with outcrops of rock. The huts unfortunately were square, chiefly built of corrugated iron; but there were a few circular straw ones, which are the real thing . . . The real wonder was the formation. In the distance, the higher hills were flat-topped, shaved off horizontally with a sharp knife; but the valley was different. Crumple a large piece of foolscap into a tiny ball, then unroll it, and try to flatten it by pressing it on a pebbly beach; paint the result green and magnify a million times, and you will have the Valley of a Thousand Hills.'

We saw more of the Briggs family. But later, we began to mingle with the more aristocratic inhabitants: Justin McKurtan, for instance, and his remarkable uncle Douglas, who invited us to more than one luxurious meal at his home. Here we found several Coldstream officers on their way back to England from the Western Desert; and it seemed as though their wives had come out to meet them (or had they been evacuated from Egypt, that summer?) It was all very civilized, very upper-crust.

I partially regret going to live amongst the toffs, now. They even got me to another night-club, where I danced with a girl, in her early twenties, who had already divorced two husbands: quite unusual in those days. However, I preserved my virginity! I still had too many inhibitions.

It was a relief, in a way, to move on from Durban: interludes are only interludes, and we were shirking. We ran the gauntlet of a famous woman singer, whose war work was to sing to the troops in all the convoys as their ships cast off; and off we headed at last, into the Indian Ocean, on Sunday, 13 December.

It was said that the Mozambique Channel was patrolled by Japanese submarines, not Germans; but we must have dodged them, for soon we were getting into Equatorial waters once again. We were running out of patience, by now. Every broiling day was more of a burden than the one before: discipline was beginning to suffer. We officers could think of no novelties with which we could keep the men out of constant petty trouble.

I remember Christmas Day, in particular. Everyone, from the OC Troops down to the dimmest private, was drunk before noon, and there were rumours about of mutiny and mayhem. On the whole, our draft was relatively well-behaved: I was informed by Sergeant Harness early in the evening that there was a sing-song on the troops' mess-deck later on, to which Peter and I were invited; and when we arrived down below, in the stifling heat, we were made welcome, and afforded drinks which were impossible to refuse. My guess is that they were 'spiked' in some way.

We listened to the singing: the hardy annuals, the choruses like 'Sylveste,' for instance:

> 'It's my brother,
> Sylveste;
> He's a row of forty medals on his chest:
> (*Big chest!*)
> It takes all the army and the navy
> To put the wind up
> Sylveste!'

There were many more barrack-room ballads, some dreary, others unprintable, and of course the old favourite:

> 'For I'm saying goodbye to them all,
> The long and the short and the tall.

You'll get no promotion this side of the ocean,
So cheer up, my lads, bless 'em all!'

Then, to my astonishment, my own quiet soldier-servant, Willie Mitchell, was called upon. He had dug up a banjo from somewhere (did he strum it himself?) and sang a recent, but outdated, song of George Formby, in his broad Lancashire accent:

'Imagine me in t' Maginot Line,
Sitting on a mine in t' Maginot Line.
Now it's turned out nice again,
The army life is fine.
'Itler can't 'urt us a lot.
'Is secret weapon's tommy-rot.
You oughter see what t' sergeant's got! –
Down in t' Maginot Line.'

Sergeant Harness, master of the revels, his great sweaty face like a full moon, then turned on Peter and me, and demanded a contribution. We had to respond. I might have expected this! I probably came up with a couple of revolting limericks – for I was (and still am) quite incapable of song – and Peter had something, I forget what. So ended our Christmas. I was glad it was over.

On Boxing Day, we passed close in to an unidentified island, just off Cape Guadafui. Could it be Socotra, I wondered? It looked very lush and lovely from the ship; but I had to remind myself that it probably harboured all the deadly tropical animals and insects that I had ever heard of.

Then, on the following morning, we were in Aden.

We were allowed ashore for a few hours; but Aden was not like Durban (maybe there was another, more westernised part of the town which we did not discover) and all was rock and sand, noise and smell. We were marched down to a bathing beach, but a swim gave us little pleasure: the shark-net prevented us from wading out beyond our knees, and all within it was warm and dirty. Peter and I found tea in some fly-blown cafe; but we were almost relieved to get back on board.

We passed the island of Perim, and then into the last stretch, up the Red Sea, and toward our destiny.

It was New Year's Eve, and I had meant to go to bed early, for there were busy days ahead. But Peter invited in a couple of 'line mob' officers, filled them with liquor, and went on to discuss religion once again. He repeated his insistence on the 'leap of faith,' I remember; but, this time, he said that a single leap was not enough. There are obstacles and doubts

48

arising all the time in the path of the Christian, and new leaps to make continually.

What was I letting myself in for, I wondered? This Christian life sounded far from pleasant! But the alcohol was.

When the others had gone, Peter and I talked again on another recurring subject, sex. Looking back on it now, I am not sure that Peter knew much more about it than I did; but at least we found the subject intriguing. By about three o'clock in the morning, we were fighting one another, somewhat drunkenly, on the cabin floor: of such unlikely ingredients are permanent friendships formed.

So we arrived at Suez, rather the worse for wear, on Sunday morning, 3 January 1943. I had learned a good deal on the troopship, and now felt a little more confident: perhaps I might be able to cope, after all, with this new life which was just about to begin. We had all come a long way to find out.

II
TUNISIA

7

THE THIRD BATTALION

We landed at Suez, and realized that the whole course of the war had changed.

It was not only that we were now in a new, strange country, after our long voyage; no longer spectators, but participants, even though it was to take a couple of months before we were to meet the enemy face to face. We were joining a force which had been in action for over two years, and which was beginning to look upon itself as a fighting elite – as indeed it was. We had heard the news of El Alamein whilst we were in the North Atlantic, and had been listening ever since to tales of unbelievable advances across the desert. It seemed now that the Eighth Army was unstoppable; and that the cunning Desert Fox, Rommel, was on the run at last.

But, in addition, we began to realize that the whole tide of war was turning in our favour. 'Operation Torch', the landings of British and American troops in Algeria, had taken place while we were at sea; and though the First Army was meeting determined opposition, it was at least easier to keep supplied. Our own Second Battalion was involved, we heard: there were rumours to come through soon that there had already been one heavy engagement. Supplies, presumably American for the most part, were pouring in to Algiers, as we could see they were pouring into Suez. A new air of optimism greeted us as we came ashore.

Further afield, there were stories of desperate fighting between the enormous armies of Germany and Russia. Had the German advance been finally halted at Stalingrad? It sounded like it.

And had the Japanese army had been halted on the Indian frontier? It was too early to be sure. There were accounts seeping through, also, of at least two great naval encounters in the South Pacific. But, to be frank, we failed as yet to appreciate any more than our parochial successes in the Western Desert; nor were we yet confident that this new General in charge of the Eighth Army would succeed in getting further into Tripolitania than his predecessors. There seemed to be an unidentifiable obstacle about a hundred miles beyond Benghazi, which we had already entered, twice. Would this 'Monty' break the hoodoo?

We were ferried ashore, and were carried in trucks to Geniefa, the enormous transit camp on the edge of the Great Bitter Lake. We pulled ourselves together, to glimpse mile upon mile of tents. But we found the officer who strolled across to meet us far more magical than anything else in Africa.

Buster Luard was a major, seconded from the Third Battalion with instructions to meet and forward the various Coldstream drafts which were now expected. In his early thirties, I suppose, he had been in the Battalion when the war broke out, and was due for a home posting soon. Clearly, the desert held no terrors for him now: even his hair was sandy! His trim moustache enhanced a face which, I felt, had seen it all: the sand, the sandstorms, the heat and cold of the greatest desert of all, the terrors, the battles, wounds and death, and had emerged unruffled and triumphant. He was wearing the traditional garb of the desert: khaki shirt and tie, khaki jersey with epaulettes to carry the crown of his rank, and a brooch on his left breast with the ribbon of his Military Cross; corduroy trousers, suede desert boots, and the inevitable fly-whisk in contrasting red and black. How could I ever aspire to heights like that? How could I doubt the Eighth Army any longer? I hardly dared speak in the presence of such a master.

He led us to the Mess, and signed us in. He was talking calmly, quietly, about the Battalion, where it was and how soon we would move on; and we, I suppose, were asking for news of brother-officers we knew. We were like new boys around a prefect.

We spent about a fortnight in Geniefa. To anyone else, it would seem a period of utter boredom, so I must not describe every day in detail. But to me, it was a new life; and I remember all the details, even today. We went to Cairo on a day trip, I remember, and had two afternoons in Ismailia; but, most of the time, we were 'acclimatising', getting used to the sand – there was a vicious *khamsin* the first night – the food, the unaccustomed space after nearly three months of confinement, the new sights and – more particularly – the smells.

Then we were on our way to join the Third Battalion, just under Mount Hermon, about fifteen miles south-west of Damascus.

That journey deserves a saga for itself. Every sight was a fresh experience, at least for me; and when we changed trains at Haifa, on to the narrow-gauge mountain railway that took us up the valley of Esdraelon, into the mountains, then to a halt at a village at the southern end of the Sea of Galilee, and then up the gorge of the Yarmuk to Deraa, I recalled the exploits of T.E. Lawrence, my particular hero at that time, and could not write enough about it all. We reached Damascus about midnight, in the rain, slept badly in what must have been a transit camp, and were well below our best when the trucks – desert-coloured dull gold – dumped us in the Coldstream camp a few miles outside Qatana. We had arrived at last.

Here, I found myself in the company of real soldiers. My draft, who had all come from Harrow with me and whom I had looked on as my own, were dispersed in a twinkling, as Peter had warned me; and were mingled with the battle-hardened veterans of the desert. Many of these were regular soldiers. They had been in Palestine before the war began, trying to keep Jews and Arabs from killing one another; and had found that fighting against Italians, and then Germans in the Western Desert was a far easier business. They were now children of the desert, 'Desert Rats', who knew every sand-dune from Alexandria to Agedabia. They must have been some of the finest troops in the world.

My first impression, to be sure, was that they had grown a little slack. True, numbers were down: only about 180 had fought their way out of Tobruk that summer, and they had had to wait six months for the new drafts – ours amongst others – before they could begin to call themselves effective once again. I cannot say that we were welcomed with open arms, for all we could offer was smartness and 'training', which they did not want or need. (It was a little ludicrous that *I* should be an advertisement for smartness! – and 'training' had almost become an end in itself amongst the bored troops in England. I well remember an officer coming out to join us later, whilst we were resting after the Tunisian campaign. His first public statement was that our next campaign would do wonders for the training! As soon as we had worked out what on earth he was talking about, he was shipped back to England, to get back to it.)

But, after a day or two, I found myself basking in the pride that came of being with these men. I saw quickly that this was an exclusive club, supremely confident of its skills. Not a few of the guardsmen sported the Palestine Medal; and there were Military Medals to be seen, as well. Both drill-sergeants, Joel and Masterman, had the MM. My old fears and prejudices about drill-sergeants were immediately laid.

Then there were the senior officers, the majors and the captains now in line to command companies. I hardly dared call them by their Christian names in the Mess. Though each had his own distinct personality, they all seemed to me to have a great deal in common: they shone with an unshakeable confidence in their own military expertise. They tended even to look rather alike – tall, lean, beautifully groomed, moustaches cut to a hundredth of an inch, outwardly slow and somewhat languid but completely in control of any situation, on the battlefield or elsewhere.

Aristocrats, in the sense of lineage, they probably were, but they were now aristocrats also of the British army, the product of a war they had not sought but now knew more about than anybody.

They would talk reminiscently with one another about the 'Msus Stakes', Knightsbridge and Tobruk, as though they had been social occasions – which, in a way, they had been.

The arrival of our draft, and of a second a few days later, signalled that the exile of the Battalion was coming to an end. The senior officers were very kind to us; but they had to tutor us quickly into the mysteries of war in the Desert. They worked us hard.

We discovered that we were a 'motor battalion' (as distinct from a battalion of motorized infantry, carried from one area to another by centrally-organized transport.) A motor battalion should have its own transport, and plenty of it: three fifteen-hundredweight trucks for each platoon, and a jeep for the platoon commander. Ours was to be one of the battalions of a motor brigade, the 201st Guards Brigade, which included the 2nd Scots and the 6th Grenadiers.

A motor brigade's proper function was to support an armoured division, as it thrust its way across the desert: 'close-support' troops, men to occupy the ground won by the armour. The accepted wisdom was that tanks could take ground, but could not hold it, for their function was, and is, movement, not defence. 'Soft' vehicles were required, though, in close support, carrying enough troops to hold the ground taken, till the main bulk of infantry arrived to consolidate. We were closer to the armour than to the infantry proper – indeed, we regarded ourselves still as 'Desert Rats' (members of the Seventh Armoured Division) for we had been under divisional command during the previous campaign; but now we had become independent.

As far as I know, motor brigades were peculiar to the Eighth Army, and did not survive the desert campaign. I can see why, I think. When we arrived in Italy, for instance, the long advances of the armoured divisions were no longer practicable; and, even in the Tunisian campaign, motor units were, all too often, used for operations for which they were not altogether suited.

We had to be extremely mobile, then: a problem for me, as I had not yet learned to drive! We also had to be able to keep in touch with one another by radio (still called wireless, by the way.) Under Mount Hermon, we were to take part in several exercises with borrowed 'No. 18' sets which, even then, I utterly despised. Were these really the best our boffins could produce for us?

I remember taking some of the old veterans on a route march through the local villages. The wintry countryside captivated me: red as Devon, the grass a brilliant green, the local Arabs cheerful, the villages untidy, with a half-finished look which only Arabs seem to achieve. The air which whistled down from Hermon (not a 'little hill' at all, by the way, but 9,000 feet high) carried a message to go farther and faster, to the snow-line and beyond. But I had a somewhat negative reaction from the men. When we got back to camp, Michael told me that they had put in a complaint: they were not used to marching, he said. In the desert they used transport to travel a hundred yards, and were almost inseparable from their vehicles.

As a kind of compensation, he drove me out that evening, as the sun sank over Hermon, on a short reconnaissance; and I thought that I had never seen anything to match it. Was his solicitude merely an illustration of his gift for leadership? I began to think that there was a deeper friendship forming. It flourished. Perhaps he appreciated my enthusiasm, my need to learn, my longing to be a good officer, like him.

We had two or three evening excursions into Damascus, part business, part pleasure. The business was to buy clothing and other necessaries, for it was becoming clearer every day that we were once again bound for the Western Desert (there had been rumours, for instance, that we were on our way to invade Turkey, or Iran, or to drive through both to join up with the Russians.) I bought a 'Hebron Coat', for instance, made from the skins of three whole sheep. We all had them – and needed them in the desert, where it was incredibly cold at night – and we also bought desert boots, still fairly new in the Middle East, but immensely comfortable and, I later discovered, very nearly silent when moving over rock and sand.

The pleasure was to eat and drink in the 'Orient Palace' hotel, to buy presents in the luxury shops, and to explore the city. The Great Mosque was a delight to me, as were the intricate covered malls of the Souk. Peter took me to walk along the street called 'Straight'; and kept on peering over parapets looking for Abana and Pharphar, the Biblical rivers of Damascus. They meant little to me, alas.

Then it was time to go.

The whole brigade was to move from South-Western Syria to meet up with the main body of the Eighth Army, near Tripoli.

An advance party was to drive ahead, to make contact with the leading formations; and, to my delight, I was told that I was to go with it. Michael, I am sure, had had a hand in it, for he had been chosen to go as second-in-command to Dickie Pembroke (who was, in turn, second-in-command of the Battalion.) One officer was chosen from each company and, to my even greater delight, Peter was picked to represent his company, as was a sprinkling of other recently-arrived young officers. I knew them all. This, then, was to be a small adventure on a magnificent scale: we were to drive for two thousand miles, and would stop only when we 'reached the front'.

Just before we were due to go, the weather broke. We awoke on the penultimate morning to find ourselves snowbound.

Each hut was fairly large, but had only a single sheet of corrugated iron to keep us from the elements (A Nissen hut had two thicknesses and, more often than not, some insulation in between.) Cold, then, at the best of times, our camp had not been built to withstand snow, and almost collapsed under the weight of this fall. The snow dissolved, water seeped through on to us, then froze on the floor. It would be good to get away, I thought.

We had a final, hilarious evening in Damascus, with Michael driving the communal truck and nearly killing us all on the way back. Then the 'advance party' stood to, before dawn on 2 February, on the freezing snow; and we were off again on our travels.

What a fortnight it had been! Michael had taken me under his wing, and made everything easy for me. As we drove off together, sliding up the small incline out of the isolated camp, I tried to tell Michael how much his tutorship had meant to me.

8

THE ADVANCE PARTY

Golly, it was cold! Michael skidded our truck over the icy track which led to the main road at Qatana, but it was not much better when we reached it. Dawn came; and before we reached Kuneitra the sun was lighting the upper slopes of Hermon, over to the right, 'cold rose-pink with purple shadows', I wrote in my diary that night. It was a fitting send-off, Michael remarked.

Then we were over the edge of the escarpment, and dropping down into the northern extremity of the Rift Valley, 'wet, below the snowline, smelling of vegetation'. On our right, Lake Huleh looked like a frosted mirror, whilst on our left, immeasurably distant, deep and tiny, Galilee shone like a sapphire. The main road, used by countless armies before us, took us down to the lake past the Mount of the Sermon; then out and up again at Tiberias, over the next hills, and down to the valley of Esdraelon. We must have passed Afula, then Megiddo, for we were to spend that first night at Tulkarm.

Paul Bowman, who was engaged to the Governor's daughter, Araminta McMichael, had obtained prior permission to spend that night in Jerusalem; and had asked if Peter, who was sharing his truck, could go too. Rather hesitant, I asked if I could go with them, and Michael agreed; but all the other young officers then asked if they could, too. We had to toss for it; and I, to my grief, drew the short straw. I had to wait forty years for my next opportunity! However, the junior officers of the Scots and Grenadiers had each to leave an officer behind; and we had an uneventful drive the following day, through Lydda and Beersheba to our next leaguer at Asluj, on the edge of the Negev, where the Jerusalem party rejoined us.

We were sleeping in the open, now, our bed-rolls laid out for us on our camp beds. It was cold, but not unbearable. With my new Hebron Coat on the top of all the bedding, the difficulty was to get up in the morning! Shaving in pyjamas – usually only pyjama bottoms – was no joke, at the beginning of February. From then on, to sleep under a roof was a rare luxury.

'But' I wrote, 'we felt very important really, as if we were in a real battle – or almost. For of course we nearly are. In ten days' time we may well be on the other side of Tripoli. It's funny' I added, 'how little one thinks of it. I don't feel frightened, or even upset in any way – just excited at the thought of going into action at last, and before everyone else in the Battalion. Life has become very simple, once again, just as it did on the day we went to sea.'

I was with Peter that day. At that time, I had not even properly learned how to drive – this came later, and rather suddenly – and I suppose that Michael wanted to be sure that we all knew one another. He should have been under no illusion about Peter and me, for we had been sharing a cabin on the troopship, and had been together in the Sixth Battalion for a year before that; but, like a good officer, he may also have wanted to get to know one of the other young officers himself. So off we drove, across the Sinai desert; and, as we sped along, we sang till our voices cracked, dance tunes, hymns, old favourites, anything else we could think of, over mile after mile of desert unending, sand and rock, with occasional black mountains towering over them, and the road stretching ahead in a dark, blue, crazy line through them, for miles ahead.

We came down to the Canal at about one o'clock, crossed it at Ismailia, leaguering there for the night; then, on the following day – with Michael again, this time – along the Sweet Water Canal, past Tel el Kebir, till we reached the outskirts of Cairo. There was shopping to be done there, and we were busy in the city till dark, when Peter and I saw a film and had a last bath, before drinks at Shepheards, dinner at the 'Auberge de Turf' and a dangerous drive out to find our transport again at Mena. We slept in the open once again. We were getting acclimatised by now.

Peter met Tim Sainthill there, the hero of Tobruk; and they went off for a round of golf. With Peter Gibbs of the Scots Guards, I 'did' the Pyramids clambering to the top of the Great Pyramid, and looking rather blankly at the Sphinx. There were one or two outstanding items of shopping in Cairo; then we dined together at Mena House, and were off before dawn next day.

The road to Alexandria is straight, along the western edge of the Delta; and by late morning we could see in the distance the roofs and minarets of the city, over what I presumed to be Lake Maryut. It was known very well by the old soldiers with us – they liked it far more than Cairo – and I have little doubt that the veterans in the backs of the trucks had stories to tell the new arrivals. But we never went there. About three miles out to the west of the city, the road forked: Alexandria to the right, but, to the left, the signpost read 'To the Western Desert'. We forked left.

It was a symbolic moment to me, and probably to us all. We were on our own now. I still remember, after fifty years, the spiritual thrill of turning off into the desert.

What has to be remembered is that, till that time, this was the only area in which we seemed able to wage successful war. We had had enough of the 'Dunkirk Spirit' in England. It was not only a couple of years out of date; but, splendid though it had been, no doubt, there was no blinking the fact that, by any military criterion, it had been a monumental defeat. Most of our soldiers had fled home to Britain with their tails between their legs, leaving their rifles behind for the Germans to collect as souvenirs. And this was not all. In North Africa, after a couple of years of careering wildly forward and backward across the desert, it really seemed that the campaign was near its end, and that we could win. We had been brought out of England to drive the enemy out of Africa, for good.

But there was more to it than that. Leaving behind us the cities of the plain, the remnant of the decadent civilization of Egypt, we knew that we were also abandoning the trappings of our old lives. I, for one, could at last afford to laugh about my overdraft. There was no further need to concern myself with the tailoring of my uniform, or even the cut of my hair. The old priorities had gone.

So now there was no need to keep up appearances – to go only to the best restaurants, to travel in a taxi, never in a bus, to take out girls only of the proper social standing – for there were no restaurants, no transport but the trucks were for using and living in, no girls at all. It may have been monastic, but at least we were all equal in the face of the enemy. But *would* I be equal, I wondered, when the shooting began? All my thousand fears were distilled down into one. I must beware lest this over-master me.

Dickie Pembroke, the major in command of the advance party, I never came to know well. I did not know if he had been with the Battalion for long, but I assumed that he was a veteran. Here, I now think that I was wrong: till recently, I think that he had been in Kenya, and that he rejoined the regiment by coming to the Battalion. His piercing eyes looked out into the middle distance, and I imagined that he was withdrawn because it was the lot of leaders not to fraternise too closely. But now, I wonder if he was shy and lonely. If he had only arrived recently, then this would have been his first independent assignment, and he may well not have seen the desert before. The party, made up from a deliberate mix of old and new, desert veterans and new arrivals, could not have been easy to control, and he may have thought it best to let them cope with one another. He had the commanders of the two other advance parties, and they could compare notes with one another, if they wished.

Michael Brodrick, then a lieutenant, I think, but soon to be a captain, was the officer who made the immediate decisions, and it was to him that we all brought our problems. As second-in-command of my own company, No.3, he kept a particular eye on me; and, more often than not, he drove our company truck, with me beside him in the cab; with the driver, and our two soldier-servants, lolling amid the blankets, food, water and petrol cans in the body of the truck.

Michael was a veteran, at least to me. I admired his MC as I admired everything else about him. Before long, this hovered little short of idolatry.

The impression of Michael which I shall always retain is that he was tall, mature, military-looking and confident. Now, I am none too sure that he was much taller than I was, though it is true that he held himself far better, and looked every inch an officer, even to his black moustache. But I am far from sure that he was a regular soldier. He may have had a regular commission in mind, of course, before the war began; but now, I am inclined to think that he was less than a couple of years older than I was – which could mean that he did not join up till the war had begun.

But by this time, he could be nothing else but a soldier. He was the infantry officer one dreams of, upstanding, alert, masterful, direct, with a hawk nose and piercing dark eyes. His clothes fitted him as though he had always worn them; and he affected all the sartorial idiosyncrasies of his seniors: desert boots, corduroy trousers, a light fawn shirt with epaulettes, and his stars of rank (we did not call them 'pips' as they were not like the quadrilateral buttons which the officers of other regiments affected, but stars, longer than they were broad, brass copies of our regimental cap badge) sometimes a khaki jersey, with sleeves, and the stars again on the epaulettes, a khaki regimental cap, and a black-and-red fly-whisk which, I think, was the unofficial badge of an officer who had already served for a spell in the desert. We young officers would never have dared to carry them; but the field officers did, no matter if there were flies to whisk away or not. To me, Michael was the most handsome officer I had ever seen. I was deeply flattered by his attention.

He thought only of the war, the desert, the regiment. It may be that my own wants – my need to be on equal terms with my brother-officers, and then to justify myself in action against the enemy – communicated themselves to him, for he looked upon me as his personal pupil and invested me with all the responsibility he could. I hope that he felt in the end that his labours had been worth-while! But more of him, later: he brought me into desert ways.

The most forceful and adaptable of the young officers was Paul Bowman. He was an Old Etonian (Michael had been to Winchester, but they seemed to know each other well) and had been one of the dozen cadets with me at Sandhurst. He was the man to whom we left any decisions we felt too lazy to make ourselves – haggling with the occasional Arabs (who came over the sand-dunes whenever the convoy stopped, trying either to buy or to sell) and chatting with the few military men we met, camp commandants, lone drivers of stray vehicles, the floating population of the desert road. I envied Paul his easy nonchalance, his readiness to grease the wheels of our westward progress, his continual good humour. He was seriously wounded in our first big battle, and I lost sight of him after that. (I believe that he eventually returned to the Battalion in Italy, survived the war, and now lives in Australia.)

Then there were Peter Daubeny and John Hamilton. Oddly, my diary of this period does not mention them much, though I knew them well enough. Michael Mitchell, of course, I knew better: we had both been in the Holding Battalion, thence to the Sixth Battalion and the troopship too, and I had always found him good company. In fact we were *all* good company, and it was a real joy to be together.

I have left Peter Wyld till last, for I felt closer to him than to anybody else. We had been in the Sixth Battalion together, of course, though our paths had not crossed much; and it was only when we shared the cabin on the troopship that we came to know each other well. It is not too much to suggest that he altered my life – as may appear later in this chronicle – for he was a friend who really seemed to appreciate my company. I had wondered sometimes – in Durban, for instance – if I were becoming too dependent on him altogether, for I would hardly leave him alone; and, every now and then, there would be days when, for one reason or another, we would hardly be on speaking terms. I would feel that he was deserting me: he knew so many people, had so many interests. But he always came back. He still does.

Off we went, then, into the desert country of Western Egypt, never, I thought, to return. (This may appear gloomy, but, surprisingly, it did not seem to matter as much as it had: I think it was because I had at last found friends.) I found this journey along the coastal road an odyssey of vast interest, for we had a running commentary on the various campaigns from men who had fought in them; and we were travelling in the wake of others we were soon to overtake. We saw the Alamein battlefield only three months after the battle had taken place (not much more than an hour's journey from the signpost – I had no idea that the Germans had come so close) and we looked over row after row of burnt-out tanks, some still stinking of human putrefaction. We spent a night at Mersa Matruh, whence the first British advance had been launched in the Autumn of 1940, Sidi Barrani (the site of our first successful battle, now probably forgotten) then the campaigning grounds of 1941, through Buq Buq to the frontier wire ('so near and yet Sofarfi!') with the steep hill to our left to Hellfire Pass. Then, in Cyrenaica, we passed the site of the tank battle at Sidi Rezegh, now reverting to desert once again.

The old soldiers were much moved by their return to Tobruk. This was scarcely surprising: they had been members of the only organized unit to fight its way out of that disaster, not much more than six months before. Michael waxed eloquent.

'It's looking a little brighter, now,' he said cheerfully to Drill Sergeant Masterman. 'Remember the smoke-cloud over the port? The Germans came in from the south-east, and it was absolute shambles for the day. We didn't get any messages, here on the south-west perimeter, though there was a good deal of ironmongery flying about. Our problem was that we didn't know the way out through the minefield, otherwise we'd have driven off before. Luckily, we picked up a stray Gunner Officer who said he knew how to get through. He did, too. Once we were through, we just drove through the desert, in another direction, and the Germans didn't bomb us because they probably thought that it was one of their own convoys. Exciting, though.'

And so on, along the coastal road through Gazala and Derna, then up the escarpment and across country – greener and better watered than the previous section – till we found ourselves dropping down again, into Benghazi.

In my diary, I did not give Benghazi very high marks. 'It's a horrible place,' I wrote, 'very flat and swampy, with no whole buildings and everything in a frightful mess. No places of amusement at all (what was I expecting – a cinema?) not even a NAAFI. Our transit camp is reputedly an old brothel. The food hasn't been too hot, and the water undrinkable.' I was asking rather a lot of a town which had just fallen into our hands – but I was very weary after nearly a fortnight on the road. The small chores of the full day we spent there, collecting stores, food and petrol, sent me over the edge, somehow, and I took it out on Peter whilst I drank far more than I should.

'I can't think why I'm here at all,' I moaned miserably. 'Did you see those trunks and crates going into the trooper, all marked "Not Wanted on Voyage"? I felt just like one of them, and I feel just like that, now. Who the hell wants me? I'm not going to make a pennyworth of difference to the war, and yet people are spending lots of money getting me to it. Why? None of you seem to want me, either. I might just as well have stayed at home.'

Peter had had to put up with a good deal of this already, but this was too much: perhaps alcohol was loosening his tongue, too.

'The trouble with you, Chris,' he burst out, 'is that you are your own worst enemy. It's not that the rest of us are finding you inadequate. You don't seem to realize that you are generally given the messy jobs because you are reckoned to be the officer most capable of carrying them out. The rest of us let you do them because you ask for them. You are over-conscientious. You're too impetuous, and simply can't relax. You seem to think that you have to *prove* something or other, both to the rest of us and to yourself.

'And, of course, we all take you for a ride. If you are willing to do this extra work, why should *we* have to bother? Why not wait, next time, till you are told? You're making us all feel guilty.'

'Damn it all. Let's have a drink.' I passed out, that night, for the first time in my life. But I remember that earlier part. In an odd way, it seemed to cheer me.

I was in Michael's truck the following day, feeling terrible; but I woke up and took notice when he began to talk about his adventures at Mersa Brega and Agedabia the previous year.

'We were on a patrol somewhere near the road,' he said. 'I've got a feeling that it was just about here. Yes! See that bush over there? That's where a German sentry peed on me!'

'Did you scrag him?'

'No, thanks. I wanted to go home to Mummy. It was only a recce patrol, you see, and it was important to get back with the information, without them knowing that we were around.'

'But what *was* the information? Just that Germans can pee?' (Yes, I *was* feeling better.)

'Idiot!'

So we drove on to El Agheila; then Marble Arch, then Sultan, Sirte and Buerat, leaguering by the roadside whenever night came; and on to Misurata, which we reached on the evening of 16 February. We found an abandoned barracks, and spent a night under a roof – rather to our relief, as we had been soaked through the night before. We spent a day here, on maintenance work; and, to my distress, lost Peter, who was carried off with appendicitis, without warning, just as we were getting within range of our destination.

The road, along this stretch, was in poor condition, partly perhaps because we were closing in on the leading troops by now. We were none too sure about minefields along the verges, and had to tread carefully when we walked off with our spades to relieve nature. We had enough food to get us to Tripoli now, but it was all out of tins and far from appetizing: corned beef hash, perhaps, potatoes from a tin (rather soapy) and tinned peas or beans.

What was the desert like, though?

The experts would say, of course, that this was scarcely desert at all. This long coastal strip had a great deal of variety: chiefly sandy along the Western Egyptian coast, more rocky along the escarpment of Cyrenaica, then cultivated in the 'bulge' around Cyrene, marshy and featureless around Benghazi and along the Gulf of Sirte. We were all aware of vegetation. In these winter months, there were flowers on both sand and rock: the seeds which the winds had blown there now had rain to germinate them. The upland areas could sustain hardy domestic animals like sheep and camels, and there were even olive groves in sheltered gullies. Elsewhere, bright flowers could be seen by the roadside, anemones and poppies amongst them. I thought the whole scene indescribably beautiful.

But this was February. Within a month or two, the fierce sun would have burned away all the greenery, and to the casual eye it would revert to desert once again.

Also, we were always conscious of vast tracts of real desert on our left. Not far in from this coastal belt, there would be nothing but bare rock and sand, stretching southward for nearly a thousand miles, with only the rare oasis to break the monotony. Once in fifty miles, there might be a camel caravan, I suppose; and even more rarely there might be a little, self-contained patrol of the Long Range Desert Group, probing ever westward to prepare our own way before us. Its officers were said to know the only route through the 'Sand Sea', a vast tract of moving dunes in Southern Cyrenaica. To us it was a million square miles of almost nothing at all.

When we came to the cultivated lands of Western Tripolitania we could no longer even pretend that we were in the desert. The coastal plain was fifty miles wide, well populated, with fields fenced with prickly pear, vicious dogs, and fly-infested children. To us, it was almost indecently fertile. The inhabitants would greet us with a *Saheeda*. Perhaps they would wonder, privately, if we were an easier touch than the Germans and Italians with whom they had previously done business. And there were Roman ruins, too. Two thousand years ago, this had been the granary of the Roman Empire, until, when that fell, the sand had been allowed to encroach.

The villages and little seaside towns were mostly in ruins – that is, until we outran the limit of previous campaigns, to and fro across the desert. In Tripolitania, west of El Agheila, there had been little fighting, except at the Wadi Zem Zem, and there were fewer signs of war. Even so, the dreary tale of ruined houses did not altogether cease; and the edges of the desert road were still speckled with abandoned, burnt-out vehicles. I suppose that this is the trade mark of running warfare. At the best of times, armies are not regarded as environmentally friendly! Let us hope that there were units coming up behind us to clear away the mess.

When we reached Tripoli, we found that we had now caught up with destruction, once again. Experts were working around the clock to move the wrecks from the harbour, and to clear warehouse space; for Tripoli was to become the advance base for the final 'squeeze' on Tunis; and German bombers were over us each night, making a creditable effort to prevent it. We spent our first night in a large hotel which our army had commandeered a week or two earlier. The Italian waiters were obsequious and the food good. We even had hot baths, an unbelievable luxury, and sank into comfortable beds, to lose consciousness in no time. But there was the inevitable air raid. When we got down to breakfast next morning, we found that the ground floor was a ruin: a stick of bombs had straddled the hotel, doing more damage at ground-floor level than upstairs; just as well, for we had all slept through it.

It now remained to travel to the 'front'. No one seemed quite to know where it was; and we were ordered to continue our journey along the road till we reached our forward troops – by now over the frontier and, it seemed, crossing a patch of desert around Ben Gardane.

In our turn, we reached Ben Gardane, but found no troops there. We eventually found them within a few miles of Medenine – perhaps a couple of hundred miles west of Tripoli – and made contact with a brigadier commanding three battalions of the Queen's Regiment, the spearhead of our advance. The enemy, we were told, had withdrawn to the Mareth Line, and was expected to make a stand there.

9

First encounters

I finished my diary at Misurata. It was meant to be the first volume, covering the 'Journey to a War', for I could foresee that the next would have action-packed descriptions of hand-to-hand fighting – far more readable, if more frightening, than the juvenile nonsense I had been writing so far. I did in fact begin a second volume but, alas, it came to an untimely, rather shameful death soon after, and caused me no little worry. From now on, dates and sequences are impossible to verify. But, on the whole, I still remember this time vividly enough to be reasonably accurate – even to the conversations, the sights, and the misgivings which came thick and fast during the next month or two.

After that night in Tripoli, then, we came up to the sharp end of the army's advance a day later: let me guess that it was 20 or 21 February. We were not in the Medenine area for more than two or three days – this is where my celebrated lone walk towards Tunis took place – and we hurried back to present a report to the Commanding Officer, who had been leading the rest of the Battalion up the desert road behind us, and had now reached Tripoli. The advance guard was absorbed into the main body of the Battalion. We were all ordered up to the front a couple of days later.

I met my Company Commander, Desmond Holmes, for the first time (he had been away on a course during my time in Syria) and liked what I saw. It was a slight relief to find that he had not the studied sophistication of the other senior officers, though he had been with the Battalion for a long time, and had plenty of desert experience. His sandy hair, disorganized eyebrows and untended moustache went to my heart; and his unexpected, abrupt turns of phrase and his wild look had earned him the name of 'Dizzy'. I was not sure that Michael, his second-in-command, and he would always see eye to eye, for Michael was a purist, a splendid soldier of a more orthodox aspect. But, as far as I know, they never disagreed, and 'Lucky No. 3' was a cheerful company to be in. Other young officers were less fortunate, I thought. One company commander ordered all his officers to grow moustaches, for instance.

The author in North
Africa.

Colonel Sir Terence Falkiner commanded the Battalion. He had been
in charge whilst I was in Syria but, to Battalion eyes, he was something
of a 'new boy', and had yet to prove himself. He had seen no more active
service than I had. Let me invent (if it did not actually take place, though
I think it must have done) a 'conference' of all officers, leaguered up in
the olive groves on the outskirts of Tripoli, the day before we moved up
to face the *Afrika Korps* in the Mareth Line.

There was a 'flap' on, and it was up to us to find a solution.

He must have begun, in the robust style that was soon to become
familiar, with the general situation: 'These bloody Americans haven't a
clue. They landed at Algiers with our First Army, and were allotted the
southern sector, on the border between Algeria and Tunisia, whilst
the First Army drove straight along the coast towards Bizerta and Tunis.
The First Army have got stuck. I don't know why: hilly country and bad

Lt.-Col. Sir Terence
Falkiner, Bt.

weather, I expect. So our friend Rommel withdrew two *Panzer* divisions, leaving his infantry to hold the First Army in the North and the Eighth Army in the Mareth Line; then, without any warning, landed on the wretched Americans and drove them out of Tunisia altogether. There's a place called Kasserine on the western border, somewhere, and as far as I know the Americans are still running all the way back to America.

'Now, the First Army is moving south to counter-attack, as it stands to reason that the Germans are quite dangerously exposed on their right flank. Also, this gives us a chance, on this side, to penetrate the Mareth Line, while the *Panzer* divisions are having a holiday out to the west. We'll probably be too late – Rommel has the advantage of interior lines – but at least we'll take the pressure off the wretched Yanks. That's the immediate intention.

'Our Brigade is to go up to the front, tomorrow, together with some other odds and sods. We are to dig in next to the Queen's Regiment, who have had a brigade with the Seventh Armoured Division for some time. So we become 'Desert Rats' again.

'Then there's the whole of the New Zealand Division coming up the road behind us. At the moment, the idea is that we all face west, more or less in line, ourselves and the rest of Seventh Armoured on the right, somewhere near this Tadjera Khir feature you will see on your maps, when they've been distributed. (Except for that and the main road, there isn't very much else on the map at all, between Medenine and the Matmata Hills, so you won't get lost among the skyscrapers.) Then the Kiwis will fit in on our left; and there are other units said to be coming up to the left of them again, probably getting ready to see if there's a

The Officers of the 3rd Battalion. Tripoli, 1943.

Back Row: Lt. E.R. Nares, Captain H.T.H. Snowden, Lt. A.P. Harbord-Hamond, Lt. M. Kinchin-Smith, Lt. N.D.T. Gardner, Lt. S.F.B. Codrington, Lt. P.H. Wyld, Lt. E.S. Skinner, Lt. D.A. Kerr-Wilson, Lt. C.H. Tuke, Lt. J. Longueville, Lt. F.W. Forgan (RAMC), Lt. Radcliffe (REME)

3rd Row: Capt. A.F. Davidson, Capt. D.E. Waddilove, Lt. the Hon. D.H. Joicey, Lt. R.O. Caroe, Lt. C.L. Loyd, Lt. J.H. Chaworth-Musters, Capt. the Rev. J.E.G. Quinn (RAChD), Lt. I.W.S. Moss, Lt. J.H.C. Venables, Lt. QM L. Rowlands, M.B.E.

2nd Row: Capt. R.J.M. Harley, Capt. J.G.C. Clark, Major R. Beck, Major D.A. Kennard, M.C., Major D.W.A.W. Forbes, M.C., Lt.-Col. Sir Terence Falkiner, Bt., Major I.W. Gore-Langton, Major J.M.G. Griffith-Jones, M.C., Major the Hon. M.V. Brodrick, M.C., Capt. A. Yates, Capt. H.K. Sweeting (Adjt.)

Front Row: Capt. A.R. McDougall, Capt. T.E.S. Egerton, Lt. D.J.R. Ker, Lt. C.H. Bulteel, Lt. R.E.W. Lumley, Lt. W.J. Straker-Smith, Capt. P.H.A. Bowman, Lt. G.A. Gidney

route around the south of the Mareth Line, when we finally go on to the offensive. But we have to deal with the German armour first. Our reconnaissance planes say that they are still busy, but they may suddenly turn back from chasing the Americans, and try to catch us as we're on our way up.

'All our gear is ready for us: just been unloaded. Chiefly vehicles, to bring us up to strength. Number 2 Company (anti-tank guns) must get a move on, for they must hand in their two-pounders straight away and get themselves the new six-pounders. If you don't know how they work, you'll have to find out quickly. The motor platoons each get three Dodge fifteen-hundredweight trucks, and a jeep for the platoon commanders. So more or less everybody will be a learner-driver tomorrow. Don't smash up these nice machines the Americans are giving us.'

And so on. We took notes busily. After the 'conference' it seemed important to sort out who was going to drive. Our 'regular' drivers were used to Bedford trucks, and did not fancy moving on to Dodges; but – more important – who was going to drive *our* jeep? I found Willie Mitchell.

'Which of us is going to drive this jeep thing?' I asked him.

'Not me, Sir. I dunno where to begin.'

'Well,' I said heavily, 'I suppose that it had better be me, then, to begin with. But you know very well that I don't know how to drive, either, and I've never even seen one of these jeep things. If you want to stay alive, you'd better start learning, yourself, as from yesterday afternoon.'

On this somewhat inauspicious note, together Willie Mitchell and I went to war.

Colonel Terence was right in thinking that we were not the only beginners on the road, that night. Things were not too bad as long as the daylight lasted, but this did not take us far (I have to assume that this was the evening of 26 February). It became more complicated when night fell. To begin with, as the Germans had not been in a hurry when they withdrew along this section – the pursuit had slackened when our army arrived in Tripoli – they had had ample time to lay mines along the roadside: a more than adequate reason for us to keep ourselves and our vehicles on the road itself. An additional handicap was that we were not allowed to use lights.

Every vehicle (not the jeeps) had been fitted with a low-power bulb under the tailboard, trained to shine dimly on its rear-wheel differential, which had been painted white. A good idea: but as the night wore on the drivers found it hard to keep fully alert to the range; and would find that they had driven their vehicle under the tailboard of the truck in front – crash! – or would lose the guiding light altogether, find themselves alone in the desert, accelerate wildly and find that the light they were pursuing had gone out – crash again! – and all this on the darkest night of the war. Of the nine hundred vehicles in our convoy, I was told later that two hundred had crashed that night.

To my astonishment, I was unscathed; and, from that epic drive onward, had more confidence in my driving skill. Willie, alas, took longer. I remember coming across him a week later, having driven our jeep on to the top of a pile of stones at the roadside, all four wheels in the air at once. I had to get four men to tip him off.

So we arrived at – or near – the village of Medenine, some fifty miles inside the frontier of Tunisia.

We bypassed this (it was said to be heavily booby-trapped) and drove on to the position we were to take up: this was just within sight of a smaller village, named Metameur, and astride a small dirt road which pointed westward, towards Toujane, in the distant hills.

I have already suggested that the days of the motor battalion were coming to an end. It was created as an adjunct to the armoured division in the desert, closely supporting the tanks as they sped across country, and providing, for them, a certain amount of 'backup' on ground which they had just overrun. A motor battalion, then, was not ideally suited for the formal defensive battle we were now expecting.

It possessed an enormous number of vehicles, to begin with, all of which needed some form of protection. More seriously, practically every man was a specialist of a kind. One entire company (No. 2, in our Battalion) held all the six-pounder anti-tank guns, for instance; whilst the 'Headquarters Company' was home for a host of other experts, on three-inch mortars, signals, vehicle repair and maintenance, and other arcane skills of which I was not even aware. Add to that a large 'B' Echelon', camped somewhere out of harm's way, but charged with supplying the 'front line' with nightly doses of food, water, and ammunition.

This meant that there were only three companies in each battalion to 'hold the line' (not that there was one, exactly) against an oncoming enemy. One of the three platoons in each company was its Carrier Platoon, often out on patrol and ceaselessly on the move. I would say, rather nastily, that its men spent more time on repairing the tracks of their vehicles than driving them.

This meant that only two 'motor platoons' in each company had actually to man the slit-trenches (which, in the Second World War, were dug instead of the old-fashioned continuous line of trenches.) These could be quite shallow ('shell-scrapes'), dug hurriedly and occupied only for minutes, perhaps, or deep enough to stand up in, with only a couple of heads protruding over the top. They were safe against anything but a direct hit from a shell. (One sergeant-major dug his trench so deep that

73

he could not see the battle at all; and, having dug below head-level, was unable to get out.) It was customary for two men to dig, and share, their slit trench. They would keep their bed-rolls and equipment there; but, if there was nothing happening, would sleep, eat, drink, and gossip with their mates, on the surface. Downwind, we would dig a communal latrine.

Looking back, I am none too sure that the platoon position I chose (or was it chosen for me?) was altogether satisfactory. We had a good field of fire – say three hundred yards of flattish ground, rocky desert country – then a *wadi* beyond that, in which I could see the tops of a few palm trees; and beyond that again, a long slope to a semi-skyline a mile away; and then, in the far distance, the unattainable blue peaks of the Matmata Hills, rocky, spiky, mysterious, perhaps twenty miles away in an arc around us, like a bow. Unromantic as ever, Desmond said that they reminded him of the under-jaw of a barracuda.

I thought that they were beautiful, especially when the shadows were long, at dawn and dusk; but, if we could see far, the enemy could also see us. The New Zealanders, when they settled in beside us (mine was the left hand platoon of the Brigade) were, I noted, more cunning. They sited their forward platoons on reverse slopes, out of sight of any prospective enemy; and they 'registered' the *wadi* before us as a target for their mortars. The Divisional Commander, General Freyburg, VC (and a great hero, to me) came over personally to make contact, and to introduce me to my next-door neighbour, his right-hand platoon commander.

We improved our own fortifications as the days went by. Our own anti-tank gunners liked the level ground in front of us, and set up several of their six-pounder guns there. There were fixed lines for our medium machine-guns. In addition, we set up an impenetrable barrier, in the form of a dummy minefield.

This last was quite easy; and, on the day, surprisingly effective. Instead of laying the mines, we merely hammered in some six-foot angle-irons, and connected them all with a single strand of barbed wire. No German tank commander could tell, from inside his tank, if these wired-in rectangles marked real minefields, or not; so he would turn off sideways to search for a gap. Brilliant! Just the kind of trick I enjoyed taking part in; but it ran me into trouble, for one night, when I was driving my jeep away in the velvety darkness, it decided to catch fire.

It is bad enough to have a car on fire at any time; but, here, I should be sworn at by the entire Eighth Army, as a good blaze could not fail to give away our position. True, at the moment, it was no more than a flicker . . . I had a look underneath, and found the small flames surrounding the transmission shaft – I had left the handbrake on, and did not realize till later that it gripped the universal coupling, not the wheels

– so, with my well-known presence of mind (I told everyone later) I blew it out. I did not know that the flames were actually lapping around the petrol tank, immediately underneath the driver's seat. More by luck than courage, honour was saved.

After a few days, Desmond called us to Company Headquarters.

'Well, the Germans are on their way,' he told us. 'Our shufti planes (reconnaissance) spotted some columns this morning, and we had better stand by. They might already have some patrols of their own out, looking for us, or coming out from the hills ahead to look for somewhere to off-load and deploy their armour.

'Now, Chris: listen. This is a fairly tall order, but I want you to go out tonight on a recce patrol, to see if you can find any Germans coming down on to the plain. It's an enormous area, I know, but you may be lucky. Leave here at sunset, cover as much ground as you can, don't get involved with anyone, and come back here before dawn.'

'Gosh, Desmond, it'll take me till dawn even to *get* there!'

'Maybe. Tell you what: George (Gidney,) can you take Chris and, say, three of his soldiers out into the desert, this evening? Find a place to drop them: somewhere he'll be able to recognize on the way back, and some-where you can recognize yourself. I can't afford to leave you out all night, as well as Chris.'

So it was arranged. George and I both had maps, almost blank; but it did seem that we could start westward, along the road to Toujane till, about ten miles out, it appeared to cross another track, running from north-east to south-west. George, not keen on driving along roads, which might be mined, said that he would take us, across country, to a spot near, but not *on*, the 'crossroads'.

From there, I intended to walk on, westwards, into the foothills, then to turn left under them and explore whatever exits there might be. The arc, such as it was, bent a little, so that, by the end of the night, I should be walking eastward, till I found the diagonal road which would lead me back to the crossroads – or rather to the rendezvous with George and his carriers. There would be about twenty miles of walking, if we met no obstacles, nor any Germans.

We set off before dark, the carriers raising the usual dustcloud. I wondered if there were any Germans watching us from the hills. Well, it was my job to find out.

George dumped us, as arranged. We both felt fairly confident that we could find the place again.

'For goodness' sake, be back here before dawn,' he insisted, as we parted. 'If you're late, you'll just have to walk.' Rather shaken, we moved off into the desert, wondering if we would ever see him again: west, toward the hills, visible in the light of the halfmoon (but that would set, during the night.) It was a strange, not unpleasant feeling, walking over the desert sand, ten miles ahead of anyone. We made no sound.

After a few minutes, we came across the lateral road up from the south-west, along which we hoped to return. It was no more than a track, of course: a stony base, with blown sand over it, scored with the tyre marks of vehicles: whose? I put my foot into a softer patch, stumbled, then saw that it was circular, about eighteen inches across: a mine.

This needed savage thinking. I came to the tentative conclusion that it was German, but that the tyre marks were British: our own reconnais-sance vehicles might well have been out here, during the day, and a crafty German had crept up, after dark, to lay a Teller mine, which would blow it up the following day. What should *this* conscientious British officer do now? Should he ignore this new phenomenon, and leave it to someone else to discover the hard way? I had a lot of other things to do that night.

The trouble was that I knew so little about German mines. On the way up, Michael had told me something about them: the 'S-mine' (to be met with, later) and the Teller, a green double soup-plate nearly a foot across, which should not explode under a pressure of less than three hundred pounds. This must be one. In a way, it was quite easy to disarm, for all that was necessary was to move the switch over at the top, rather like the switch of a standard lamp. But there was a catch in it: the mine could be booby-trapped.

I dredged my memory to recall what Michael had said. The trick was to find a protruding arm – in fact, another detonator – screwed into the side of the mine and attached to a large stone, say, with a length of string. If there were no detonator inserted, there would be a small hole in the circumference of the mine, and all would be well. But wait a minute. I had forgotten something.

Yes: there was yet another recess, somewhere underneath the body of the mine. There could be a detonator there, too. It could be attached to a stone, or, possibly, to another Teller mine below.

I sent my three companions off to shelter behind a pile of stones, and got to work. It was easy enough to scrape the sand off the surface, and to expose the mine: yes, a Teller. I found the central 'switch' and, sick with fright, pushed it over.

Breathing rapidly, I then tried to dig away at the circumference with my hands; only to find that the sand kept running back. This was going to take hours, I thought. It did. Eventually, I felt fairly sure that there was no detonator at the side. Now for the bottom.

The sweat was running down my arms so much that I could use it to build a tunnel underneath the mine, kept firm by damp dough. I felt around underneath, despairingly, while the sand poured in again over the original hole, and the minutes fled by. I began to feel sure that no German would be likely to booby-trap a single Teller mine in the middle of the desert, but I did not want to be the person to find that I had been wrong . . .

One quick pull decided the matter. We left the Teller mine on the heap of rubble beside the road; and went on to do what we had come for. It took me some time to regain my equilibrium; but at least I was still in one piece.

I have gone into unnecessary detail about this little incident, chiefly because it was, in a way, the first test I had had to undergo. It is, perhaps, worth adding that, as we passed the spot on our return journey, the mine was not there. Had the Germans put it back again during the night? I did not try to find out. And when? The uncomfortable thought came to me later that the man who had 'planted' the mine had been hiding, close by, and had watched me take it out, only to plant it back again as soon as we had moved off. The desert can *seem* deserted; but it is not always empty.

After miles and hours of walking through the silence, we came to the edge of the plain, and turned to our left – south – under the steep escarpment. Does my memory play me tricks, or did we cross a railway line? I might have been a little light-headed by this time, for who in his senses would go to the trouble of building a railway-track in the middle of the desert? It seemed to go from nowhere to nowhere, and to have no conceivable purpose.

As the line of hills began to curve eastward, I decided that there was still time enough to scramble up into them: we would be more likely to find observation posts on the higher ground, with German troops looking through their field-glasses at the dustclouds swirling round our British vehicles. We had to step up our own pace, though. Perhaps we were becoming a little careless.

I stopped abruptly. Willy Mitchell, just behind, cannoned into me. About fifty yards ahead, somebody had coughed.

He went on coughing. It was not a wild goat, then. We crept off, right-handed, into the hill, for I had to locate him precisely, and see what he was up to. He *might* be a shepherd; but it was far more likely that he was a German, doing exactly what we had come to find out. We tripped over a length of signal cable. This confirmed it.

Willie Mitchell and I crept closer to one another.

'Just right,' I breathed. 'See the signal cable? We'll just creep round and get a bearing from the other side.'

The observation post was just where it ought to be, beside a prominent crag, looking down over the plain below. It only remained to creep away, find our way on, taking more bearings as we went, and locate George Gidney again. We found the lateral road, walked along beside it (not *on* it) for innumerable miles, met up with George, and drove home to report to Colonel Terence; then wearily back to our platoon position, to catch up on sleep.

A couple of hours later, I was summoned by Colonel Terence who said: 'Look, Chris, it seems worth while trying to capture a prisoner, who may be able to tell us who he is. Billy Straker-Smith is taking out a fighting patrol tonight. But it's a long way, and there's an awful lot of desert, and he doesn't feel quite sure that he can find the place.

'I'm not asking you to *lead* the patrol: Billy will do that. But I really think that you'll have to go as his guide, and make sure that he gets it absolutely right: it'll save an awful lot of time, and I don't want his gang of thugs wandering around in the mountains for the next week. Now, don't get involved in any shooting, yourself: I'm prepared to risk one officer, not two. Just get Billy up within spitting distance, then sit around and wait for the bang.'

So Willie Mitchell and I had to do without another night's sleep. But it was fair enough: I did not have to take any great risk, myself, and I was sure that I could find the place again.

Into the dusk we rattled, once more, in the carriers; and once more, after miles of plodding, we found the tell-tale pillar of rock above us. I thought it best to lead Billy in behind it, to set the telephone cable in his hand and to let him find his way along it. Off he went, leading his gang, in their stocking caps and their blackened faces, carrying their Tommy guns. Willie and I stayed.

Billy seemed to be taking a terribly long time. I had imagined that he would have charged down on the Germans within seconds; but half an hour went by; and then another. What was going on?

Willie and I must have waited, in complete silence, for over two hours. We were within feet of a German post – or thought that we were – and completely paralysed. I suppose that I *could* have followed Billy down the wire; but, for all I knew, there was a German ambush at the other end of it, and Billy, with all his patrol, had already been scragged or strangled. Anyway, I thought, where did that telephone cable actually go? It might be miles – then *we* should get lost; or rather, Billy would not be able to find us.

We had to be out and away, eventually. Very weary, utterly mystified, and at a loss as to what to tell Colonel Terence, we limped unhappily all the way back to the rendezvous.

'Where the hell have you been?' George Gidney asked, irritably. 'I'd just about given you up for good.'

'Oh, George,' I wailed, 'I've lost Billy, and all his patrol. Do you think I ought to go back and look for them?'

'You'll find him when you get back to the Battalion,' George said, perhaps a little tartly. 'He wouldn't wait for you. I had to take him back a couple of hours ago, swearing blue murder about you. At least, you won't find him straight away, as he's gone to sleep it off, I expect. He said that he was absolutely worn out.'

'Did he find any Germans?'

'Not a whisper, he said. He thought that you had been taking him for a ride.'

What on earth had happened? True, I had not heard the coughing, that night; but surely there must have been *somebody* at the end of that telephone line? Billy simply could not have missed him altogether. I went off, to sleep at last, hurt and exhausted.

When we had both made up our ration of sleep, and could face one another again, Billy told me that the cable he had followed had simply petered out fifty yards further on. He had crept on with his patrol, though; and after a few hundred yards had sent one of his men back to find me. I could not be found – nor, for that matter, had we heard his approach – so Billy was left in the same condition of total isolation as I. He refused, now, to believe that there had been any Germans there. There, the case rested. I was looked upon as a romantic dreamer, not to be relied on.

So ended one of the unsolved mysteries of the Desert War. To be honest, no one was any the worse for it, except for loss of sleep; but I was to brood on it for years to come: it was yet another instance of my own shortcomings. Many years later, though, it occurred to me that I *might* have been justified, after all: if the Germans had heard Billy coming (and this was not impossible, for Billy's men were not completely silent) they could easily have disconnected their field telephone, and taken it with them to hide behind another rock. Just how many people *were* playing hide-and-seek with one another in that howling wilderness? As I said earlier, the desert is not always empty.

I was less than delighted to be told that I must go out on yet another patrol a couple of nights later. This time, though, it was to be a 'standing patrol' and a Company affair: Desmond had been warned to expect the enemy attack and, very practically, was keeping a small outpost on watch, day and night, about five miles to the west of our 'line', beside the road to Toujane. During daylight hours, George was keeping a section of carriers out there; but at night it would be wiser to replace them with a small party with a jeep: they would be more mobile, and less of a risk.

My turn came on the night of 5 March. I took three men with me, so that two could sleep whilst two kept watch. Five miles of telephone cable had been run out behind us, and every so often we would contact Company Headquarters to whisper that we were awake.

Early in our watch, there was an alarming and inexplicable phenomenon. The telephone went dead.

There was little we could do about it. There must be a loose connection somewhere, or a fault, either in our own machine or at the other end. It was the job of the signallers to put it right.

After an hour, the signals jeep crept up in the darkness.

'Sorry, Sir,' the sergeant told me, 'but I have to report that somebody has cut the cable; only about a couple of hundred yards back from here. Not one of your blokes. I suppose?'

'Good Lord, no.'

'Well, we've repaired the break. Your phone's OK now – till someone does it again. Permission to get back, Sir, out of harm's way? It's a bit dodgy, right out here.'

I felt the same. In fact, the more I thought about it, the less I liked it. Surely, the Germans must have done this? I could sense them creeping up on me over the sand-dunes, getting ready to charge down upon us with an unearthly yell.

But the long night wore on, with no more alarms. Some time in the small hours, I walked off alone, only to relieve myself by a small bush of camel-thorn. There was an earth-shattering explosion. I jumped a foot.

It was only a desert thrush! It flew out of the bush in which it had been roosting, as if it were a *Panzer* division – which only went to prove how tense I was, myself. In fact, I have never forgotten the amazing *silence* of the desert, where the flight of a small bird could frighten me so much. (Yet, as I was standing in this silence, two entire *Panzer* divisions were passing beside me, not more than a couple of miles away; and I never heard anything at all. Perhaps this sand is sound-absorbent?)

10

THE BATTLE OF MEDENINE

Most of this chapter is cribbed from my contribution to *No Dishonourable Name*, a series of stories collected together and edited at the end of the war by David Quilter (who, it is worth noting, came under Cuthbert Fitzherbert's umbrella in the Sixth Battalion, then followed me into the Third.) I am very glad that he bullied us all into writing a section or two each. I keep the book by me, still: a precious possession.

At dawn on 6 March, George Gidney, with Sergeants Pring and Pratt, came out in their carriers to relieve us; and we drove back to our platoon positions. Breakfast had been prepared for us by the Platoon Sergeant, Hartley. (Where did he come from, and what happened to him afterwards? Sergeant Reg Brewer became my Platoon Sergeant a few days later, and I came to know him well. Perhaps Hartley put in for a transfer: I can hardly blame him.)

Not more than a few minutes later, we saw the George's three carriers coming in to roost at about fifty miles an hour. They disappeared in the direction of Company Headquarters; and, a minute or two later, the telephone rang.

'Stand to at once!' came the voice of Desmond Holmes.

'Why, what's happened?'

'That man Gidney has brought the whole German army in after him' said Desmond, as if that were just the annoying thing that George *would* do to upset a pleasant morning. 'He was chased by about a hundred German tanks, and he says that they are forming up just the other side of the hill, in front of you.'

I did not believe that this sort of thing could happen to civilized people like ourselves. But I told everybody to stand to, while Platoon Headquarters continued to eat breakfast in the open. We were just sharing out our sausages, when someone said 'Look!' and disappeared from sight.

I looked. George – or Desmond – had exaggerated. About thirty German tanks had just come over the brow in front of us, about a thousand yards away, and were coming straight for us. Our sausages fell to the ground, and the mugs of tea stayed where they were. There was a combined running jump for shelter as Hell broke loose, and the Germans opened up with everything they had. Speech became impossible. More by luck than anything else, Hartley and I landed together in the same slit trench which, again by good fortune, turned out to be the one with the telephone in it – not that there was much that we could do. I could not help wondering how we were supposed to stop these tanks: it seemed perfectly obvious that they would all come on until they reached us, then stop, and give their infantry time to come up and kill us all. Not for the biggest bribe in the world, would I have put my head over the top of the trench to see what was happening.

The din must have lasted for about five minutes. At the end of that time, the noise seemed slightly less, and a colossal black cloud was mush-rooming up in front of us.

I eyed Hartley. 'What do you think we ought to do now?' I asked, trying to look brave.

'Don't move, Sir!' he said, to my relief. With tremendous care, he balanced his steel helmet on top of his rifle, and raised it cautiously into the open air. Nothing hit it. Perhaps, then, the entire German army was not just outside.

It was an unforgettable sight. Of the thirty or so tanks, only five were now visible. These five were in the little *wadi* just in front of us, and all were stationary. From each issued a dense cloud of oily black smoke, a hundred feet high, flecked with flame. In the distance, on our left, were the New Zealanders, their positions looking like an ant-heap which had just been kicked. Just in front of me, I saw one of my section commanders, Corporal Batty, stalking about in the open, picking up and eating the sausages which his section had dropped when they bolted for safety.

Desmond rang up, and told me that most of the undamaged German tanks had turned to their left, northward, from in front of us, and were now being faithfully dealt with by the Scots Guards on our right. It seemed that the few angle-irons, which we had hammered into the ground in front of us and strung together with a strand of wire, had fooled the German tank commanders – as we had hoped – into believing that we had laid a real minefield.

I reported to Desmond that we had suffered no casualties and, ringing off, had just time to ensure that everyone was comfortable before it all began again. This time, a number of German machine-gun teams had installed themselves on the distant ridge in front of us; and now they began to spray us busily, and rather accurately. In the relative comfort of our slit-trenches, we had to hope that none of them would be stupid enough to advance too close. In the middle of all this, the telephone bell rang again, and Desmond asked:

'Can you see Point 140?'

'No,' I said.

'You aren't looking.'

'Well, no, I'm not,' I answered truthfully. 'What is it, anyway?'

'It's a point on the map, of course. Look at the map, and then at the ground; then ring me back and tell me if you can see it. The Germans are supposed to be re-grouping there, or something.'

Hartley and I got out the map; and, after some careful thought, decided that this point would not be visible, even if we did look over the top. I rang up Desmond, and assured him of this, with some difficulty; and thereafter we were left in peace.

The noise continued till about midday. What had happened was that the Germans had come forward without having the faintest idea that there were troops to bar the way. They had used considerable strength, with three *Panzer* Divisions, and infantry to follow up. But the tanks had been diverted by our dummy minefield; and had turned to run the gauntlet of the entire front. The supporting infantry could scarcely be expected to advance over ground littered with the wrecks of their own tanks; and had confined themselves to plaguing us with long-range machine-gun fire. They eventually drew back, allowing us an undisturbed lunch, and a chance to saunter forward, in relays, to have a look at the wrecked tanks, still smoking sullenly in front of us.

During the afternoon, there was yet another alarm. This time, not content with the lesson they had learned that morning, the Germans laid on a pure infantry attack; and, to crown the blunder, they did not arrange supporting artillery fire.

It was sheer suicide. I suddenly saw a large number of tiny figures appearing over the crest of the distant hill in front of us, all in extended formation, coming in our direction. I wondered if we should open fire; but it was not necessary. With a shriek and a thud the entire Corps artillery came down on these miserable creatures; and, as we stood in the open and watched, the dust and smoke pillared up from the slope where we had seen them. I would never have imagined fire more devastating. After a few minutes of it, the massacre ended; and, when the smoke cleared, we saw other little figures, with stretchers, coming to bear the casualties away.

As far as we were concerned, that was the end of the battle. During the evening, there was sporadic shooting, here or there; and every now and then Desmond or Michael would ring up from Company Headquarters to warn me of some impending attack, which did not materialize. In fact, the Germans had had enough. They had lost over fifty tanks; and only they knew how many of their infantry had been killed and wounded. On our side, the casualties had been negligible. The heaviest fighting had been to the north of us, where 131 Brigade had fought many tanks at close quarters. The Scots Guards had suffered about ten casualties, and the New Zealanders had lost a few. In our battalion only one man had been wounded. The story was that he became so excited, firing his anti-tank gun, that it was only when he saw blood on his tunic that he realized that he had been hit.

So ended my first battle. When night fell, I went back to Company Headquarters, and found Desmond and Michael, Reggie Mytton, and the other two platoon commanders, George Gidney and Peter Daubeny, all very pleased with themselves; and as we drank a celebratory glass of whisky under the stars, we were joined by Guy Knight, who commanded No. 4 Company, and two of his officers, John Harley and Oliver Breakwell. Everyone was delighted. For us, it had been the perfect defensive battle, when everything had gone our way.

But I did have the grace to wonder what the German survivors were saying at that moment. They were seasoned troops. They must have been thinking – even saying – that their brilliant general had made a big mistake this time, in sending them against good troops in prepared positions without prior 'softening'. I also had to wonder if all our future battles were going to be as easy as this. Would we, not the Germans, be at the receiving end next time?

And what about the wounded, and dying, and the dead? What about the mothers, the widows, the orphaned children? It did not do to think too much about this. I tried to keep at the back of my mind the agony, the loss, the destruction that men seem so often to inflict upon each other, for if I were to brood on it I should find it always harder to continue.

As for myself, I was relieved, in that I had survived my 'baptism of fire' without completely losing my head. The fear had been almost overmastering, but I had expected that, of course. I was a realist as far as my own weaknesses were concerned; but I had not panicked, this time. I felt a little more confident already. Perhaps, after all, I should be able to disguise my horrors, surrounded as I was with so great a cloud of witnesses.

11

THE HORSESHOE

Now it was time for the Eighth Army to go on to the offensive. Preparations were already in hand for an assault on the Mareth Line, a formidable barrier built by the French, in the days when Tunisia was a colony, to prevent encroachment from the Italians who had colonised Cyrenaica and Tripolitania to the east of them.

When the Italians were being expansionist, the French had had an unswerving belief in defence. These were the days of the Maginot Line, said to be impregnable (and it might have been if the Germans had not quickly marched round the flank in 1940, through neutral countries.) They must have felt the same about the Mareth Line. It was certainly very strong.

There is a gentle bend here in the coastline of North Africa: whereas the general line is, of course, east-to-west, the line of the Tunisian coast is generally south-to-north till, beyond Bizerta, it turns west again toward the Algerian frontier. In the first bend is the Wadi Zigzau, a stagnant inlet which bites deeply into the desert country of Southern Tunisia to the foot of the Matmata Hills, which, in their turn, bend southward to continue the barrier. Beyond these hills, there was said to be an impassable salt-marsh, continuing the line southward for yet another hundred miles.

General Montgomery had, long before this, sent out patrols of the Long Range Desert Group, who had discovered a route through the salt-marsh; and now, unknown to us (or to the Germans, it seems) units of the Eighth Army were pushing towards this passage. The pace was set by the First Armoured Division; but it was closely followed by the New Zealanders and by the Fourth Indian Division.

It seemed to us, though, that the main attack would have to be along the coast; and we were told that a frontal assault would soon be launched on the Wadi Zigzau by the Fifty-first (Highland) and the Fiftieth (Tyne and Tees) Divisions, with the Seventh Armoured Division on stand-by, to break out when the German line had been pierced. We did not yet know if our Brigade would be involved.

Not yet, it emerged. There was another small task for us to do, first.

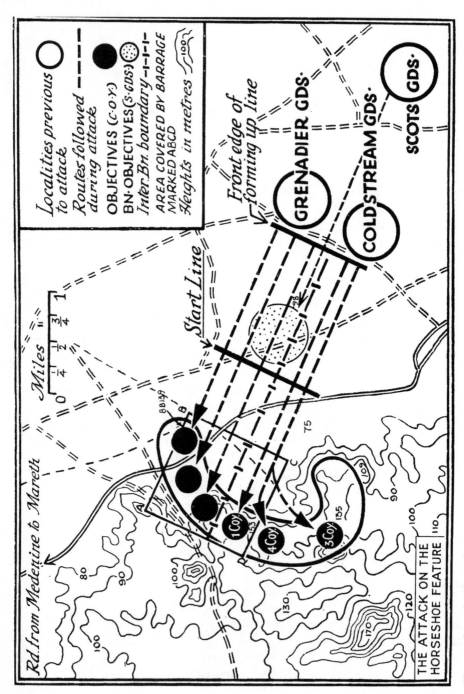

The attack on the Horseshoe.

There might be a weakness in the defences, between the head of the Wadi Zigzau and the northern outcrops of the Matmata Hills. The main road to Tunis ran here; and possession of this road might mean that our armour would be able to get through, towards the next obstacle thirty miles beyond, the 'Gabes Gap', yet another bottleneck to be attacked, in due course, when we had disposed of the Mareth Line. The Fiftieth and Fifty-first Divisions held back their assault across the Wadi Zigzau (not without some relief, for it was going to be expensive) because, at worst, a prior attack along the road itself might draw away some German units, and enable them to complete their own preparations.

Our 'shufti planes' reported that there was little German movement along and beside the road. Just to the left of it, on a craggy mound, labelled Hill 153 on our rudimentary maps, it seemed that the Germans had set up an outpost. It was not looked upon as a part of the Mareth Line proper; but it would be a useful tactical feature to occupy ourselves: a good prod there might suggest to the Germans that we were contemplating cutting their defences into two. Our Brigade was ordered to occupy this little 'horse-shoe' of high ground, rising up from the Wadi bou Remle which, when there was a flash-flood, would carry storm-water down from the hills, and across the main road to the Wadi Zigzau, and thence to the sea.

A night attack was decided on: good training! The Brigade was virtually untried, and would learn some useful lessons, about finding its way

The scene near Mareth before the Horseshoe action, taken through a slit in a concrete bunker.

across desert country under the moon, behind an artillery barrage. There was a clear objective, only limited opposition, and an excellent feature to put, once occupied, into a state of defence.

We drove off from our positions at Medenine, round Tadjera Khir, and across country to the east of the main road, till we came to a sheltered valley, the Wadi Hachana, about three miles to the east of the 'Horseshoe'. All was quiet.

Our patrols reconnoitred the route; and, on the night before the attack, marked it with white tape so that we could not get lost. (But could the Germans see it too?) The Grenadiers were to be on the right, their start-line to the east of the road, and the Coldstream on the left, crossing the road before they reached their start-line, then scrambling down and up the steep walls of the wadi, to advance to the main feature, Hill 153, and a subsidiary hill to the south-east of it named (after its height in metres) 135.

We were a little bewildered when we were told that we were to advance under a barrage of 30,000 shells. It sounded a little extravagant for a minor operation of war like this.

By this time, I knew my platoon fairly well. Sergeant Hartley had been posted elsewhere, but I was getting to know Reg Brewer, a regular old soldier who had been with the Battalion since before the war. (We stayed together till I was carried off feet first; and when he, too, was sent home. We were to have a good time together, at Pirbright, till the war ended.)

We had extra officers in the Company, once more. There was Desmond, of course, and Michael as second-in-command; then George Gidney, Peter Daubeny and myself as the three platoon commanders. But what was Dick Ker doing there? He must have had some important function, for he was awarded the Military Cross that night (though, at the time I was lost, and did not see what he did.)

So we set off, on foot, as dark fell on 16 March. Number 1 Company was to be on the right, and would have Hill 153 as its objective. Number 4 Company, on its left, would aim for the ridge between this and Hill 135, to the south-east of it; and No. 3 Company, I was relieved to note, would be in reserve, under the eye of Colonel Terence, who would send it off to Hill 135 when the other two companies had reached their objectives.

We reached the main road without incident; though the moan of innumerable shells far above us was disconcerting. Once over the road, though, things began to go wrong: there were louder noises now, close by. Still following one another in single file, we went forward into a minor runnel beyond the road, only to find that this was an obvious registration mark for German mortars. There were some dreadful bangs. Then came the casualties, carried back past us, now. Julian Holland-Hibbert, Paul Bowman, and Simon Phipps were all wounded, severely I think, with some of the men; and others were detached to carry them away.

I thought that they had trodden on 'S' mines. These were fiendish anti-personnel mines, dug in below the ground with only a cluster of thin, stiff wires above the surface. Anyone who trod on one would depress a tin can beneath, sitting within a larger, open-topped bowl, with a small explosive charge in between, enough to blow it into the air. When in the air, the can would explode, scattering a lethal, more or less horizontal hail of metal pieces all round. Mercifully, I never discovered for myself how far this shrapnel could travel! But others discovered that night, to their cost: every depression in which men could take shelter was, literally, a minefield. (One of my men trod on one later, just beside me. I can still remember him looking at me, rather stupidly, either wondering what had happened, or counting his chances of survival. By some incredible fluke, the can failed to explode in the air.)

Digging a shell-scrape beside the main wadi, I was aware that a full-scale battle was developing, just ahead, as our two leading companies disappeared into the gloom. This, surely, was no enemy 'outpost'! the whole German army seemed to be shooting, whilst both shells and mortar-bombs fell around us, too. Number 1 Company, it seems, was almost immediately enveloped in a hail of fire. A few hundred yards beyond the wadi, they stepped over a single strand of wire; but, this time, it was no dummy minefield. Sergeant Brock, my section commander in the Sixth Battalion, had his guts ripped out, fell against the wire, and died yelling for me to help him. Michael Mitchell had his leg blown off. (He was rescued, still alive, the next day; and by the following June, was back in England and fit enough to be in the Guards Chapel when it was hit and destroyed by a doodlebug. So died a good, unfortunate friend.)

Very few members of No. 1 Company came back to us, that night. Many were killed on the minefield, and many more, I suppose, by machine-gun bullets. Unable to go back through the minefield they had penetrated (the Germans thought that they must have dropped by para-chute) the remnant went forward, captured quite a few prisoners, and stormed Hill 153. It was at this moment, though, that they ran into their own artillery barrage; and Mike Wills, the Company Commander – so far unwounded – fired the success flares with his Verey pistol. This worked, in the sense that our shelling stopped. But it meant, to the others in the Battalion, that he had achieved his objective. Number 4 Company plunged deeper into the minefield on the left, and met even more resis-tance. Guy Knight, the Company Commander, was wounded, and over half his men were casualties. He went back to find Colonel Terence and to ask him for help; but, on receipt of the success signal, No. 3 Company had already been sent forward to secure Hill 135, and there was no way to reinforce No. 4 Company, stuck in the middle of the densest minefield found, so far, in the war. Eventually, some came back, but many of these were wounded. David Kerr-Wilson, who commanded the Carrier Platoon, had one carrier blown up under him, moved to the next, which was blown up too, then to a third, which also struck a mine. Very badly burnt by this time, David was carried off the field. It was left to Billy Straker-Smith, also wounded, I believe, to extricate the pitiful remnant of the company.

Meanwhile No. 3 Company, believing that the others had reached their objectives, set out for Hill 135.

Though the din of battle was unbelievable, yet for the first half-mile or more we were to some extent protected in the lee of a low ridge, over which the tracer bullets from the German Spandau light machine-guns were coming in a 'waterfall' (and what we could see was only the tracer, perhaps one in every six bullets emerging from each Spandau.) At the top of this rise, perhaps half-way to our objective, we found ourselves bathed in this amazing stream, the crack of literally thousands of bullets every minute sounding like lengths of tarpaulin torn by giants. There was shellfire too, I expect, but that was nothing to the Spandaus. They were firing from our right front, which No. 4 Company should have taken.

Michael beckoned to me. When I came up, he had to yell over the din.

'We can't go forward with those Spandaus on our flank,' he shouted. 'I've no idea where No. 4 Company have got to. We can't raise a whisper on the 18 sets.' (I have mentioned these already: each needed two men to handle them, one to carry and the other to speak and listen. They were quite useless, that night.) 'Now, here's a job for you. Take your platoon off to the right, there, silence those Spandaus, then report back to us on Hill 135.'

I shouted back, somewhat rudely, I think. But off I ran with my platoon, forming a line as we went, each man fixing his bayonet. I entirely forgot even to pull my pistol out of its holster.

We galloped unsteadily into the line of the 'waterfall' (more like a hosepipe squirting lead, I thought to myself.) We had about half a mile to go. For the first quarter, we may not have been spotted; but then we went over another small rise and down a gentle slope at the enemy positions. What did it feel like? Not many people live to answer this question.

Though terrified out of my wits, I felt quite lucid. I remember, mostly, talking to myself and giggling, stupidly: 'Oh God, this is the end . . . Just as well I put on my tin hat . . . They simply can't miss, though . . . What a *bloody* silly way to die!' – And so on. I wished that I could lose myself

90

in the fiery lust of battle that is said to exalt warriors as they move into action. My brain continued to function quite rationally, despite the hysterical giggles.

I saw that we were stumbling past a whole line of little pits. I did not find it difficult to realize that the Germans were laying yet another mine-field, but had not yet put the mines into their holes. Just as well, I thought. I yelled at my ragged line of heroes:

'**CHARGE!**' Even at the time it sounded ridiculous. I seem to remember that my voice broke as I shouted.

Every German in Africa turned his personal hosepipe on to us. My wonderful soldiers yelled their defiance over the din: perhaps some of them felt lit by the fire of battle, then? Not I.

Then, fifty yards short of the German slit-trenches, I stumbled into a double-apron barbed wire fence.

It was in a shallow hollow. The Germans were on the gentle slope opposite, secure in their slit-trenches, still firing as though they could never stop. We had no chance. Up against this impassable barrier, we all lay flat on our faces, awaiting the *coup de grace*. The stream of bullets, fired at point-blank range, flowed, cracked, whined all round us.

I had led my men to suicide. Certain death, anyway. The only miti-gating circumstance was that I was going to die with them.

In my horror, I even began to giggle, once again. Any moment, now . . . At least, they won't shoot my bollocks away . . . Or, if they do, they will have shot a hole right through me first, so it won't make any difference . . . I wonder how many of us have bought it, by now? Odd, that they haven't knocked *me* off, yet . . .

I began even to look at the streams of bullets whipping towards me. Were they leaving me till last? Or was I, by some accident, in one of the 'gaps' between the streams?

Then I began to notice that, though the first few bullets in every burst spat all round me, after a few rounds the direction of the stream began to go upwards, till, by the end of the belt, the stream was several feet over my head. Did these Germans not appreciate that the recoil of a light machine gun, fired over a bipod, would tend to lift the muzzle of the weapon in the course of each burst? They should have an NCO to check this, surely? If I lay doggo, and acted dead, they might not know that I was still alive. Was there just a glimmer of hope?

No. Not a chance. Any moment, now.

Seconds are hours, minutes are days when one is waiting for the end: I have no idea how long I lay there. But there came a time when I thought that I should take the initiative. Prone, I shouted, when the hurricane had subsided to a strong gale:

'When I get up and run, all of you run, too. Gather, over the top of the slope behind us.'

This, as I expected, provoked a fresh holocaust of fire. But eventually, even Germans had to put fresh belts into their Spandaus, and firing eased from a million a minute to a mere ten thousand. This was the moment, then. With a curious reluctance, I got to my feet, and ran as I had never run in my life.

As I ran, I realized with dreadful clarity that I was running away from the enemy – and, what was worse, running away from my own shattered troops. For all I knew, they were all dead or wounded; and my conception of chivalry dictated that I should have stayed with them. But I wonder. If only *some* of the men followed me, I thought desperately, that would be justification, of a sort – but this was not the moment to turn round and count heads. I galloped over the brow, found a little depression in the ground which might just offer temporary shelter, and heard panting behind me.

To my enormous relief and utter astonishment, every man was still with me.

I do not suppose that any German will ever read this; but if, by any chance, an ex-soldier of the Ninetieth Light Division (one of the crack divisions of the *Afrika Korps*) reads and remembers that night, he might know how many rounds were expended by his Spandaus – ten, a hundred thousand? – and refuse to believe that none found a target. Almost every bullet had gone over our heads. I began to feel better myself. It was not easy to run away, as I had; but with no possibility of going forward, it seemed that I had been right to withdraw, temporarily. Now, for another shot. What was I to do?

The answer was not long in coming. I was thinking that I should report back to Michael, before trying to find a way round, when my ears just caught a tiny whistle. There was no time even to shout a warning; but I managed to get flat on to my stomach before the mortar bomb landed, eighteen inches from my head. Fortunately, for me anyway, German mortars do not explode as they touch, but make a small crater. The crown of my steel helmet was on the lip of it.

I was not wounded, then, in any technical sense. But it seems that the incredible bang of the explosion blew in my ear-drums, and caused some mechanism within my fuddled brain to short-circuit. It was all too much. When I next became aware of what I was doing, I was breaking the sound-barrier, running faster than any man has ever done, and on my way back to Cairo, two thousand miles away. I should have been there in about ten minutes.

I must not seek excuses for this. In fact, I have no real idea how far I went, or indeed how I came to be where I was (to be more honest, I do not suppose that it was more than fifty yards; but it *felt* like fifty miles.) Somehow or other, I collected myself; felt myself all over for wounds; realized that, once again, I had led my men into a trap (that little piece of dead ground must obviously be a registration point for German mortars;) and came to the conclusion that I must go back and get them out of it.

Utterly shattered by this time, I tottered back. I am not sure, even now, if the men realized that I had run away. They could have thought that I had been vapourized.

One of the men, called Turner (not my old Willie Turner from the Sixth Battalion) was desperately wounded. The bomb had landed on his legs, and he had lost a good deal of the lower half of his body. He was still alive, but I am none too sure that he was conscious. Now aware that another mortar bomb would land here at any second, I got some of the men to help drag his body for a few yards, till we all found a little more cover; and we set to work on the hopeless task of putting shell-dressings on the worst of his wounds.

There was no moving him further. Did we all have to wait about, for him to die? Guardsman Haigh, one of my most reliable men, came up with a suggestion.

'If you want to take the platoon back to join the Company, Sir,' he said, 'then leave me here with Turner for a bit. He won't last long. Then I'll come back and find you – that is, if you can't find a stretcher party.'

Reluctantly, I left Haigh with his unconscious charge. I am not sure that I was right to do so, but I promised to send a stretcher, if I could find one – I was not thinking very coherently – though I privately doubted the need. What mattered now was Haigh. We were still only two hundred yards from the enemy, and I did not want him captured. On the other hand, the platoon was probably needed, to carry on with the battle. (Mercifully, Turner died a few hours later; and Haigh rejoined us.)

We rejoined the Company. We were fortunate to find it at all, more or less where I had previously parted company with it; but, this time, moving in the other direction.

I reported to Desmond. We had to shout above the din: those terrible Spandaus were still ripping over our heads.

'We couldn't make it, Desmond,' I yelled. 'Minefield. Double apron fence. Mortars. Half a dozen Spandaus, at least. Not a hope.'

'How many casualties?'

'Two. Can I take a stretcher party back to collect them?'

'No. Sorry, Chris. They'll just have to take their chance, I'm afraid.

They may be better off in the bag. We've had orders to report back to Battalion Headquarters in the wadi, straight away. No dithering.'

'But, Desmond . . .'

'No. Do as you're told, for once. We've had our problems, too. And the other companies are in even worse trouble.'

I never found out what these 'problems' had been; and was too shattered to ask. Before long, we were reporting back to Colonel Terence in the wadi.

As we waited for news of the two missing companies, we listened to him, trying to collect together the remains of his command. It seemed that almost all No. 1 Company was lost to us for ever. (A few months later, we were to hear – from our own German prisoners – who had been killed and who taken prisoner: Mike Wills, the Company Commander, dead, Michael Mitchell wounded but back with us, Johnny Proctor and Stamp Brooksbank prisoners.) Number 4 Company was still an entity, but most of its officers were wounded, and Oliver Breakwell was dead. Number 3 Company had – as usual! – suffered least. All the same, ten officers and 126 other ranks in the Battalion were casualties, that night. When it is remembered that the 'bayonet strength' of the Battalion – three motor companies, with only two non-specialist platoons in each – could not have been much more than 150, then there were not many of us left. Our colleagues in the Grenadiers had fared worse.

In his memoirs, Monty suggests that our attack had been a ruse, to divert the attention of the Germans from his proposed 'left hook', due to come in from the south a few days later. Perhaps it was. Battles cost men, of course, and even ruses can be expensive. But this thought did not help us very much, as we tried to come to terms with our failure. I imagine that we felt aggrieved, in that our hard-earned specialist skills had been ignored: that we had been used to undertake a task for which we were not suited.

I came to admire Colonel Terence more and more, late that night and during the few days which followed. Once more, the Battalion had been decimated. It would not regain its usefulness for months, until reinforcements came in at the end of the campaign. Questions would be asked about his competence – there is little sympathy shown in the army for those who fail – and the fact that it was not his fault made no difference.

Before dawn, I discovered, to my horror, that I had committed an unforgivable crime.

When I had been trying to bandage Turner's wounds, I had been using shell-dressings, which I was carrying in a canvas shoulder-bag. In my confused state at the time, I had fumbled with these (how does one put them on to a man with hardly any legs left?) and had used up all the stock

I had been carrying. But, before the battle began, I had put the current volume of my diary into this bag, too.

To keep a diary at all was forbidden. I had compounded the felony by writing down all I knew about the progress of the Eighth Army, and how it proposed to attack the Mareth Line . . . and now, I had left the bag beside the wounded man.

I am sure, *now*, that the Germans knew far more about the battle than I did. But, at the time, I could see myself as the man who was about to lose the war. What was I to do?

During the battle, George Gidney had been told to get the Company Carrier Platoon across the Wadi bou Remle; but had found the sides so steep and the bed of the wadi so broken that all the carriers were still stuck in it, most of them with their tracks broken. His men took days – nights, rather – to repair them, and then to bring them back, less than a mile from the Germans; and, every night, bodies of armed guardsmen were being sent out to afford a little protection. I volunteered, more than once, for this gave me an opportunity to go a little further.

It stood to reason that, as I had found my way back to the wadi from the wounded Turner, and had also brought the platoon back with me, then I should be able to go back yet again. A single man can creep around the desert much more safely than a crowd. One night, I crept forward along the well-known route till I reached the spot. I heard the Germans talking to one another in their slit-trenches, checked that their new minefield had now been laid and buried, and found Turner's body, now beginning to decompose. He cannot have survived for long, then: the Germans had not moved him.

My canvas bag was still there. But it was empty.

So the Germans *had* come, then. They had found my diary, and their experts were already evaluating its contents. My juvenile observations on the course of the war, so far, would not be worth much; but my predictions about the course of the present battle could be of vital interest. What *had* I written?

Perhaps it did not matter, I kept telling myself. Even as I was searching, the battle had been joined, both to east and south, and, in the days that followed, it seemed that the Germans were beginning to pull out of the Mareth Line. By the end of the month, they were to be taking up a new defensive position along the bank of the Wadi Akarit, and the war was moving on. But it was a major discomfort to me, all the same, as my own personal miseries increased during the next six weeks; and it even bothers me, now. Did my inexcusable behaviour cost lives?

But this was not my only worry. I knew that, in the battle itself, I had been at fault: I had been tried in the balances and had been found wanting. I sensed that my brother-officers were looking at me, quizzically, partly because I was one of the few who had emerged from the battle without a wound to show for it, partly because I had suddenly become 'twitchy': I would start at a noise, and I have little doubt that my eyes were bright with fear. The phrase we used was 'bomb-happy'. Alas, it was not bombs which made me jump, but Spandaus; and I was emphatically *not* happy! However, the phrase applied. The worst had happened. Jumpy, deaf, and once again as lonely as I had ever been, I knew that I had descended to yet another of the depths of my little life.

12

WADI AKARIT

Our sojourn in the Wadi Hachana continued till the end of the month. Our orders were to 'maintain pressure' whilst other, more serious attacks went in. I believe that the assault over the Wadi Zigzau was launched on the night of 20/21 March; but my impression is that it was not successful.

Every day, we would drive out over the hill and show ourselves to the Germans on Hill 153 – always choosing a different route to the skyline, so that the German artillery had no time to register before we had found another fold in the ground; and, every night, our patrols would go out, to recover our wrecked carriers or to make loud noises, ostensibly to fool the Germans into imagining that we were about to attack them again. We could not have been very convincing. Poor Geoffrey Sowter was killed at about this time. I hardly knew him: he had just arrived – after the 'horseshoe' battle, I thought – and I only met him once.

I do not suppose that we were in an entertaining mood, anyway. It takes a long time to get over the aftermath of a defeat, and others beside myself were 'bomb-happy', I expect. My own misery was illustrated by the arrival of a NAAFI truck, with a consignment of good things. They were brave men, these drivers – not members of the army themselves, but taking little luxuries into territory which was completely unknown to them or even to the High Command – determined to get supplies through to the 'men at the front'.

The easy part was to drive along the road: there was only one, after all. But it was more difficult to know when to stop.

The drivers were warned not to listen to soldiers who told them that they had already reached the front line. (This was always one of the hazards of desert warfare: no one ever knew where this mythical 'front line' was, except the men who were actually doing the shooting.) There came the inevitable truck, whose driver continued on, disregarding all shouts, until he found himself surrounded by grinning, voracious Germans.

It was a pleasant surprise, then, to find a NAAFI truck at our own front door. I forget how we paid, if indeed we paid at all; but, at least, the officers of No. 3 Company received a small consignment of alcohol – not enough, of course, but a wonderful change from the brackish water which had been our lot recently. I 'made' a small tin of pineapple chunks, I remember. In the darkness, I disappeared into my slit-trench, and ate the lot myself. Perhaps the others did the same; but I still remember that incident with shame.

Meanwhile, the outflanking column – the New Zealanders, with the First Armoured Division and the Fourth Indian Division, – had found the narrow route between the mountains and the salt-pans to the south, and were racing to surround any Germans who remained in the Mareth Line. Monty writes that the enemy saw the danger on 20 March, but that they were too late: General Horrocks, in charge of X Corps, had excellent liaison with the RAF, and the decisive battle, it seems, was fought behind a 'barrage' of fighters, on the afternoon of 26 March, 'the most complete example of the close integration of land and air power up to that time'. Within a couple of days, we were facing the enemy across the Wadi Akarit.

This particular 'left hook' seems to have wrong-footed the enemy: there are many pundits who insist that the Wadi Akarit would have been a better line than Mareth for the Germans to defend in the first place. This was the narrow waist of Southern Tunisia. The wadi itself was another deep salt-water inlet, very difficult to cross; and, inland from it for about a hundred miles, almost to the western frontier of Tunisia, there was a series of salt-pans and lakes which must have been almost impassable. There was only one dry crossing-point, the 'Gabes Gap', where the main road ran through; and, a week later, the Highlanders were to break through it in a day.

The Battalion – what remained of it – arrived on 31 March. We must have driven straight along the main road, now open to us. We took up our new positions within a mile of the Wadi itself – a little too close for comfort – with my platoon on the extreme right of the army. I had the beach and the sea just beside me.

It was the dullest stretch of coast I had ever seen. We dug ourselves into the sand-hills, covered in marram grass (or the equivalent) in which it was not too difficult to move without being shot at. Strangely, it was easy to get lost, too. I remember showing Michael the way to Company Headquarters – he must have arrived late – and being sworn at for getting it wrong. (At this time, he may have taken temporary command of No. 4 Company, in the absence of Guy Knight. It did not matter very much: the two companies had virtually merged at the time, and were performing the same tasks, burrowing into the sand-hills.)

'You're swanning, Chris!' He complained. Well he might: we were very close indeed to the wadi, and to the enemy on the far bank.

'No,' I defended myself. 'I marked the way in.' Between our positions and the wadi was a rectangular wodge of minefield, laid by the Italians; and it was important not to stray on to this. (This reminds me that I have hardly mentioned the presence of the Italian army, which may well have been larger than the German. Rommel had thought little of them, it seemed, and neither did we. As they were not well armed, he had tended to place them in defensive positions whilst his *Panzers* did the mobile fighting: at least, they could occupy territory. However, it has to be admitted that the Italians had held large sectors of the Mareth Line; that the Germans had thought it worthwhile to withdraw them before they were all encircled; and that we were faced by Italian troops now, along the coastal end of the Wadi Akarit. They must have been there for some time, for it was they who had been responsible for laying the minefield.)

Our patrols found the forward edge of it. It must have been marked, with the usual single strand of wire. We considered that it would be suicidal to penetrate it.

Frankly, our tenure of this sector of the front was not very heroic. We were doing exactly what the Italians in front of us were doing: occupying territory, whilst the chief participants prepared themselves for the next action. I was not the only officer who had not recovered from the previous battle.

One afternoon, when I was out in front of my platoon, watching enemy movement on the far side of the wadi, a German Junkers 88 flew over, very low, to investigate.

Sergeant Hammond, one of my section commanders, opened up with a Bren gun, firing from the hip. Either he failed to see me altogether, or I was hidden in the grass; but he practically sliced me in half. Flat on my face in the sand, I yelled:

'Stop that bloody firing, Sergeant Hammond!'

Sergeant Hammond stopped. But the rear-gunner of the Junkers saw him, and let him have a burst. He did not seem to realize that, once again, I was in the way. I was nearly sliced again.

The attack went in, on our left, on 6 April: the Highlanders, together with the 50th and the 4th Indian Divisions, more or less along the line of the main road. I hope that they were able to keep their feet dry! It must have been an overwhelming attack, for they were through in a matter of hours, and our two armoured divisions were soon burning up the miles to Sfax, Sousse and the north, the enemy in pell-mell retreat.

Our part had merely been diversionary, of course. We had been told to make a loud noise, and to keep the enemy thinking that we might ourselves be about to cross the wadi. For the whole night, we kept firing; and all our officers were leading patrols, not in any attempt actually to cross the wadi, but to fire across it continually from as close as they could get.

This meant attempting to penetrate the Italian minefield.

David Helme, in his diary, writes that there was every mine dreamed up by the combined ingenuity of both the Italians and Germans: our old acquaintance the Teller, the German 'S' mine, the Italian 'Red Devil', and one, at least, which we had never come across before: being wooden, it did not register on a mine-detector. Almost all mines seemed to be booby-trapped in one way or another. The Italian 'Red Devil', for instance, had a pin not unlike our own hand-grenade: when the pin came out, it released an arm which, in its turn, activated the detonator. If the pin were tied by a length of green string to the pin of another of these things, and then pulled taut, the cocktail would be deadly. The string was almost invisible even in daylight, stretched out at shin-height; and there were enough fragments of metal, from ball-bearings to rusty nails, to cut legs to smithereens, even to kill. David was not the only one of us to become aware, at some time or other during that night, of the gentle pressure of taut string on his shin-bone. Ian Dickinson, and others I believe, lost legs that night.

When I emerged at first light, green myself with fright, whom should I meet but my Commanding Officer, coming forward to tell everyone that the main attack had been successful.

'What the *hell* is the matter with you, Chris?' he barked. 'You look as though you've spent the night in a pig-sty. You haven't even shaved! Go and report yourself to Desmond, straight away.'

Nearly in tears, I went to report to Desmond: at least, he must have known what it had been like. But I collected little sympathy; only, once again, that enigmatic, calculating look. I was losing more marks every day.

13

ENFIDAVILLE

We sped north behind the tanks. But it took a day even to emerge on to the road; and the road itself was so clogged with other transport – tanks, tank-transporters, trucks and all the gear which follows in the wake of armour – that we found it simpler to drive across-country. We were beginning to reach more cultivated country, now: by our standards it was densely populated. The desert had been reclaimed, for wheat, barley and olives; and further north, we were to find acres of fruit trees: figs, pomegranates, apricots and the rest, not yet ripe, but needing the care and attention of the local people. They could hardly welcome us: we were threatening destruction at a critical time.

I was ordered to take a truck to a local bakery, to collect bread. There was a long queue – maybe the German authorities had, after all, been starving the civilians – and there was much shouting when we arrived. When we emerged with our loaves, there was a near-riot; and I had to withdraw quickly, for fear of a lynching.

Returning to the Battalion, I found to my disgust that a drill parade had been arranged.

All available officers had been ordered on to parade, and there was no chance of avoiding it. Willie Mitchell had prepared what remained of my khaki drill uniform – he could not find my ash-plant walking stick, I seem to remember, and I collected yet another rocket for being 'naked'. When the men had been marched off, then, following tradition, the junior officers were 'chased' by one of the drill-sergeants – Masterman, I think – and everyone except myself was satisfied that it had been very good for us. For goodness' sake! Did the establishment *really* believe in all this bull-shit? As far as I could see, this was the most exciting entertainment the local Arab boys could ever remember; but for us, without a chance of washing the sweat off afterwards, it was purgatory.

Northward again, past Sfax, well into the pregnant belly of Tunisia, we stopped, some miles to the south-west of Sousse.

We heard now that the Eighth Army had been halted just beyond the town of Enfidaville, where the Germans had decided to make a last stand. About sixty miles south of Tunis, Enfidaville was at the eastern end of a quarter-circle of mountains, which protected the two main cities of Tunis and Bizerta. After this, the north-going coastline turned westward once again towards Algeria.

It seemed that it was up to the Eighth Army to punch a hole in these last defences. According to the pundits of the desert war, the First Army had been hammering in vain since November at the north-western rim of these encircling hills (true enough, I expect) and now the Eighth Army must come to the rescue, by breaking through from the south, along the main road, beside the coast.

Our Brigade got ready, once again, to take up its position in the line, just beyond Enfidaville, astride the road as it wriggled between the mountains and the sea. The rumour went around that the attack should go in there. The road would have to be cleared. It did not need a genius to guess who was going to have to do it.

I cannot say that we viewed the prospect with much enthusiasm. Everyone knew that we were desperately short of men. We were *not* infantry, everyone kept repeating, but a motor brigade, supposed to support the armour, not to 'punch holes' for the tanks to go through afterwards. The generals suggested a combined attack, then: our troops advancing in the wake of 'I' tanks (which were supposed to be heavily enough armoured to tackle the enemy infantry head-on, and to sit on them until their foot-soldiers came up, to dispose of them or take them prisoner.)

There were two classes of 'I' tank, the Churchills (but I do not think that we had any, in our sector) and the Valentines. Everyone knew, though, that Valentines were obsolescent by now, and that they only carried two-pounder guns. The exercise would be hard on the Valentines and their crews; hard, too, on the infantry coming up under their poor protection. But rehearsals began. Was Monty overreaching himself? – we asked one another. It seemed out of character that he should sacrifice his army only to prove that he could succeed where the First Army, so far, had failed.

It must have been on 16/17 April that the Battalion moved forward, to face the Germans once again. Enfidaville itself was full of soldiers: New Zealanders and Indians for the most part, I believe, for bloody fighting was going on to scale the mountain wall just to the north of the little town. Our Brigade, though, forked right along the main Tunis road, and took up positions on the flatter ground near the sea, ready (everyone presumed) to lead the forlorn hope which was intended to bring the rest of the Eighth Army through to end the war in Africa.

Everyone who waited in Enfidaville disliked the place intensely. There must have been marshy land round, somewhere, for we were to encounter mosquitoes for the first time; but a more savage grouse was about the poor food, and dreadful water.

We had outrun our lines of communication. Water, of course, came from local sources, wells and reservoirs, and was brought up by tankers, treated with liberal doses of chlorine and other chemicals, as the Germans were said to have dropped dead camels into the wells. The ration was down to half a gallon per man per day – and the sun was now getting hot. This meant three pint mugs of tea, each day. (The fourth pint was for washing and shaving.) I still remember the condensed milk which went into the tea. The water was so foul that tinned milk would not dissolve, but lay on the surface in circular oily globules. Shaving soap would not lather, either.

The food was in tins, of course. Bully was acceptable, and made a reasonable 'hash'! cooked and stirred in half a 'flimsy' (the four-gallon double cube which had once held petrol) with a length of wire for a handle. The other half of the flimsy was the 'stove'. Pierced here and there with a bayonet, three-quarters filled with sand (there was still no shortage of *that*) and impregnated with a liberal splash of petrol (no shortage there, either,) these makeshift stoves would burn for up to half an hour, with an occasional kick to separate more petrol from the sand which trapped it. Every vehicle in the desert would carry these two half-flimsies, rattling on the tailboard. They were more familiar than the vehicles themselves.

'Slinkers' were an abomination to us all. I hope that the American who invented them eats them for ever in hell. They *looked* vaguely like sausages when taken out of a tin, but even the Americans had the grace to label them 'soya links', as a warning to their own countrymen. My personal hate was directed at the tins of potatoes, which looked like little pellets of soap, and even tasted like them. There was something to be said for the occasional tin of baked beans; but there was no bread, only biscuits, 'hard tack', which broke the men's teeth if they failed to 'dunk' them first. Small wonder that many of us suffered eruptions of 'desert sores'! I carry the scars on my forearms, still.

More deadly than anything else, though, was the dearth of tobacco.

Long afterwards, I would declaim in the Mess at Pirbright that the advance of the Eighth Army was finally halted here through lack of cigarettes. We had all been used to regular issues, ever since we had joined the army; and whenever a truck came to a halt, its occupants were all smoking within seconds. Perhaps they did soothe the nerves of men in constant danger. Lack of them wrecked the nerves of almost every soldier, in danger or not. We had reluctantly accepted the disagreeable

'V' packets which had come up with the rations – thought to be the dried dung swept off the highways of India – but now, to be deprived even of these was little short of disaster. The men were making their own now, of dried grass wrapped in lavatory paper.

I have taken a long time to get to the battle. The reason is that I have nothing to describe: In the end, our Brigade was to take no real part in it, after all; and, as for me, I was not even with the Battalion. My worst expectations had come true: I had lost the command of my platoon, and was relegated to 'B' Echelon.

All the spare officers, and all the spare vehicles too, were camped in an immense olive grove, which must have covered more than a hundred square miles. Hubert Snowden must have been in charge: his task was to keep the Battalion supplied with a truckload of food, ammunition and equipment for each company, every night, carried up by each of the quartermaster-sergeants.

There was little for me to do, save mope, and read the few scraps of literature I could find. I remember memorizing Julian Grenfell's 'Into Battle' and coming to the conclusion that he must have written it before he reached the front at all. 'In the air, death moans and stings' was just plain *wrong*. The death which came to meet us at Mareth had sounded like the cracking of a thousand whips.

I could hardly bear to think of my brother-officers, running these terrible risks, in which I was not allowed to share. Personally, I had no more liking for Enfidaville, and the prospect of an agonizing death, than had anyone else; but I was convinced that, if I did not make my presence known, all the time, I was likely to be forgotten. It was not merely that I was terrified. I was so terrified of *being* terrified that I actively sought more terror. I began to go up to the Battalion, on most nights, with the rations, partly to meet my brother-officers, partly perhaps to persuade myself that I was one of them, for some of the time at least.

Peter had come back, after his operation. I was surprised, and perhaps a little envious, that he had immediately been given a platoon; and astonished that he seemed to be enjoying himself.

I could voice my fears and doubts to him. His reply (to be frank, this may have been on a later occasion, but it might fit in here) went rather like this:

'Surely, Chris,' he would say, 'you must see that we must all be given a chance to justify ourselves. You have had more battle experience than I have, at the moment. Let me catch up with you.

'Your trouble is that you spend all your time trying to convince yourself that you're brave, even when you say that you're scared. Either you're brave – in the sense of not having a clue what fear is at all – or you aren't. If you aren't, it's just too bad: you just have to work at it when the time comes. You certainly won't be any braver if you get yourself shot.'

A visitor to 'B' Echelon (in fact, it may have been his base, but he was generally touring the Battalion in his truck) was Gough Quinn, the Chaplain. I had had few dealings with him, as yet, and would have looked upon him as a scruffy non-soldier, 'a bit of a yob', whose very presence in the Battalion was unnecessary. I was none too sure that I wanted to be 'professionally' involved with him, as yet: it seemed to me that it was my own business to sort out my salvation. But there he was, in his thick glasses, friendly, yet anxious not to impose himself; and we would gossip together about our friends, about various academic matters which I had forgotten about since I came down from Oxford, and about books generally. A mutual favourite was *Cold Comfort Farm*, which I had with me in paperback (and still have, somewhere.) It amused us to identify its characters with our brother-officers. Hubert Snowden was cast as Aunt Ada Doom; and the four quartermaster-sergeants as Adam Lambsbreath's four cows. I forget the other tie-ups: Amos the hot-gospeller, Seth the sex-pot, and all the rest; but it was cheering to find that many officers had read the book, for the game soon became known by several others, not only at 'B' Echelon but up in the Battalion itself.

After a while, I took a plunge, and began to bully him. It was 'camou-flage', in a way, for all the other things I really wanted to discover. He probably realized this before I did, but, for the time anyway, he refused the bait. I had found it strange to discover, for the first time, that parsons were human beings after all; and that they had interests other than the care of souls, some of them quite earthy, secular, and investigative. Gough had a hearty disrespect for all matters military, for instance. He looked at our stiff, tidy, regularised world, all our 'bullshit', with a derisive humour, which earned him low marks from the senior officers but which went to my rebellious heart. Perhaps it was this which led me on: I began to rail at his religion.

'I can't understand why you are here,' I began rudely, one evening. 'I can see that someone has got to bury corpses; but does it have to be a parson? At sea, it's up to the Captain to throw them overboard decently. Why don't commanding officers hold mass funerals after a battle? After all, they are responsible for writing them off.'

'I hope that priests have other duties, too.'

'They must find the going a bit rough. We're a bit short on spirituality, in these parts.'

'What makes you think that?'

'Isn't it obvious? Soldiers are trained not to think, only to do what they are told. How many of them have ever asked you for spiritual help – whatever that is?'

'You'd be surprised,' said Gough, refusing to be drawn.

I tried another ploy. (looking back on it now, my rudeness horrifies me; but I imagine that priests are trained to look upon juvenile insults like these as signs of the Spirit at work.)

'I have a theory,' I began. 'Shoot it down if you like, because it's only a tentative one. Why do some of us get killed, but not others? My theory is that God wants his favoured ones up in heaven with him as soon as possible. But he doesn't really think that they ought to come until they've been through some sort of "test". Didn't I read about this in Christopher Isherwood's autobiography? When God thinks that one of us is ready – that he has "solved the riddle of existence", perhaps, whatever *that* means – then he reckons that it's about time for him to move on.'

'Who decides *who* moves on, where?'

'God, of course; deciding who dies and goes on to heaven.'

'I don't think that it's all as simple as that.'

'I don't see why God makes it all so *difficult*,' I said. 'It isn't only that he's the referee: he *makes* the rules, as well, and changes them when he wants to. Then, not content with that, just when we're getting used to them, he moves the goalposts. And what is all this rigmarole about creating man in his image, and then letting him go off the rails? If we are really made in his image, then we should act, and think, as he does. There would be no more sin.

'Then, surely, if he had made a bosh shot, why didn't he just pack it in and start again? This stuff about sending down his only son, to redeem men from sin by allowing men to kill him, all sounds so *cumbersome*. Surely God could be a little more efficient? It doesn't seem to have worked all that well, anyway.

'But then, it seems to me, sometimes, that everything to do with God and man is too complicated to be true. Look at the incredible mess he makes of everything. Look at the millions who die of starvation. Look at the incidence of mental illness, and cancer, and downright human wickedness. Look at war. Look at anything you like, and you see no divine plan. Is this really the best he can do?'

'Do you really expect me to answer all this?' Gough was getting a little irritated, I thought. On what mental level could he find any suitable comment? 'You have a lifetime to find some answers for yourself. I'm not going to solve the riddle of existence for you in a couple of minutes.'

'But how long is a lifetime? That's just what I want to know. It may end at any minute.'

'You know, Chris,' Gough said, obviously rattled by this time, for it was becoming clearer to him now that he had a tortured soul before him, really wanting to know how to conduct the remnants of his life with what little dignity he could muster, 'You really ought to think a little more about the Christian life before you write it off as a waste of time. There is a lot which I can't answer, I'm afraid, and a lot which we can't go into now. But don't despair, will you? Try saying some prayers. Perhaps you do?'

'I do, sometimes, when I'm getting more panicky than usual; but, quite frankly, I don't see much point in praying *for* anything, if God knows all about it anyway, and knows what's going to happen. But just in case, I always make it quite clear that there are umpteen religious problems I haven't solved, yet. I don't want God to take me aboard under any misapprehension: I'm not ready yet. Nor, quite frankly, am I in a hurry to get myself killed.'

'Aren't you? You don't seem particularly keen to stay alive, just now. I hear that you had quite a close shave last night, when you went up to the Battalion. Colonel Terence would *not* be amused if you get yourself written off.'

Gough was changing the subject. I could see that I was not going to get anything out of him, at that time; and I think now that he was right. My mind was leaping about like a squirrel in a tree. We talked instead about our friends in the Battalion.

'Did you hear about George Gidney, on patrol last night?' I asked after a while.

'I hope he got back all right.'

'Ye-es. Just. He said that the countryside was alive with Germans, all moving around, and he thought that they must be looking for him, personally. Anyway, he got behind a sand-dune, or something, and raised Battalion Headquarters on one of those little send-and-receive wireless sets we've just been issued with – what are they called? – and he whispered into it: "I'm almost surrounded by hundreds of Germans. What am I to do?"'

'He found that he had got Mervyn (the Adjutant) on the other end. But all he got from Mervyn was his well-known drawl: "We are not, er, interested in your, er, activities."'

We both had a laugh at this. Mervyn's drawl did indeed become famous in the Law Courts, after the war ended. I was to experience it myself, long before that.

I had a final remark for Gough. He must have remembered it, for it was to bring developments.

'I've said already that I'm not particularly keen to get myself killed,' I remarked, conversationally. 'But I'd be willing to risk it, if it means that

I can get back to the Battalion. My brother-officers, and my old platoon, mean a tremendous lot to me. I had simply no conception of the meaning of friendship, till I joined this crowd, and shared their dangers. Any chance of you being able to persuade Colonel Terence to have me back?'

'You really mean this, don't you?'

'Oh, yes. If I have to stay here in 'B' Echelon when the next attack goes in, I'll go crazy.'

'I don't think that there's much that I can do. Colonel Terence and I haven't got much in common, I'm afraid. But I'll see if there's an opportunity. One might turn up.' We left it at that.

Our projected attack kept being postponed, much to the relief of those who were to take part; but postponement only meant putting off what seemed inevitable. Then some unbelievable news came in, and spread like wildfire. The Brigade was to be relieved.

An entire division (the 56th London Division) was on its way up from the Delta – from the frontier with Iraq, some said – and would take over not only our positions, but our planned attack. We would be moved round, to join the First Army and to take part in yet another attempt at a break-through, further to the west and north.

I had not realized, myself, how much everyone hated Enfidaville, and dreaded the projected assault. At the news, there was an almost palpable, communal sigh of relief from the entire Brigade: perhaps everyone realized that it was doomed to failure. We got ready to welcome the newcomers.

Though I did not see it, I guess that our guardsmen were rather cruel to their replacements when they arrived. The men were tiny. Our hulking soldiers had dug deep slit-trenches for themselves, and when the little Cockneys jumped into them, they could not get out again. Then there was the farcical hand-over from one set of brass-hats to another: it was the best laugh we had had for weeks.

It seems that our Brigadier decided to give his successors a panoramic view of the battlefield, for he arranged a 'conference' on the top of a hill, just forward of the line of slit-trenches. This involved a fair number of people: our own Brigadier and his immediate staff, the incoming general, *his* three brigadiers, their staff officers, and the motley crowd of signallers, drivers and bottle-washers without which no divisional headquarters would be complete. Our Brigadier may have been surprised to see such a crowd. But the newcomers were just as surprised to see our Brigadier, resplendent in his desert gear, his badges of rank shining in the sun and his fly-whisk at the ready, in his corduroy trousers, desert boots and red tabs. There was not a steel helmet in sight, not a gas mask, not a round of ammunition and not a weapon to shoot it from. (I may be romancing, but this is how I heard the story.)

We all knew well enough that the German gunners were desperately short of shells, and were keeping them for emergencies, only. It was generally regarded as perfectly safe to wander about in the open, at this time, even in full frontal view of the German army.

But there were limits. The Germans in the mountains looked through their field-glasses at this immense, shining cavalcade; and some officer must have decided, possibly against orders from on high, that he must issue a 'warning'. One single German shell was dispatched to break up the party.

Now, a single shell is not difficult to dodge. As soon as it is fired, those at the receiving end are immediately aware that it is coming towards them; and, by the time it is coming in to land, all those who are in the target area know only too well, within feet, where it is going to land and in what direction the blast, and the shell-splinters, will go: always forwards.

There was not much doubt about this one. All the veterans, from the Brigadier downwards, found convenient holes in the ground and lay low. But the newcomers were also new to enemy shellfire; and by now the shell was shrieking down on them. They had to run. All the nearby holes were full of guardsmen, of course, so they had to search further afield. But two of their signallers, still using the infamous 18-sets, which one had to carry and both had to 'receive' in both pairs of ears, were still upright, unaware of what was going on, till they looked up, to find themselves alone on the top of the hill. Tearing off their earphones, they were deafened by the shell, which was just about to land on their heads.

One of the curious phenomena of this part of the world is the propensity of the local inhabitants to dig their wells at the top of hills, rather than at the bottom. There was a well here. It was surrounded by a low, stone coping, and possibly by a small gantry which, in its turn, would have sported a windlass and a rope, with a bucket to let down into the depths. It was not said whether or not the two signallers knew what it was; but they were in a hurry; and the crash of the shellburst was accompanied by a long, enduring scream as the two signallers fell all the way to the bottom. Luckily for them, the well was full of water.

Everyone picked themselves up; and it was decided to continue the conference in some less conspicuous place. The Brigadier summoned up a few guardsmen from their slit-trenches nearby, and had them drop a stone into the well, secured by a length of signal cable. One of the unfortunate signallers tied himself on, and was pulled up towards the surface by a posse of sulky guardsmen.

But this was too much for the German officer, who decided to disobey orders, once again . . . Another shell was dispatched, as accurate as the first . . . Another crash, another scream. It was one of those stories which have no end. Eventually, all was well. We giggled for days, as we sped away. Possibly, this was with relief.

14

ROUND THE BEND

Morale now miraculously restored, we all drove away from Enfidaville, to join our brethren in the First Army.

We all guessed that Monty had been overruled by the Commander-in-Chief, Alexander, who had taken command of the whole operation. To this day, I am not altogether sure of the truth of this; but Alex seems to have been right, to concentrate the final attack on one small sector – *not* Enfidaville – and to 'rush' Tunis with an overwhelming assault, on a narrow front and by the shortest route. He chose the valley of the River Medjerda, less than twenty-five miles from the city across reasonable tank country. The troops for the assault could be assembled in the deep valleys to the west. This country was well known to the units of the First Army, of course: rolling downs, with the wheat now turning from green to gold.

So the 'Desert Rats', the Fourth Indian Division, and other formations which included the 201st Guards Brigade, were withdrawn from the Eighth Army front and secretly brought 'round the bend' to reinforce this final push. Our Brigade was to come under command of the Sixth Armoured Division (of the First Army) and, for the last time, to exercise its proper function as a motor brigade. It suited us well. Not only could we make use of our own mobility, stifled at Enfidaville; in addition, we could fight alongside our 'sister' Guards Brigade, which included our own Second Battalion.

We took our own 'B' Echelon along with us, of course – and that meant that I could at least remain in touch with my friends. Even though it was not suggested that I should get my platoon back, I was able to share their feeling of release.

On our first evening, we leaguered a few miles out of the holy city of Kairouan, its minarets just visible over the marshes and the call of the *muezzin* in our ears. Then, next day, we were off across secondary metalled roads to the south-west, away from the war, till we turned right, and northward once again, at Sbeitla.

I have always wanted to return to Sbeitla. I simply had not realized the greatness of the Roman empire till I saw its ruins: Sbeitla, after all, is miles away from anywhere nowadays, and even the ubiquitous tourist trade has not found it. Possibly, it is not worth seeing anyway – we did not stop – but my impression was of miles of ruins, two thousand years old, yet still in a remarkable state of preservation, out on the fringe of the Roman empire, in the days when it was holding back the onrush of the Sahara sand.

The First Army had travelled this road before us, on their way down to lend a hand to the raw American army, a couple of months before. In convoy, we now followed them, north into the mountains, peacefully, not knowing what new trouble we were to meet but confident that it could hardly be worse than Enfidaville.

From the heights, we now looked down upon a plain below; and I remember the wonder of it, still.

We found suddenly that we had left the desert behind us for ever. We saw fields below us, the crops in their artificial squares, the perspective as of a landscape by Uccello, one square red with poppies perhaps, another blue with anemones, a third square gold, where the corn was ripening. I suppose that the sight was particularly vivid to us nomads in from the desert; but it entranced me, and let me think a little of home. There was a touch of magic in it, too. Beyond these fields, over the hills and far away, a fairy castle – no, not a castle but a white, walled town, we saw – awaited us at the end of the road. This was Le Kef.

It lost its magic as we drove in, of course. There had been a certain amount of fighting there recently, and the soldiers – now mostly Americans, whom we had scarcely encountered, so far – were very much in evidence; and a campaigning army is not a pretty sight. Still, it was pleasant to meet up with our own kind once again, and to know that we were getting to the place where we should be. Peter found more to interest him in the birds than in the soldiers: here were golden orioles, bee-eaters, and great grey shrikes for him.

We must have met with the Second Battalion during the following day: let me guess at 4 May. There were many greetings, and mild chaos, as we found places for ourselves on the grassy hillside, a few miles south of Medjez-el-Bab. It was an evening for celebration. Several of us junior officers had been together in the Sixth Battalion; and the memory of our previous good times together gave to us a sense of comradeship for the final, decisive battle, for which orders were now being distributed. As dark fell, we came together with a 'jerrican' of the local wine.

The officers of the Second Battalion, it appeared, had not had an easy time. They had landed on the Algerian coast whilst most of our drafts had been on the high seas, on our way to Suez; and their heaviest battles had been fought over Christmas in the area of Longstop Hill, not far away, on the north bank of the Medjerda and on the other side of Medjez. They had suffered heavy casualties. We compared notes about our respective battles.

We, in the Third Battalion, had had the advantage of the weather: the Second had had to endure rain, mud and even snow during the winter, whereas we boasted that we had never even slept in tents. The Second Battalion scored, however, in the supplies they received. Whereas the Third had been almost out of touch with England – letters might take months, tinned rations did not come from England at all, and the cigarettes had been unspeakable – the Second Battalion had received regular letters and parcels, unlimited tins of twenty Benson and Hedges cigarettes, British ration food, supplemented by frequent additions from the NAAFI, fresh vegetables obtained locally, even some meat, and unlimited jerricans of local wine. We had to work hard to catch up. We tried very hard, that night.

They told us about the Americans. At that time, it would have been almost a crime to speak kindly of them. (Things were very different in Italy, when the American army proved itself.)

'Did you hear,' someone said, 'that they've been issued with their campaign medals already?' (Our left breasts were virgin.)

'No, really? Are they going to give them to us, too?'

'Maybe. They seem to be fairly free with them. One of their troopships was driven ashore on Long Island or somewhere – just out of New York, anyway – and when the soldiers were pulled out on to dry land, *they* were wearing their African campaign medals already.'

'We were listening in at an 'O' group, by an American battalion commander, down near Kasserine at the end of February,' one of the more senior officers broke in. 'Then, when he said "any questions?" one of the company commanders just said, "Oh shit, Coynel, Ah'm tah'd!" The colonel had to call off the attack.'

'I was on a road-block down there, near Thala,' another one said, when we saw a whole convoy coming at us, with all their headlights blazing. I stopped the leading vehicle, and all I could see in the cab was a set of brilliant white teeth. The driver was an American negro. When I asked him where he was going, he said: "Guess I'se ree-treatin', boss, and I ain't stoppin' heah!" Whatever do you *say* to these people?'

'But they've got some good food. And they're good with their vehicles.'

'I don't suppose that they're all that different from our soldiers, really,' said one of the Third Battalion. 'When I was in Cairo, an officer came up to me in the bar at Shepheard's, and said: "Chippie, chippie, Guardee, I'm Tanks!" I wonder if he had ever been inside one.'

113

And then there was another, this time about a young officer in the Marines, who had a lisp, telling another: 'I thay, I think my helmet'th made of pith!' The party was warming up.

'Tell them about your war wound, George!' shouted one of the Second Battalion. It was obviously a familiar tale to them. (I am inventing the name, but not the story.)

George was a character (and still is, I hope: hence the alias.)

'Well, I got in the way of a shell-splinter at Longstop,' he began, 'in what is politely called the lower stomach. They took me off to the local CCS (casualty clearing station) and the surgeons there deprived me of my left testicle. I was then shifted back to a general hospital to get over it.

'But you don't actually "get over" an amputation, you know. You just have to learn how to do without; or – in my case anyway – satisfy yourself whether one will do the work previously done by two. I didn't like to ask the nurses in the hospital; so I had to find out for myself when I was let out.

'I did the obvious thing. I went into the bar of the Aletti Hotel in Algiers, and found one of the "hostesses". They are quite a good crowd there, and I wasn't the only man on the prowl. I gave her a good dinner; and then we went up to the room I had booked.

'But there we had a problem. The Aletti was very full that night, and after I had booked a double room for myself a whole crowd of American officers had come in behind me. The receptionist thought I wouldn't mind if I shared my room with one of these Americans. There he was, reading a book in an armchair, not best pleased to see us, I thought. Awkward.

'This girl was quite friendly, but she had a job to do, and didn't want to hang around all night. So we hopped into my bed and got on with it, while the American just went on reading his book. But, somehow or other, I felt a little embarrassed. So, after a while, to preserve a little order and decency, I jumped up and put the light out. There was a shuffle of discontent from the American. But all he *said* was "Can't a fella *read?*"'

This brought up one of the Third Battalion. 'Roger had the same trouble,' he said of one of our company commanders. 'Do you have any shite-hawks in this corner of Africa?'

'I expect so. What are they?'

'Kites. Big carrion birds. All over the place in Egypt, and out into the Desert, too. Anyway, Roger was carted off to *our* local CCS – a sort of marquee, a few miles behind the front, with red crosses, and a big queue at the door whenever there was a battle going on.

'The doctors didn't have time to fool around; so when a foot or an arm was taken off, they just threw it out through a tent-flap to a sort of dustbin just outside. Well, all the shite-hawks in Egypt would collect round this bin, of course. One lucky one was there to gobble up Roger's lost ball. He found it so delicious that he's been hanging around Roger ever since, hoping that someone will throw the other at him. He's probably still here, just outside.'

It was *that* sort of evening. Everyone enjoyed it.

Somebody reminded us all of a brother-officer, prim, pious and pretty useless.

'Do you remember John Green at Pirbright? He kept on saying in the Mess: "Oh, for a crack at the Hun!"'

We all found this hilarious. Perhaps there was a hint of hysteria in it, as well.

'We'll be having our own crack in the next day or two, I expect,' someone else observed. It sobered us all down; and the party broke up.

15

In the bag

This 'crack at the Hun' was not for me, I completed a circuit of the Battalion next day, tackling everyone who might be able to help. Desmond Holmes refused quite categorically to have me back into No. 3 Company. I can see his point: his platoon commanders had been at the head of their soldiers for over three weeks, now, and it would be a gesture of no confidence to deprive any one of his command on the eve of his biggest battle. (Michael, independently, had pointed this out to me.) I tried other company commanders, without success; and eventually summoned up the courage to beg Colonel Terence for a 'reserve' place in the 'team', up at the front.

'Wouldn't it help, Sir,' I asked, 'if I were to be handy, ready to take up a slot which suddenly becomes vacant?'

'Not a hope, Chris,' he answered, quite kindly really. 'You *are* in reserve already, and I want you where I can find you. You know perfectly well how the Battalion operates. If a platoon commander stops a bullet or something, then his platoon sergeant automatically takes over, at least till there's time for the company commander to apply to me for another officer. I shall have quite enough to think about without having you in the way, tripping over myself and everybody else. Be sensible.'

I could only creep off, disconsolate and rebellious. The real trouble was that I was sure that I had been consigned to the regimental scrap-heap. We were expecting a bitter battle, it must be remembered – far worse than it eventually turned out – and I could not bear the thought of standing by, unwanted, whilst all my brother-officers were risking their lives. To be in their company was almost more important than life itself. I *must* find some way of joining them, legal or not.

I found an ally. I had come as far as this with Gough Quinn, and my bed-roll was still in his truck. Why not go on with him?

Gough must have been wondering what to do with me, when he went forward into the attack; and he did not need much persuading to let me go on with him. Gough was no respecter of persons, no stickler for rules, not a military man; and he was about the only free agent on the battle-

The Rev. J.E.G. Quinn,
MC (Padre) 23
September 1943.

field. He knew what I wanted, and saw no harm in offering me a lift. I do not think that either of us thought beyond that. What I should do when I got there, what the senior officers would say when they saw me, did not occur to him, or to me. He told me to keep my head down in the back of the truck, lest I should be spotted; and off we went.

The battle began before dawn on 6 May, with two divisions, the Fourth (First Army) and the Fourth Indian (Eighth Army) assaulting on a narrow front, a few miles east of Medjez and more or less along the course of the River Medjerda, as it wound to the sea near Tunis. One good push should do it: only about twenty-five miles, we thought, and we would be there. Each of the 'lead' divisions had an armoured division just behind it to exploit any break-through; and our Brigade (together with the First Guards Brigade, we were pleased to hear) would be part of the 6th Armoured Division which, I had assumed – incorrectly – would be on the left of the advance.

Our convoy wound its way down from the hills and on to the plain, stopping every few minutes as the battle developed ahead. We went more and more slowly, for we were, in effect, shuffling across the main line of advance. The noise was shocking, bewildering, and continuous, as we all struggled to find our places, from which we could push our way through the hole which, by this time, should have been punched to the east of us.

By noon, we had come to the main road from Medjez to Tunis, and were crossing it. I was a little surprised, for it seemed obvious that we must include this road in our plans for advance – and indeed we had been told that the Battalion would reach a village called Massicault, further down this very road toward Tunis, that evening. Gough and I were now completely stuck. There was sand and dust everywhere. Where were we going? Surely we should be turning toward the east now, not continuing this miserable shuffle toward the north?

'This is pretty boring,' Gough said, over his shoulder to me. 'I wonder if there's a short cut?'

'Well, there *is*, of course,' I said. 'We could just drive along the main road, and pick up the Battalion when we all get to Massicault. It can't be more than a few miles. Surely the Germans know that they have to withdraw now, if our armour has really got through the gap?

'There must be two gaps, by now,' I continued after a pause. 'If our Brigade is crossing the front to join the Sixth Armoured on the left, then the Fourth Indian, and the Seventh Armoured behind them, must have punched *their* hole on the right, *here*. They've probably cleared the main road. It's the obvious thing.'

We were completely stuck in the queue, now, less than fifty yards from the main road. We had been motionless for nearly half an hour, by this time.

'Tell you what,' Gough said, 'let's hitch a ride. Saunders (the driver) can stay in the queue; and we'll rendezvous at Massicault this evening. It looks a tiny place, on the map.'

There were several snags about this plan. One golden rule we had picked up in the desert was that it was always wrong to be parted from one's bed and breakfast, and nearly always wrong to be parted from one's transport; and I was totally wrong, also, in thinking that the contingent from the Eighth Army was attacking on the right – in fact I had no real idea at all where any of the attack was going in. All that we both knew was the intended stopping-place for the Brigade, Massicault; but objectives are not always attained at a predetermined time.

So we left the truck, stood by the main road, and thumbed a lift. There was a fair amount of traffic, to begin with at least, but no tanks, no tank-transporters and not many trucks; a pleasure to be free of that smelly, motionless queue. In about five minutes a staff car pulled up, going our way. It was driven by a major, his driver standing in the back, his head through the sunshine roof.

'Going east?' Gough enquired.

'Yes. I'm trying to catch up with the Derbyshire Yeomen. Any idea where I can find them?'

118

I said, 'If you take us to Massicault, our Brigade staff will know where they are. They're leading the pursuit for the Sixth Armoured, aren't they?'

'Maybe they're in Tunis by now.' (They weren't.)

Gough and I clambered into the back of the staff car, one of the square-ended Humbers, unfamiliar to us at that time; and we stood up, partly to get some fresh air, but more particularly to watch out for German aeroplanes which might strafe the road. After a couple of miles, the road, which had been taking us in a south-easterly direction, rather away from the battle area, crossed a wadi and began to take us north-eastward, towards Massicault, we thought. This, it seemed, was 'Peter's Corner'.

'I'm feeling a bit naked, out here,' the major shouted up at us. 'What's happened to all the other traffic?'

We passed some burnt-out Churchill tanks, beside the road.

'Well, somebody's been here before us, I see,' he continued. 'But it must have been some time ago. It seems that they didn't like it, much.' This was an understatement: we could smell the stench as we drove by. I was looking forward along the road, and saw that the tarmac surface was pitted with holes, filled in with earth and sand. I knew what this meant.

'**MINES**!' I shouted. 'Don't drive over them!'

Then, suddenly, came the tearing, continuous cracking of German machine guns, zipping past us. With German aeroplanes in mind, I was sure that a Messerschmitt was coming up behind us. 'Keep weaving!' I yelled, as we subsided into a huddle on the floor of the car. We were in a mess, and no mistake.

When one is under machine-gun fire – and I seemed to have had more than my fair share, recently – time goes into slow motion. It seemed that we were being shot at for whole minutes, but I suppose that the entire drama was over in a matter of seconds. Even so, it began to dawn on me that a Messerschmitt could not go on firing for as long as this: it would be half-way back to Italy by now. Also, it was not hitting us. Now, aeroplanes do not fire on vehicles to miss them. There was something wrong, here: we should be dead.

At moments like this – never forgotten! – the passage of time may slow down, but the sequence of thought seems to accelerate. It became blindingly clear to me that I had made yet another howling mistake: I had failed to distinguish the 'crack' of the bullets as they broke the sound-barrier beside us with the 'boom' of the explosion as they left the gun.

This always matters, when one is under fire. But it is easier to write about than to experience, and make the correct deduction: the 'crack' is far more insistent, far more terrifying; but *it does not reflect the path of the bullet,* or where the fire comes from. It was stupid of me: the fact that the stream of fire was missing us ought to have told me that this was Spandau fire. We are being shot at by men on the ground. We were driving straight into them.

The next development was a pulverising **BANG**!

It took about a millionth of a second to work this out. I saw that we were driving straight at the enemy: our attack had not come this way at all. Not only were we driving into an enemy position, along an empty road, dead straight for miles ahead, with no chance at all of turning; now, they were firing an 88-millimetre anti-tank gun at us. They might miss with the first shot, for we were travelling fast; but they would fire again in a second; and that would be the end. They were the best guns the Germans had.

There was another ear-splitting crash, a cry of pain from the major in the driving seat, and a blast of air between me and his driver, as we lay huddled on the floor. The car sailed on. I expect that this solid round had come right through the engine, through us, and out at the back.

The heavy car was still on the road, but coasting, the engine not working; and the major lay slumped on the wheel. This terrible gun would fire again at any second.

'**GET OUT**!' I screamed. Gough opened the left-hand rear door, and jumped, though the car was still moving at over thirty miles an hour. On the right, I raised my arm (my left arm, for some reason) to my door-handle; but, at that moment, a bullet must have come through the handle, and jammed the latch. (I still keep a fragment of that handle, embedded for ever in the fleshy 'web' between the first and second fingers of my left hand. Why bother to shift it? It warns me of rain.) The major's driver was between me and the left-hand door, still in the foetal position. I did not think that he was wounded, though I did not even think about it. I gave him an almighty kick in the posterior, and the way was clear for me to follow him. The car went on.

I did not judge that jump very well, for I seem to have landed on the backs of my wrists, somehow: it had been a dive, more than a jump, I think, but there was no future in lying on the road. In another second, I had found my way into a shallow ditch at the roadside, and was flat on my face, Spandau bullets still zipping above me. Before long, they stopped. An unearthly peace followed.

Crawling back along this ditch on my stomach, I found the driver, then Gough. We were all relatively unhurt.

'Well, what's to do, now?' Gough asked. I seemed to be in charge of the venture – I do not understand why – and, to that extent anyway, felt responsible for the mess we were in.

'We'd better start crawling down this ditch.'

'All the way back to Peter's Corner?'

'Well, can you think of a better idea? Not many taxis round here, I don't think. Let's go.'

'I'm a bit uneasy about that major,' Gough said, rather typically for him. 'Is he dead, do you think? If he's still alive, then I ought really to administer the last rites.'

'Well, yes, but who will administer yours?' I said impatiently. 'He's a German responsibility, now. He was last seen driving in their direction, as though he didn't mean to stop. I don't actually think he was dead at the time, but I didn't wait around to see.' This was not the time for theological or moral arguments, I felt strongly. We had to get back.

We were too late, anyway. I saw now why the firing had stopped. Two large figures, clad in field-grey and with coal-scuttle hats, jumped into the trench ahead of us; and two more behind. They were all pointing their Schmeisser sub-machine guns at us.

They need hardly have bothered. Gough had no weapon. The driver had left his – if he had one – in the car; and I had once again forgotten to load my pistol, that day.

'Hande hoch!' One of them said. I wondered then, as I wonder now, about the need for an umlaut, and whether it were 'Hande' or 'Hander.' I had forgotten.

16

OUT OF THE BAG

'That's torn it!' I said to Gough, hands in air. (I had been reading Dorothy Sayers.) I was dreaming of an endless stay in a German prison camp, and a return to England when the war ended to face a court martial. What would I be charged with – deserting my post? A bit odd, surely, as I had not had one to desert.

'Don't think only of yourself,' Gough said, rather tartly for him (but he was under strain, too.) 'Let's ask these Germans if we can lend a hand with that Major.'

With a little gesticulation, we persuaded our guards to take us along the road to the staff car. (They had to check, too, of course.) It had come to a halt a few hundred yards further on, miraculously still on the road; and in it the major lay slumped over the steering column. When we began to move him he yelled in pain.

We all, German and English, eased him out of the car and on to his back in the shallow ditch. There was not much of his leg left. We stanched the arterial bleeding, but there was little else we could think of, for the moment, and the Germans decided that he must stay where he was till, perhaps, they could find a stretcher party. Then we were marched up a hill to the right of the road, and deposited in a large vehicle pit, where we found about ten Germans, and about a dozen British prisoners, all rather the worse for wear. They greeted us gloomily.

'How did you get here?'

'We drove our bloody staff car along the bloody road, right into it. I thought that we had cleared the main road, long ago.'

'We thought the same. Where the hell has our bloody army got to, do you know? We were told that it was making for Massicault.'

'Perhaps it's been held up.'

There was not much else to say. It seemed that everyone had done exactly what we had, assuming that the road was clear, only to drive straight into a cascade of Spandau fire. One of them, a colonel in the Gunners, had a bullet through his elbow; and I still remember looking with fascination at the bright white tip of his funny-bone, chipped off and shining in a bed of blood. One man had a nasty wound in the thigh. The others merely looked shattered, as I suppose we did. I do not think that there can be many worse situations: being shot at by Spandaus is at best demoralising, and it is not helped by being shot at by an 88-millimetre as well – and *then* to be captured, taken off into custody, watched over by Germans with their Schmeissers slung over their shoulders, and wondering whether they would use them to get rid of the encumbrance of having to deal with prisoners at all. All these things added to the sum of human misery, from which there seemed no chance of emerging.

But it could – and did – get worse, that afternoon. It would seem that the British army *was* advancing; and that its cheery band of Gunners was looking for more targets. They found us.

Our big pit must have been easily visible. It was large, to begin with, on a forward slope, and, being some kind of company headquarters, was frequently visited by officers, runners, and all the rest. Obviously, a battery of four-point-fives (larger than twenty-five pounders, and with greater penetrative power) was told to polish us off; and, for a couple of hours, salvo after salvo would crash down amongst us.

We could hear the bang of the shells as they left the guns; shells travel more slowly than the speed of sound, and the muzzles which were pointing in our direction had, as it were, a personalised bang about them. Then, coming down at us from the upper atmosphere, the sound of their approach became a screech; and they landed all around. One shell even clipped the far side of our dug-out, deluging us with smoke and cordite fumes. Another direct hit would finish us all off. There was little any of us could do, except wait for the next salvo. An odd way to die, I thought, once again: killed by our own guns in a German position which I had come to by disobeying orders.

While the shells were crashing around us, I looked round at my companions. The British prisoners were cowering – not that wrapping themselves into a ball was likely to help them, much – whereas the Germans seemed almost to be enjoying themselves. Well, they had not been through what we had, lately. All the same, I had to admire their cheerfulness and fortitude. This was the Hermann Goering Division (I believe that there were several.) I was told that no one in this particular unit, whatever it was, platoon, company, or battalion, was over twenty. Some looked less than eighteen.

I found this out from a friendly corporal, with whom I had already established an extraordinary rapport. He was the son of a bank manager in Cologne, he told me, and had had a good secondary education. We spoke together in French, remarkably fluently, as neither of us had to make any attempt at a French accent. I wish that I had asked him his name! I suppose that it did not occur to me that we could ever meet again; but, as it turned out, he must have been our prisoner, locally, a week later, and probably survived the war.

Gough saw that I had established contact, and came up.

'I say, Chris, can you ask if I can go back down to the road, to cope with that Major? Do these people know that I'm a non-combatant?'

'I'll ask. *Ecoutez. Mon ami dit qu'il est pretre, vous comprenez. Il ne porte pas les armes. Il a une carte,* (Haven't you, Gough? Show it to him.) *Et il demande s'il est permit, s'il est possible d'aller en bas, tout pres du chemin, et conforter l'officier la, qui est bien blesse, et peut mourir, tout de suite.'*

'Je vais demander a notre officier. Un moment.'

Gough received full permission to attend to the material and spiritual needs of the wounded officer; and was told, through me, that if they failed to collect him that night, he would be entitled to get him back to the English lines, in any way he could. He went.

'All the best, Chris. I'll pass on your news, if I get back.'

Now I was alone, to collect my own impressions, and to come to terms, with life 'in the bag'.

Strangely enough, the first feeling was one of relief. Although I could not claim to be safe, with British shells exploding all round me, yet at least I no longer had to make any decisions. It was now up to the Germans to take the initiative. Was I merely being cowardly? Privately, I suspect that most newly-taken prisoners of war have to go through this phase: we, for instance, had just been through an intense, nerve-shattering ordeal and were down to the last of our spiritual reserves. There can be no doubt that, at this moment, the captive is at a great psychological disadvantage, and his captors need not bother overmuch about keeping him strictly under control. In a world peopled with heroes, this would be the time, then, for the prisoner to make a break for it. On the face of it, it must be easier to escape from the battlefield than from a camp in the depths of enemy country: it is less far to go, for a start, and the escaper can bank on a certain amount of confusion even amongst his captors, let alone the 'fog of war' which envelops every battlefield. But alas, he is not ready. He has found someone to look after him.

My circumstances were more complicated, though. In the course of that awful afternoon, I began to appreciate more fully the real depth of the pit I had dug for myself. I was not supposed to have been anywhere near the 'front line' at all. I really must get back, if only to explain myself.

During daylight, in this open veldt country, there was clearly nothing to be done: it would mean running for a couple of miles across the open, under intense machine-gun fire. There might be a chance after dark, though.

The interchange with the German corporal had brought the other prisoners around me. So far, I had tended to neglect them. But they had been watching, of course, and had seen Gough walk away, after a discussion in which I had been involved; and I was still present, yet, it seemed, able to communicate with their captors. Perhaps I had some magic formula for them, too.

They crowded round, as best they could in a pit which was crowded enough already – and liable to disintegrate at any moment.

'Sir, ask him what's going to happen to us.'

'*Il dit, qu'est que vous allez faire avec les prisonniers?*'

'*Moi, je ne sais pas. C'est pour nos officiers de decider. Mais je crois que nous allons, tous, en retraite, quand il fait nuit.*'

'*Et la bataille? Tout va bien?*'

'*Pour nous, ou pour vouse?*'

He told me that the British attack had gone in, to the north of us, and that he thought it had been successful. As a result, he thought that the German position, here beside the main road, was becoming too exposed; and that the British would be likely to widen their front during the night, for they would be needing the road to continue their advance. To the south of us, though, ran a line of hills (the true right of the Medjerda river valley;) and he imagined that his unit would be withdrawing to them during the night, either to prevent the British from expanding their front any further, or possibly to prepare a counter-attack from the flank. As for the prisoners, he imagined that they would be flown out to Italy. There was little room for them in Tunisia, now.

What a charming and intelligent young man he was! We talked together for hours in our schoolboy French: about the folly of war, the need for Britons and Germans to fight together on the same side, about the relative uselessness of Italian troops to the Germans, and American troops to the British – topical military gossip, chiefly, though there were hints of deeper thinking which I should have liked to explore. Eventually, the British guns fell silent. Perhaps they had run out of ammunition, or they thought that we had been exterminated by this time; and as the evening came, an uneasy peace descended on us all. I began to wonder when, and how, we were all going to retreat. My own rudimentary plans depended on it.

So as darkness fell, we all prepared to move. It was difficult to follow the sequence of orders, and where they came from, for everyone was busy and the language used was – obviously – German. My friend the Corporal had a moment to come and say goodbye, both of us a little more emotional than the occasion warranted, perhaps. But I missed him. We had been able to talk together of normal, harmless things, but now had to come to terms, once again, with the revolting facts of war. I still wonder what happened to him.

An officer detailed four German privates to guard us on our way. I suppose that they were told where to go; but they were not very bright, and I am not sure that they really knew what they were doing. It was not long before we had parted company with the rest of the retreating column, and were stumbling through the cornfields without much sense of direction. We began by going east. Before long, though, I noticed that the direction was more southerly, which, to me, made a little more sense – in fact, I have a vague memory of helping them in their route-finding myself.

I had learned a little German at school, five years before, but my vocabulary had by now completely deserted me. My grammar had always been shaky. All the same, I was already dubbed interpreter, for the guards had nothing but German, and the prisoners nothing but English. It was up to me to do the best I could.

It would have been quite easy to bolt for it, into the darkness, and risk a bullet. But I made the mistake of asking the Gunner colonel for permission, before I made off: I did not want yet another charge of disobeying orders, hanging over me when the time eventually came for a reckoning.

'No, no!' the Colonel was horrified. 'We must stick together, I'm sure. What are these German thugs going to do with us? Did you hear (I hadn't) that the other day, when one British soldier was captured and then escaped, the Germans shot all the rest?'

I refused to believe this. 'Sir, I don't think that these guards even know where they are taking us,' I said. 'Have you noticed that we are beginning to turn south? Could it be that they will be marching us west, before long, towards our own people?'

'All the more reason for keeping together, then.'

I saw that I was losing this particular argument. In a way, the Colonel may have been right. It was impossible for our group of prisoners to scrag these guards, kill them with their own rifles and then return to our lines: we were an indifferent bunch, still demoralised, and at least two were wounded. But, all the same, I began to feel that if I did not do something positive soon, then before long we would all be in an aeroplane heading for a German prison camp.

It was a black night, in more senses than one. The colonel could walk without assistance, as could most of the other prisoners. However the one seriously wounded man had to be carried, on a groundsheet, held at each of its four corners by a bearer, usually with a slight wound of his own. We made very slow progress. I shared the burden for a while, but both my wrists were giving me almost intolerable pain by this time, and I had to withdraw my share. At about midnight, we came to a farm building, on a small hill.

'*Bitte,*' I tried my terrible German on the guards. '*Darfen wir ruhig hier?*'

Everybody stopped. It was pitch dark – no moon – and we were sheltered by the wall of an outbuilding. Cigarettes were lit up. I tried to work out my next request. It was not easy.

'*Hier ist der Verwundert,*' I began. What on earth was the German for 'stretcher'? '*Er ist sehr schwer.*' That did not sound right, but would have to do, for the moment. '*Darf ich eine Planke suchen, eine Tur, etwas zu tragen?*' It was the best I could do; but it was a million times better than anyone else. The Germans shrugged their shoulders, and I went for a hunt in the ruins of the farmhouse. There were some loose pieces of timber about – roof-timbers, I think, far too narrow for the wounded man but much easier for his bearers – and I returned with two or three. The buildings had come under shellfire, that afternoon, and some were smouldering still.

'I say, Sir, what about a fire?' One of the prisoners asked.

Well, we were all extremely cold, even in the North African spring: shock, perhaps. I went and collected a few more pieces of timber; and it was an incredible morale-booster to us all, to sit around a real fire, as it was to me to feel that, for once, I had actually done something useful. I began to feel that I was beginning to take charge of the motley group of soldiers, colonels down to privates, English and German. Later on, the legend was to grow in the Battalion that I had cheerfully set fire to a farmhouse because I was feeling chilly! How this percolated through I have no idea; but it is true that, somehow or other, I think that I was becoming a little crazy at this stage, almost unaware of the perils with which we were still surrounded, and ready to tackle everything and everybody myself. I blush as I remember it! But it was good while it lasted.

We shuffled onward through the black night. I kept my eye on the stars, and saw that our general direction was still southward. Perhaps, I thought, the guards knew where they were taking us, after all, but it no longer seemed important. By dawn, we were coming up to the line of hills, now well off the direct line of the British attack and, just possibly, the last redoubt into which all German troops were to make a stand. Down to the south of us was the misty spike of the Djebel Zaghuan, the highest mountain in those parts. I had last seen it from Enfidaville.

There were troops about. Soon after dawn we staggered up to a small party of German officers, waving their map-cases, and wondering what on earth to make of our party.

'Where do you come from?' This was an intelligent-looking major, who recognized our uniforms, and spoke English fluently. I nearly

127

hugged him. Perhaps he thought that we were the vanguard of the advancing British army. I looked at our Gunner Colonel, for he was officially in charge; but he merely said: 'Tell them, will you? Tell them we need a medical unit.'

'Are you holding this line of hills, or are we?' I asked.

'Oh, we are, for the moment. You had better report to headquarters, I think. You must be about the last to come in,'

Not long afterwards, we found our way through a nick in the line of hills, where several hundred weary Germans were resting. I could see at a glance that they were not ready for a counter-attack: they were beginning to man observation-posts along the line of the ridges, looking north, where an attack was soon to be expected. But they did not seem too energetic: morale amongst them was no longer high. These were not members of the Hermann Goering Division.

I reported to another bunch of officers. Fortunately, one of them spoke a little English, and could translate for me.

'What is the situation, do you know?' I asked, before anyone could ask me anything.

'It seems that the British have broken through to the north of us, on a fairly narrow front,' I was told (more or less.) 'We were going to counter-attack from this line of hills; but another order has just come in, that we are to withdraw deeper into the hills. It will be difficult, though, to collect all our men together.

'I have two wounded men, here. Have you got a medical post?'

'No. I am sorry .'

'Have you seen any British troops yet, on the plain? They must be advancing in this direction, by now.'

'No, not today. Not yet.'

'I think what I had better do,' I remarked (odd, again, that I seemed able not only to contribute to the discussion, but even to make suggestions) 'is to march my lot back, to find medical attention. You are withdrawing, aren't you? You won't want to be saddled with more wounded than you can cope with; and you certainly won't be able to hold on to this line of hills.'

There was some discussion about this. 'It will not be easy, for you. Our forward detachments have orders to fire. We have no longer any communication with them.'

The talk became desultory, for a while. I did not want to push my plan too forcefully, lest they should think up more problems. These officers, to do them justice, were almost as much in the dark as I was. They scarcely knew each other. They had probably spent the night bringing isolated groups of Germans over the fields, heading towards relative –

and temporary – safety, without any specific orders; and were now waiting for someone to take the initiative and tell them what to do next. For some unaccountable reason, it seemed that they were prepared to listen to me.

Looking back, I can begin to appreciate their need. They, and their men, were weary beyond belief, punch-drunk, peeled off on to one side like wood-shavings, discarded, leaderless, knowing that there was little anyone could do now to save the German army in Africa. On the other hand, I had passed my low moment, and was thinking clearly. I have no idea where this sudden sureness had come from; but I could see the whole battle in my mind, the British divisions rushing for the city of Tunis (they arrived later that day, I believe, Thursday, 7 May) and mopping up any German units which failed to give themselves up. I was on the winning side, I knew, even though I was gossiping with the losers. It was a heady feeling.

I did think of advising them all to come along with me, to give themselves up; but came to the private conclusion that they were not ready for this, yet. I distrusted my own motives, too. How grand it would be to bring a few thousand Germans over to the British lines! Perhaps I could have done; but I think now that I was right to be cautious. For all I knew, there were whole formations of Germans over the next hill, preparing a counter-attack; and for all I knew the British advance had been halted. Best, I thought, to bring back my own bedraggled little band. This should not be too difficult.

'Look,' I said, 'I don't think that you have much chance of holding this line of hills, here. The British are past you, and closing in on Tunis. Another British army is fighting its way up from the south. I hear that the French are advancing in between them. If you want my advice, it would be to escape from the jaws of this trap, and make for the peninsula of Cap Bon, to the East. You should meet up with the rest of your army, there.

'But you must hurry, or the jaws will close. We would be holding you up; so I think I'd better carry our wounded back towards the British army.

'I shall try to get them out to the westward, through your forward positions, and then down on to the plain. These men need doctors, as soon as possible. I'll just have to take a chance with your outposts. They shouldn't fire on a stretcher-party, coming out from their own lines.'

'Okay, *Britisch Offizier*. God be with you. If you speak with our men on the hill, can you tell them that we are now about to withdraw? They should follow, in haste.'

So, after a mutual pull at a mugful of wine from a jerrican, it was all decided; and I set off with my weary band on the next stage of our travels.

We had parted company with our guards. We were free, even though walking through Germans. They greeted us as we went by.

We saw our first observation post on a distant hilltop, and waved at the Germans there, frantically.

They must have wondered why we were taking our wounded in the wrong direction (and even who we were, for khaki drill does not immediately identify its wearer, in a battle.) But, as we came closer, I saw Spandaus pointing in our direction.

'*HALT!*' I yelled at them (mercifully, a word common to us all.) '*Sie mussen nach Ost gangen. Schnell! Sehen sie die Andern?*' I wondered if I had got that right, but in the distance, we could all see the long column of Germans moving sadly eastward. We were invited in. After a generous hand-out from another jerrican of wine, they packed up, and we went our separate ways – we to the westward, along the crests, for I had spotted the next observation post a mile away.

It happened again and again. By afternoon we had cleared the entire ridge of Germans; so we edged to the north-west and staggered down on to the plain. I guessed that, by this time, we were about level with Peter's Corner, on the main road, but well to the south of it. We were moving very slowly, now.

Our stretcher-bearers were coming to the end of their strength. The Gunner Colonel and I – and, I think, a third man with a wound – had not been carrying, so I had organised two teams, to relieve each other at stated intervals; but, all the same, they had been carrying this man on one miserable plank for about eighteen hours. The Colonel, too, was stumbling; and I felt completely drained, myself. Very slowly, we approached some farm buildings.

'HALT! Who goes there?' came a shout from an outbuilding.

'Friend!' A gust of immense relief. We watched, as an armoured car bounced through the cornfield towards us. *They* could take over, now. An officer called up an ambulance on his radio set. Then the commanding officer drew up in his vehicle.

'What's it like out there?' he asked. 'Have you seen any Germans around? My regiment has orders to clear these hills, just ahead.'

'I think you can tell them that it's safe enough, Sir. The Germans have all retreated now, from the whole line of hills. It seems that they are going east.'

'Have you been helping them on their way?'

'Not exactly, Sir. They were helping us, if anything.'

'Well, you'd better all get in to that ambulance and go to the CCS for the night. We're going to be a bit busy here, I expect. You all look as though you need patching up. But you seem to have done what *we* were sent here to do. Thank you very much indeed. We'd better get along, though, and take possession.'

We were dumped at the CCS bathed, covered in plaster and put to bed. The adventure was over. I suddenly found myself utterly spent, physically and mentally, unable to think for myself, let alone the whole German army. And what on earth was I to say to Colonel Terence?

17

The battle of Potinville

I slept like a dead man. I was discharged on the following morning, 8 May (or was it the one after? I seem to have lost a day somewhere) when a truck from the Battalion came to take me away. With an arm in plaster (but I must have borrowed a razor) I looked even less guardsmanlike than usual.

Tunis had by now been entered, and what was left of the German army was retreating to the Cap Bon peninsula, to the south-east. There were rumours that it would be evacuated. The two Guards brigades had been shunted to the right, somewhere south of the city, either to block the evacuation, or to keep the retreating Germans under pressure. Here, there was a narrow corridor between the sea and the mountains, across the bay from Tunis, and this must be cleared before we could be sure that the German army had no more resistance to offer.

The First Guards Brigade was now tackling the corridor, and was making some progress, into the village of Hammam Lif. (The hills, by the way, may have been about 1,000 feet high, fairly steep and craggy; and the main road, which would complete our circle and bring us back to Enfidaville, went through it, and along the corridor on to the Grombalia Plain.) Resistance was a little more dogged than had been expected: it seemed as though our brigade, in reserve behind the other, might have to leapfrog through later.

Colonel Terence, then had time to deal with me.

I had been dreading this moment. There was no question about it: I had disobeyed explicit orders, had been taken prisoner, and had now turned up again just when – and where – I was not wanted. I dare say that he would have preferred me to remain a prisoner, preferably on the other side of the Mediterranean.

'Now, what the hell have you been up to?' He began. There was no simple reply to this. I could only stand to attention, scruffy, sheepish and demoralized, looking straight before me.

'Stand to attention, boy!' he shouted. (Difficult, this, with an arm in a sling.) 'Don't you realize that I'm supposed to be giving you an imperial rocket?'

'Yes, sir. I'm very sorry, sir.'

'My orders were that you were to remain with 'B' Echelon, and to be there in reserve, in case we had casualties amongst the officers. Fortunately, we haven't had any, yet. I simply can't have my valuable officers swanning loose around the battlefield, fighting their own private war. Did you know that two other officers, those idiots Wyld and Brodrick, nicked a Bren gun carrier to go out and look for you? I'd have looked pretty silly if they had been put in the bag, too. But I'd have blamed *you* for that.'

'However did they know, sir?'

'I haven't a clue. It must have been when that fool of a Chaplain came back in yesterday morning.'

'So he's back. I wonder how he got on?'

'Ask him. He's here, somewhere. But you're changing the subject. I'm supposed to be giving you a rocket. But this Chaplain character will keep on saying that he takes responsibility; and I've given *him* a rocket, too, for corrupting my young officers. However, he says that you did very well, when you both got caught.

'I've also had some fool colonel on the blower. Says he commands a recce battalion. Can't remember his name now, or his unit. Says that you cleared the Germans off a whole ridge single-handed, and seemed to think the world of you. What's all this about?'

'Well, it's not true, sir. I may have saved him a little work, I suppose, but that was all.'

'And what's all this he said about you bringing a crowd of our soldiers out of the bag?'

I had to think quickly. I collected the impression that Colonel Terence was bluffing: that his bark was going to be worse than his bite. Perhaps I had given him a pleasant surprise! (I had certainly surprised myself.) But what he had heard was all wrong, and I was deeply embarrassed to be looked upon, falsely, as some kind of hero. Whatever should I say, now?

I was given no chance. 'Look here, Chris,' said my Commanding Officer. 'There seems to be people here who think you deserve a medal; but there is also a good case for getting you court-martialled. Take a major rocket instead, and just think yourself fortunate. What you had better do now is to go and find Michael Brodrick; and I'll tell him to keep you on a chain for the next few days. You aren't fit to be trusted out on your own. Just stick around, and behave like a civilized human being.'

'Yes, sir. Thank you very much, sir.' I ran for cover.

Of course, the first person I had to meet was Sergeant Harness, my old platoon sergeant from the Sixth Battalion, marching some men off, on fatigues. He could not stop, of course; but he gave me a grin which stretched from one ear to the other, and raised both hands in surrender. Damn. *Everybody* knew.

It was the same wherever I went. It seemed that my behaviour had tickled the whole Battalion; and I had to put up with a storm of good humour. I was not prepared to cope with this at all. I had been prepared to feel sorry for myself, and to apologise for my dreadful lapse; but everyone crowded round to hear about my adventures, and I saw that I had achieved a reputation for dare-devilry and cunning which would take months to go away.

I found Gough Quinn first of all. 'I had an easy time, really,' he told me. 'Yes, the Germans let me go all right, as you saw; and I went down to the road to find the major. It wasn't too difficult, really. The important thing was to get him into an ambulance, and then on to proper medical treatment.'

'You got an ambulance out to him? Surely not!'

'Well, it wasn't quite as easy as that. I had to do a lot of walking. But then I found somebody who was prepared to drive me back – very grateful to find that the road was clear. He sent up an ambulance, and I went back with it.'

'And what about the major? Did he survive?'

'I think they carried out a proper amputation when we got him to the CCS. They said that he ought to be all right.'

Then I went round to find Michael Brodrick. (Was he back in No.3 Company by this time?) He had heard that I was on my way. We had rather a typical upper-class English encounter: Michael drawling about the state of the battle, I trying to mask my delight at coming under his wing once again. He said that I had better find myself a place in the armoured car he had somehow picked up. His soldier-servant would make contact with mine, and they could carry our heavy gear in another truck.

'And what's all this about you and Peter coming out to find me?' I asked. 'Where were you looking?'

'Who told you about that?'

'Colonel Terence.'

'How did *he* find out, for goodness' sake? Peter and I will be in dead trouble about this, now.'

'I don't think so. He was blasting about a bit, I suppose, but he seemed to be quite pleased, really.'

Michael then told me where we were, and what we were doing. The officers of the Second Battalion, in front of us, had had a hard day, though they had not had many serious casualties. There was a regiment of Lancers, in Sherman tanks, just ahead of them now, keeping up the pressure along this narrow coastal corridor.

We were off before dawn the following morning – it must have been 10 May – and we drove past our friends in the Second Battalion amongst the houses of Hammam Lif; then out along the main road, running east now, more or less, but due to bend to the right when it was clear of the mountains. Down here by the sea, there were small fields, ripe with crops, orchards, and trees lining the road – walnut I guessed (or guess now) – and date palms nearby.

It was very cool and peaceful, I thought. There was nothing stirring till we came to the tanks: Shermans, with their hatches battened down. I wondered why. (We heard, later, that the men had been having their breakfasts, when they were fired on by German Tiger tanks, each mounting an 88-millimetre gun. The Commanding Officer had been shaving in his tank, with only a couple of inches showing of the top of his head, but that, too, was shaved off by the first German shell.) On we went, into the sunrise.

BANG! Caught again! We were being shot at by armour-piercing shells. The Spandaus ripped all around us, and we were in a battle, once again.

A small secondary road opened up, half-right into the mountains, and we all jinked into it. Vehicles were a disadvantage here. We all drove behind the trees and bushes, jumped out of our armoured cars, trucks and jeeps, and sped for cover as we tried to find out what we were facing. The only solution was to run on and find out.

There were plenty of Spandaus still ahead of us. This side-road seemed to be a cul-de-sac, leading us only to a village called Potinville, at the entry to a steep side-valley running into the mountain chain. By chasing the Germans up here we were, as it happened, cutting them off from their retreat, and separating them from their Tiger tanks, which were forced to withdraw beyond the 'corridor' altogether to regain contact with their main body, now swarming all over the plain beyond.

This became clear as we ran forward. The Third Battalion must have been leading the Brigade when the firing began; and, no doubt, the other two battalions remained astride the main road.

Michael had jumped out of the armoured car almost as soon as the firing began: I am pretty sure that he saw in a flash that this was no place for a vehicle, even if it were armoured. I was in a hurry too. I never had much faith in armour at the best of times, and now I could see that our vehicle would be the first target for a Tiger tank; and, being the passenger,

I had to sit beside a forty-gallon petrol tank. I was sure that I should be safer on my two feet.

'Come on!' shouted Michael through the din. 'Let's see what the forward platoons are doing.'

They had left their vehicles under trees, beside the road, even in the middle of it, some with their engines still running. Without anyone, as far as I know, giving the order, No. 3 Company fanned out on one side of the village as they approached it, and No. 4 Company on the other. Everyone was running, Bren guns firing from the hip. Behind us, I believe, other companies had 'de-bussed' and were now fanning out further to the left again, among the vines on the slope of the eastern hillside. We, with a few others, were running along separately, catching occasional glimpses of the others amongst the buildings, the orchards and the fields.

'Hang on a second!' Michael suddenly realized that we were surrounded by German soldiers, emerging from the buildings and bushes.

'Hell!' I shouted back, 'I don't want to be taken prisoner yet again!' But none of them were firing on us.

'For God's sake tell them to surrender. They must see that they're surrounded. What's German for 'surrender'? *You* ought to know.' (Rather an unkind remark, I thought to myself.)

Luckily, the Germans forestalled us, by dropping their weapons and holding their hands up. Was our Company Sergeant-Major there? I have a vague memory of him calling a hundred or two Germans to attention, and marching them off along the road along which we had come. He must have surprised the following troops no end. But everything seemed a little crazy, that morning.

Michael went storming on past the village, waving his pistol in the air, till we came to a small rise beyond it, where the road began to peter out. There, we watched two platoons rushing forward on our right, two more trampling through the vineyards on our left, and other groups labouring up the steep slopes, further to our left again. We could also see untidy groups of Germans, mustering in the open and getting ready to be led into captivity.

'Maybe some of these characters will try to stage a demonstration,' Michael observed. 'It just can't all be just as easy as this. Where's your pistol?'

'I haven't got one.'

'My dear child, don't you realize that there's a war on? Officers are supposed to lead their troops into action, you know. Did you leave it behind in the Dingo?' (This was the armoured car.)

'No. I gave it away last week.'

'Who on earth to, for goodness' sake?'

'To a German. He seemed to want it. He was quite nice about it.'

'Well, I've never heard of an unarmed officer leading his troops in a charge against the enemy.' This was a slight exaggeration, for we were not personally leading anybody, at that moment. To be honest, I did feel a little naked, out on that hill, at least until the platoons on both sides were well ahead of us. Some fairly unprecedented things had been happening to me during the past week, I thought; and here was I, alone with Michael on a hilltop, weaponless and with an arm in plaster, watching the collapse of an enemy army. It was not a view that I was likely to see again.

Behind us, in the village, and in the vineyards and orchards around it, Germans were swarming now. Even Michael was surprised. 'Did we really walk through all that lot?' He asked. By all the rules, we had been crazy to walk through this enemy army as though we were in command of it. But nothing mattered, now.

Seeing Michael, some platoon commanders came across to report, and to ask for further orders. Everyone was wild with excitement. There had been no casualties; and I refuse to believe that our Bren guns, fired by breathless, running men, had inflicted any. It was becoming clear that the Germans had little fight left in them.

'Well, let's all wander up that hill on the left,' Michael said to anyone who was listening, 'you on the right and you on the left. Our main job, remember, is to clear the corridor by the sea, all the way along, till these mountains give way to the Grombalia plain. We'll see how far we've got when we get to the top.'

Before long, both companies had collected on the crest above the Potinville valley; where there was only a little mopping up still to be done. It seems that we had taken five thousand prisoners so far that morning, and had not had breakfast yet! It was only about 8 o'clock, according to the History. I thought that we had been at it for hours.

So ended the Battle of Potinville. To be honest, it was hardly a battle at all, but a walk-over; but we were not to know that when it all began. I wished that all battles were as exciting and enjoyable as this had been! In its small way, it was decisive, though, for from the hilltop we looked down on the Grombalia plain, and found that we had finally cleared the 'corridor'.

Hundreds of the local inhabitants had been hiding in caves on the hillside. Had we 'liberated' them, or captured them? – not that there had been any suggestion of active ill-treatment by the Germans, by the way. They seemed delighted to welcome us, and saw that we were supplied with wine. I imagine that our own quartermasters came up with rations, for we were to remain on that crest for some hours, resting, boasting a little, comparing our varied experiences. I have seldom felt more pleased with myself.

Far below us, we could watch our tanks debouch on to the plain below, and carry on the advance.

Not many people have had an opportunity to watch a tank battle as it develops. The men in the tanks can see very little, if anything; and the senior officer who co-ordinates the many manoeuvres can only listen to voices on the radio. But we, safely above it, could see it all.

Our Sherman tanks looked like slugs. They moved across country almost too slowly for us to be aware of their progress. Sometimes, a tank, or a troop, would meet an impassable obstacle, like a deep ditch, and would have to reverse away from it. (I had not realized, till I saw this, that tanks must always *face* the enemy, even if they are retreating from him: all their heavy armour is in front of them, and their engines, at the rear, are vulnerable.)

I had heard already that it took six Shermans to deal with one German Tiger tank; and it was interesting to watch how they would try, not always successfully, to circle one like hounds round a wild boar. I preferred my own two feet, I thought. The local legend was that it took six seconds for the crew to evacuate a Sherman, but only five for a Sherman, when hit, to 'brew up'.

To me, this did not look like good 'tank country'. There were too many houses, too many trees and ditches to allow free movement – but it must be remembered that we had just come in from the desert, where tank commanders had faced different problems.

Michael and I discussed all this, as we sat in the sun and waited to be called back to our vehicles. Clearly, we were going to be wanted, soon. It was our function, as part of a motor brigade, to exploit the break-through of the tanks when they had eliminated the tanks of the enemy and driven their infantry out of any 'line' they had managed to form. Neither of us imagined that we would have to wait long.

18

VICTORY

Orders came in the late afternoon. We were to reclaim our vehicles, and drive in convoy along the main road to the south-east. This meant crossing the isthmus of the Cap Bon peninsula, till we reached the sea again at Hammamet. This faced south-eastward; but here the road bent right again, along the line of the coast, through Bou Ficha to Enfidaville, Sousse – and Cairo.

The armour was still ahead of us (we must have passed through it later, – during the night, for tanks do not fight in darkness.) Our difficulty, of course, was that we should have to stick to the road. Cross-country driving was virtually impossible in this cultivated country, particularly at night.

We were to find that even driving along the road had its hazards. To begin with, it was extremely difficult to get on to the main road at all. Our side-road, coming out from Potinville, was very small, and the main road was already carrying more traffic than it could take. Behind the tanks of an armoured division, there always has to follow a stream of 'soft' vehicles, carrying fuel, supplies of ammunition, food and drink, repair parties, experts of all trades, all trying to catch up with the tank formations when they leaguer up for the night. If there is a call for tank transporters – enormous vehicles which seem to have about five hundred wheels – the road can be blocked for hours.

But our orders now were explicit: to get to the front and close the entire peninsula. It would be useless to try to argue the toss about this with the drivers of each of the vehicles in front of us. We must just drive them off the road.

Fortunately, we could tell the support vehicles of the Sixth Armoured Division by their colour. They were all painted olive-green, with their 'mailed fist' logo on their tailboards. Our desert-sand vehicles had the measure of them.

None of our drivers were given any orders, but these old sweats knew exactly what to do. Our first truck would overtake a young driver, then cut in, forcing him to use his brakes. Then would come our second,

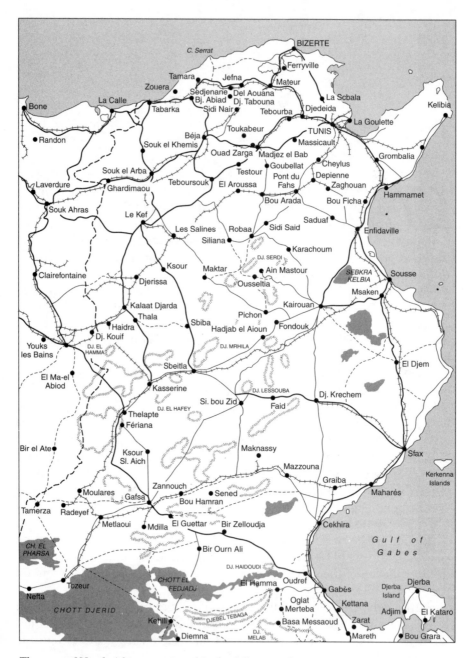

The area of North Africa mentioned in the following chapters.

cutting in even more closely; and then the third, who would clip his offside wing, and terrify him into pulling off the road altogether, till the rest had roared by. It was a treat to watch this. The tails of our trucks were far less vulnerable than the engines of their victims and so, before long, all the vehicles in our Brigade had cleared the road for themselves.

Two or three miles out into the plain, there was another minor hold-up. A bunch of German gunners had elected to go down fighting; and a couple of guns had been trained on the road.

'Well, we can't stop, just for a couple of guns,' Michael said, as we free-wheeled in to join the queue. 'The thing is to wait for the stonk, then drive like hell, to get through before the next one.' It seems that he, and many of the other drivers, had often had to handle situations like this before. I was told to time the arrival of the salvoes – not difficult – and then tell Michael, who would drive our Dingo up a place. Our turn came. My breath shortened or stopped altogether. Michael's foot went on to the accelerator; and we were through. The Germans, we knew by then, are a methodical people, and all they do can be timed in advance. (It is easy to write this, but not quite so easy to bet your life on it.)

As we drove on, the darkness fell, and our speed slackened. I have no idea who was in front of us, breaking the trail, and I did not particularly care. Large groups of demilitarized German soldiers marched past us, in the other direction; and, for hours on end, we would wait for our own forward movement to continue. The sky was rent with flashes – no one knew what they were – and every now and then there would be an enormous bang in the distance, as of Germans blowing up a bridge or a culvert. By the time we arrived at the scene of the crime, our own Sappers would have organized a diversion: we would leave the road, bounce and tumble around what was left of the obstruction, then clamber thankfully back on to the tarmac. But then there would be another long halt. So the night wore on.

Some time into the small hours, we must have gone through Grombalia, about half-way across the isthmus. Goodness, I was tired! I had had only one night's sleep in the past seven, and had been having an eventful time, all things considered. Michael, too, had been driving, fighting a battle, and driving again since four o'clock the previous morning; and these protracted halts were a trial to us both. Suddenly, our radio came to life.

'Sunray to all vehicles!' A familiar voice barked out of the machine. We made our appropriate response, but there were some silences: others had succumbed, more deeply even than ourselves. The voice of Colonel Terence rose by several decibels. ('Sunray' was the accepted code-word for the commanding officer, almost everywhere, it seemed. The Germans knew this as well as we did.)

'For Christ's sake, wake up, all of you. Don't you realize that you are surrounded by Germans? How am I supposed to run a battalion of zombies? Now answer me, and in the right order . . .' Colonel Terence rattled off the code-names of all the company commanders, and made them each report personally on their respective situations.

'Doesn't the man realize that he's given away our entire battle-order?' Michael grumbled, sleepily. 'Suppose the Germans are listening in?' (They were. They told us later that they had picked up all the names – they had known them well for months – and had greeted them with grins, and comments between themselves on the abilities of each. To our shame, they also knew the names of most of the platoon commanders, too. But it scarcely mattered, now.)

We found out, when we reached it, that this longest hold-up had been the result of some monumental demolition, of a road bridge, some miles ahead. Our Sappers had been rushed forward to deal with it, and we found ourselves diverted yet again, down a steep slope, across a wadi and up the other side. That woke us up, a little. We had not even heard this particular bang, amongst all the others.

Dawn found us within a couple of miles of the coast, halted yet once more, under a railway bridge. We dozed off.

I was sleepily looking up at the lattice of girders over our heads. This bridge seemed to be held together by bits of string.

'Funny,' I observed to Michael. 'Are all railway bridges wired for sound?'

'Don't be an idiot.'

'I'm not. Look above you, man.' Michael looked up, and froze.

'My God, this bridge is *mined*! Let's get out of here!'

He shouted to the drivers before and behind, then raced onwards along the column, shouting as he went. Soon, a Sapper officer came along in his truck, and pottered off to deal with the problem. I hope that that bridge lived on to a ripe old age.

We came to rest again, a few hundred yards further on. It seemed that we had come almost as far as we could, for, about a mile ahead, we were to find a road junction, the main road continuing to the right, towards Bou Ficha (where there was still some fighting) and, eventually, Enfidaville; and a secondary road to the left, to Hammamet, then north-eastward along the coast toward Cap Bon.

Some sort of order must have come down the line that we could 'stand easy'. We emerged from our vehicles, dizzy and aching, and walked along beside them to meet up with our friends. On our left ran a wide, shallow wadi (which, in winter, would carry storm-water, in flash floods, down to the sea near Hammamet.) Beyond it were orchards, where fruit hung ready for picking; whilst on our right were groves of olives. We had cut the peninsula off from any Germans who were still crazy enough to fight.

There were German troops all around us, coming out on to the road to find someone to whom they could surrender. They seemed quite happy. I thought to myself. They must have known that, for the past month or more, they had been fighting on only because they had been told to; and they were pleased to find themselves alive, now, their war over, their pride more or less intact.

Gough Quinn walked vaguely up, beside the road.

'A bit different from last week, Chris!' He said. 'Would you like a pair of field-glasses? I've been given five pairs already, and don't like to say no.'

'Do you think we can all go and look around for loot?'

'I really don't know. No, I'm sure we shouldn't, but it may be all right if we are actually given things.'

'Who can tell if we have? It would *look* like loot, surely?' I could hardly face these moral questions for the moment. Someone came up with a jerrican of wine, and we all took a generous swig. (I am not sure that this was the first one, for some of us.) There was a polite cough behind me. I looked round, to face a little man in a smart uniform, medals flapping on his breast, a little Biretta in a leather holster, and a fore-and-aft cap with gold braid tassels at stem and stern. He had half-a-dozen spruce officer-midgets in attendance. Where on earth had they all come from?

'My God, it's an Italian general!' Michael shouted. He must have seen one before. 'Give him a drink!'

They all had drinks, longing to speak but obviously unable to cope with a word of English. 'We no spik Inglese,' one of them managed, eventually.

I said: '*Vous parlez Francais, mon General?*' My linguistic skill seemed to be unique in the British army. Nobody else would volunteer a word. So much for an education at Eton, I said to myself, tartly; but went ahead, as I had with the Germans the week before. The General beamed, delighted that I had addressed him by his rank, and even more delighted to be his own interpreter. His French was, if anything, worse than mine.

'*Monsieur, il faut vous dire que ma division se trouve dans les montagnes, la-haut, en arriere. Les Allemands nous ont ordonne a defendre la route vers Cap Bon.*'

'Michael, this General says that his division is posted in those hills, with his guns pointed up our backsides.'

143

Battalion HQ near Hammamet at the base of the Cape Bon Peninsular. On the right of the tree can be seen the tent and staff car of Sir Terence Falkiner. The hills in the background formed one of the last German positions.

'Too bad,' Michael said. 'If they were serious they would have opened up long ago. Give him another drink.'

Just at this moment, Colonel Terence walked up, swishing his fly-whisk, at ease with all the world. I suspect he had been offered drinks from several other jerricans.

'Come and meet this Italian General, Sir,' Michael invited him to join us. 'Chris says that he has a division getting ready to shoot us up. They're in that range of hills, there, holding the way into the Cap Bon peninsula.'

'What's all this about, Chris?'

'Well, Sir, that's what he says. They could start shooting, I suppose. do you mind if I tell him that you are in command of all the troops, here?'

'Oh, say what you like, Chris. It doesn't matter. How come you're fraternizing with the enemy, again? Tell them the war's over, or something.'

Oddly enough, this was not too difficult. Companies, battalions of cheerful Germans were marching past us down the road on their way to captivity. I think that the Italians had come along to find someone to whom they could surrender, too. The Italian General saluted Colonel Terence (who, if I remember rightly, patted him on the back,) gave some orders to his officers who sped off to bring in the troops; and, before long, hundreds more cheery groups of scruffy Italians were to be seen in the distance, emerging from their hide-outs and descending on to the road.

'So far, so good,' Colonel Terence said, as surprised as we were at the size of the multitude we had driven into. 'There are some Germans still fighting a war down the road, I hear. Michael, can you and Chris go and have a look? We'll all stay here.'

Michael and I clambered back into our Dingo, none too happy about our instructions. Everyone else was settling down to enjoy themselves, the campaign as good as over; but we were being sent to cope with a few suicide-merchants who were determined, it seemed, to kill as many of us as they could before they were overwhelmed. Germans seemed to make a habit of this.

We drove south-westward, down the main road towards Bou Ficha, coming down towards Enfidaville from the north, this time. After a few miles, we were stopped by a sentry, who directed us on to a hilltop where a small party of British officers were standing, looking through field-glasses to a slope opposite, where some of our shells were landing. We asked what was happening.

'I suppose that we're waiting for someone to show a white flag,' the colonel in charge said. 'Quite difficult to know what to do, really. These Germans all know perfectly well that they haven't a hope; and we know

145

they haven't either. But we aren't in touch on the blower, so we just have to go on shooting at them. It's all a bit pointless.'

'I hope you won't be wanting infantry to mop it up,' Michael said, cheerfully. 'Anyway, Sir, we're just up the road behind you, near Hammamet.'

'I hope not. They ought to pack it in, surely? But you'd better tell your boss to remain on stand-by, just in case.'

We drove back to Colonel Terence with our message. However, the surrender came through next morning, and we could all relax, at last. What better place than the beach at Hammamet? It had been the most exciting week of my life.

19

INTERLUDE

So we lay on the beach, at Hammamet, for the rest of May. We felt – some, anyway – that we deserved a break.

But there was a certain amount to be done from time to time. Our main function, at first, was to look after some of the prisoners we had captured. In due course, they were all taken off our hands, and found destinations in Britain, Canada and the United States, I believe. But there was a long queue; and with a couple of hundred thousand to dispose of, we all had to administer to their welfare and security till their times came for embarkation.

We looked after some thousands ourselves, in a 'cage' in the very wadi where we had first come to a halt, before Hammamet. (Just as well there were no flash floods at that time!) We were delighted to find that they included large formations of the 90th Light Division, our old opponents from desert days, for they could talk with us about our mutual experiences, and reminisce about the battles we had fought. They virtually built their cage themselves. We supplied roll upon roll of 'Dannert' wire – each roll would be pulled out like a concertina, then clipped to the end of the next – and, while we patrolled outside, they patrolled inside. There was strict discipline there. They even asked permission to set up a cage within the cage, into which they would plunge their own defaulters.

It fascinated me to watch their lavatorial arrangements. They would detail a fatigue party to dig a long, deep trench; and at all times we could watch a row of squatting backsides, followed by an interval when a layer of earth and sand was laid; then the row of backsides, once again. Germans can organize everything. They caused us little trouble: they knew as well as we did that there was nowhere for them to run to, at this stage of the war. We commandeered a nearby building for them to convert into an officers' mess; and they managed to lay their hands on a piano. We spent many friendly evenings with them, drinking the local wine together. Thank goodness, many of them could speak respectable English, so I was seldom called in to make myself useless once again as an interpreter.

There was little for me to do, with an arm still in plaster. Somebody

147

had me posted to Brigade Headquarters – I was not to get my platoon back, yet – and I whiled away the time sitting under an olive tree, delivering messages, and gossiping. Here, I may have heard a little more about the progress of the war.

During that summer, the Russian army was chasing the Germans back across the western steppes. The American navy had begun its counter-offensive, and the Marines were island-hopping through the archipelagoes of the central Pacific. It seemed that another Japanese army had been halted on the eastern frontier of India; and that though the allied convoys, battling across the Atlantic, still suffered terrible losses, they could inflict them, too, on the packs of U-boats they encountered. Factories, in Britain of course but particularly in America, were pouring out staggering quantities of aeroplanes, ships, tanks, guns, weapons and ammunition, all the paraphernalia of modern war, as our own heavy bombers increased the scale of their bombing till German production faltered. The tide must be turning, now.

Even so, we were not yet ready to invade the continent of Europe. The main invasion would be on an unprecedented scale; and it would have been silly for the allies to gamble, at this stage. It would be a disaster to fail through lack of preparation.

But our leaders, under great pressure from the Russians, felt that it might be possible to give the Italians a fright.

We did not have a high opinion of the Italians' military – or naval – skill. We had already deprived them of their entire colonial empire, and there were rumours that Mussolini would be willing to sue for peace. There might, then, be something to be said for a prod at the 'soft underbelly' of Europe; and our own troops, already spread along the North African coast, could make their preparations there.

We did not know precisely where we would be going, of course. The obvious target was Sicily, as it was very close to us, and would lead us into Italy. But there were other rumours of possible landings on the European shore. Perhaps they were circulated deliberately.

During this rest period, though, we were recapitulating the immediate past, rather than peering into the future. There were old battles to discuss with the German officers; there were stories to tell the new officers, who were now flooding in straight from the training battalions, by Gibraltar and the disembarkation ports of Algeria (we could only tell them of the desert, of course, and that particular form of warfare was unlikely to come again – but, possibly, our experiences had some value;) and we may have been getting the previous campaign into perspective, ourselves.

There was no doubt that it had been successful. Not many armies clear an enemy out of a continent. Back in England, we were told, the exploits of the Eighth Army in particular (the First Army had less publicity) were said to be on the heroic scale; and our general, Montgomery, was for the time the most famous of all our leaders.

(For some reason, we did not share this enthusiasm. He had certainly done well for us: he had turned us into an elite, self-confident force, and had led us for two thousand miles against an efficient, well-equipped enemy, led by a cunning, professional general; and he had not thrown many lives away in the process. We probably thought that he was 'showing off'. It is true that he seemed to have an exaggerated view of his own importance, but I fancy that there was a little more in it than that. Perhaps he lacked the ability to 'identify' himself with his followers.)

For, during this period of retrospection, we ourselves were beginning to appreciate that we had been taking part in what was, alas, only a minor 'side-show' in the war. True, it had been the first major success to be claimed by the British army; but it did not seem important, when compared with the victories of the Russians and the Americans elsewhere – nor was it to be half as important as the invasion of North-Western Europe, a year later. However, we found it easy to imagine that we had won the war, so far. It was a cheerful thought.

More personally, I had to consider my own contribution. It had not been very glorious, I thought: a few moments of terrified action, set off against three months of depressing inactivity.

I had first to remind myself that it had been no longer. The war seemed to have been going on for ever, and I felt that I had been in the Eighth Army for years. But I had to be careful: others could hardly remember any other life. They had been see-sawing up and down the desert for nearly three years.

Now though, a good many of the old regulars, who had done five years or more, were to be repatriated. They had taught us, the newer arrivals, a good deal about the desert, and about war in general, and it would be up to us to pass the lessons on. Even I could lecture on patrols, for instance, as I had led quite a few. I could stress the need to 'dig in' when held up by enemy fire; and I could pass on my own observations about the curious inaccuracy of Spandau fire. But I could not tell them what they *really* wanted to know: how were they going to control their own fears? I did not know, myself.

I had to confess – privately, of course – that the horrors which had plagued me since I was a child were still there. It was more than a mere animal terror. Trying as best I could to analyse it, I had to assume that imagination played a not inconsiderable part: I could actually see myself writhing in agony, unable even to die. On every occasion when there had been Germans about, the gooseflesh would rise in different areas of my body preparing, as it were, for the impact of the bullet or the shell-splinter which would bring unbearable pain. With all the metal that had been flying around recently, I did not see how I was going to avoid being hit much longer. So far, each foray had tapped some spiritual reservoir, and I did not see how it would be possible to replenish it.

Did my brother-officers feel this, too? I had no idea – it was not a question which could be asked, for obvious reasons – but to me they all seemed certain of their own invulnerability. If not, then they saw no point in worrying overmuch. If they were going to be hit, then it was pre-ordained, and there was no mileage in worrying about it till it happened. They could work out the chances as easily as I could, the heavier the 'stonk' the greater the chance of 'stopping something'. But, in their outward lives, they seemed free of this continuous nagging.

My fears were compounded by yet another weakness, which I can only term self-deprecation. I still could not identify myself with my brother-officers, could not see how possibly I could match their superb ability, ease and nonchalance; and I could never be sure that they were anxious to keep me with them.

There was nothing new about this, of course: I had felt an interloper ever since I had joined the army. The brittle confidence which I had built up since had plunged once more when I met with the magnificent men who had actually been doing the fighting in the desert. How could I possibly match them? When the test came – in the Horseshoe Battle – it seemed that I had been found wanting, for I had, in effect, been deprived of my command in the field.

But, it appeared, I had redeemed myself somehow, by getting captured, and escaping. I was now a 'character', and had earned my place. I should have been satisfied, I suppose, but all the same I wished that I had not established myself with a gimmick. I was still ludicrously self-conscious about it.

Peter, who had befriended me from early days, and seemed to be aware of my difficulties, once warned me of this, not unkindly.

'I think that your trouble', he was to say (perhaps later) 'is that you seem to have to go on proving yourself. Can't you take yourself for granted? If you spend all your energies trying to enter some mythical magic circle, then the people whose circle you are trying to enter will think that you are altogether too intense, too eager, and will be frightened off. Surely you know that everyone here loves you? Why can't you just accept us all for what we are, and treat us normally? Relax!' So I did – for a time.

About three weeks later – perhaps early in June – there was need to collect stores in Tripoli. I forget what was wanted, if indeed I ever knew:

150

vehicle parts, perhaps, for, though they were American and could now come direct to a port in Algeria, they had originally been sent out, with their spares, to the Middle East. I was put in charge of a small convoy, of three or four empty trucks, and a few knowledgeable experts.

It was good to be on the move, once again. The weather was hot now, of course, but not unduly oppressive, and the journey presented no real problems. Willie Mitchell and I managed to get hold of an old, battered jeep, which raised a few doubts; but, surrounded as we were with mechanical wizards, the long journey down the coast road to Tripoli was virtually trouble-free.

My old platoon sergeant, Harness, was with us, I remember, and when we stopped that night, in the bowl of Tadjera Khir, we told each other stories of the Horseshoe Battle three months before; and reminisced about the old days with the Sixth Battalion.

It was humbling to discover how little I had known of the men under my charge.

When I had been in the Sixth Battalion, there was still a great gulf fixed between officers and 'other ranks'. Perhaps I had broken it down a little, thanks to encouragement from Cuthbert; but I had no idea of the men's home backgrounds, and could scarcely look upon them as normal human beings. Class distinctions were rigid; fraternisation would have been frowned on; and the men would not have welcomed personal enquiries about them from their officers. Now, a very slight thaw had come into our relationships.

Harness was telling me now that, before the war, he had been a policeman on Tyneside. (I had thought that he had been a regular soldier throughout.)

'Aye, times were rough then,' he was saying, round the fire, that evening. 'Ever heard of t'Hunger Marches? All the lads were out, no matter if they 'ad jobs, or no. Real bitter, they were.'

'Was everybody really hungry?'

'Ay, some were. Seventeen bob a day ain't much for a man and all 'is family. Then there was fights atween t'police and t'marchers. You ask Corporal Lacey. 'E was on t'other side. People say that them black pock-marks on 'is face are coal, which blew into 'im when there was an explosion in t'pit; but there's others say a copper 'eaved a lump of coal at 'im. Real tough, is Lacey.'

'Ee, boot 'twas rough i' Lancashire, too,' Willie Mitchell broke in, unexpectedly. He came from Nelson, and had worked in a cotton mill. 'That's why most of us joined oop. It was t'war what give us full employment, oop North. When I joined oop wi' this job, it meant that I could get married.'

151

'Good Lord, *are* you married? I had no idea. Are there any children?'

'One girl. I've never seen 'er. She was on t' way when we was shipped out 'ere.'

(Ten years later, I was to spend a night with the Mitchells in Nelson. They did not tell me, till I arrived, that this daughter had lung cancer, and had only a few days to live; but they could not have been kinder, or more hospitable.)

We reached Tripoli on the second evening; and, on the following day, Willie and I made our number with the authorities, and carried out various commissions for our friends. This was the headquarters of the NAAFI, and we could stock up a little for ourselves, as well: items of food and drink (though by now supplies were reaching us more directly, of course) and any good bargains from what was already a diminishing market. I bought a pair of brown shoes – I had hoped for desert boots, for mine were wearing out – and Willie, surprisingly, bought as many two-foot lengths of Lifebuoy soap as he could carry. I had no idea what he meant to do with them.

That evening, the technical men reported. They told me that they might have to wait several days to collect their equipment.

Was there any reason for Willie and myself to stay around? The others were just as capable of getting back as I was – there was only one road, after all – but, for myself, I did not much want to stay longer in Tripoli. I guessed that some of the men were hoping for a holiday: they had had no leave for months, and would prefer less supervision; and perhaps, like other British soldiers, they had found women for themselves, or had been told how to obtain them.

I wanted to get back because there had been a rumour that the Battalion would soon be on the move; and I did not want to be left out, again. There was little in Tripoli for Willie, or for me. So we set off, along a road which was now, to both of us, becoming familiar; but it was strange to find it so empty. The summer sun had burned the wayside grass to dust, and the flowers of spring were, of course, all dead. Just over the frontier, it was particularly desolate: only a few tufts of camel-thorn, which looked as dead as everything else, relieved the monotony. Why had I found it all so beautiful?

'Just the place for this wretched jeep to break down!' I said to Willie, not altogether as a joke.

'Ee, boot it might, at that.'

It did. The engine had been sounding rough for some miles, but this time it stopped as though it really meant it. For a while, we both played with the starter button, but we did not want to exhaust the battery. We opened the lid and looked vaguely inside, to find no loose wires, or any sign of damage. What was there to do? The situation was not desperate for, sooner or later, *some* military vehicle would come along, and we had reserve supplies. We found some shade under the vehicle, and dozed off for an hour or two.

We were roused by a distant hail. A couple of Arabs had appeared over a sand-dune, with a donkey, and were walking through what I had guessed was a German minefield towards us, all smiles. It is quite extraordinary to find the desert so well populated! I have seldom seen an area more parched; yet they were carrying water-melons, which we bought and ate with relish.

I let Willie do the bargaining; but I was not too happy about the freedom with which they went on to examine our belongings, and kept a close eye on the pair of them. However, they did not intend any theft. Willie was very pleased that they offered him cash for cakes of his Lifebuoy Soap – far more than he had paid in the NAAFI – and I was offered three times what I had paid for my new brown shoes. Both parties, then, were fully contented.

Late in the afternoon, another vehicle came along the road, and stopped for us. The two soldiers in it could not make our jeep work, either (rather to our relief, for it would have looked a little shaming if they had shown us that we had forgotten some elementary reason for the malfunction) and in the end it was agreed that they should tow us back to Tunis. This was about two hundred miles, but we had no choice. I learned all about being towed, during the next two days! It is not as simple as it looks; but at least we did not have much traffic to worry about.

We stopped near Medenine that night, I remember; and I was able once again to see the sunset and the sunrise on the Matmata Hills, clear, spiky and blue in the far west. Relaxed and idle, I thought again that I had never seen anything more beautiful.

So the desert 'bugged' us. That evening, I remember, I became aware that the horrors of the previous campaign had now almost left me; and that I was able to look back upon our previous travels through Tunisia with a detachment which was little short of romantic. So it has remained. Those of us who fought in the desert were often said to be 'bushed' – an inappropriate word, perhaps, for a land where there were so few bushes! I think that we were made crazy by the silence and the emptiness; and if craziness is also the right word – and if it is a weakness – then I suffer from it still, and am not ashamed.

When we reported back, we found that the Battalion had indeed moved on. But all was well: Brigade had an order for me, that I was to proceed

back to Sousse, and then embark, under care of the embarkation authorities, to – of all places – Pantellaria.

I had no idea where it was. The Mediterranean has more than its share
of islands; but I was to discover that this had been Italian, more or less
to the east of Cape Bon, and more or less halfway to Sicily: maybe about
sixty miles from each. Willie and I reported to the skipper of a battered
landing craft, taking supplies out to the garrison; and, to my intense
pleasure, went to sea again, after an interval of about six months. It was
all very companionable: I was invited to join the 'wardroom', such as it
was, and was allotted a spare berth.

I was a little suspicious about the qualifications of the two RNVR
lieutenants who worked the ship; and was shaken when they woke me in
the small hours, to tell me that they had strayed into the middle of a minefield. There was little I could do about it, of course, except encourage
them to get out of it; and we all spent the rest of the night on deck, asking
one another how the Germans laid mines, and at what depth. However,
we found our way to the island, thanked our hosts, and disembarked.

Pantellaria is a small, rather unexpected island in the middle of the
'narrows'. It must have been seen from the decks of countless ships, on
their way from Gibraltar to Malta; but the vulnerable Malta convoys had
had to creep by at night, till now, for it had housed an Italian airfield,
which we had now appropriated. I suppose that we were now the leading
allied troops (if that meant anything) and that there could be some danger
of raids. The highest point on the island is about 3,000 feet, and it is about
seven miles long by four broad, steep-to, possibly volcanic, rather poor.

We found No. 3 Company on the southern cliffs of the island, and were
made welcome there. Once more, I have the impression that there were
more officers than there were platoons to command; but we were able to
share duties – posting guards and sentries at night, clearing out Italian
strong-points and pillboxes by day. We were not overworked.

Our only enemies were fleas. We were told that among the chief
exports of the island were the large, acrobatic, and venomous fleas, sent
before the war to flea-circuses in Britain, but which had now made the
lives of our Italian predecessors so unbearable that they were only too
ready to surrender to anyone. Before we entered one of their pill-boxes,
we would strip down to our underpants and gym shoes (bare feet were
unthinkable,) collect an armful of hardware and get it out into the open
air; then – assuming that we were by the shore – dive quickly into the sea
from the nearest rock. Even in those few minutes, the fleas would have
blackened our legs to the knees.

The other export was sweet white wine. There was a little less to export
when we had had our fill, of course; and there can have been few markets

154

for the wine of these enormous Muscat grapes, excellent to eat off the vine but heavy, glutinous and treacly when fermented in a bottle. I used to think that John Masefield's quinquereme was wasting cargo-space, in carting that stuff around the Eastern Mediterranean.

Gough Quinn was busy on his pastoral rounds, here; and, amongst the officers at least, he had some ready listeners. I should guess that he had bible-reading sessions, and conceivably some prayer groups; but, as I cannot remember them, it is possible that I was reckoned, spiritually, too delicate as yet for devotional exercises; and that the more experienced Christians were warned to treat me gently. The one exception may prove the point.

Hugh Venables was now one of our Company officers. I remembered him from the Sixth Battalion, though I had not known him well, and he had preceded me into the Third, arriving soon after the Battalion's escape from Tobruk. He had not been in No. 3 Company, before, and as in the desert the Companies had separate messes, and usually specialist duties, we had seldom met and talked together. Here he was now, in our Company mess at Scauri, and my first real memory is of chasing fleas together through the Italian dug-outs.

It was after one of our afternoons in the pill-boxes that we went back to our requisitioned villa, to wash the salt off under a shower. It had been a good day. We had done a good deal of clearing, and had had a refreshing swim or two; but then, for no apparent reason, we began to talk about religion.

It did not take me a moment to discover that I was totally out of my depth, once again. Hugh must have come from a church-going home (was I the only exception?) and had obviously been educated at a school where the faith was actively taught. (Like Peter, he had been to Harrow, I was to learn later.) He really believed in all this mumbo-jumbo, I thought to myself morosely. Why had I been left out? This must be God's fault. Well, I had better go along with it, for the moment. It seemed to me that Hugh's brand of religion was a good deal more evangelistic than Peter's: he really wanted me to join him in prayer, or something.

So, privately protesting, I found myself on my knees beside him, listening as he experimented in extempore prayer. It was all a hideous embarrassment: I did not know what Hugh was praying for, could not follow his train of thought, and could not make myself believe that God – his own or anyone else's – could really be interested in bunk like this, or in people like us. When Hugh had finished, I fled. I must have hurt Hugh. Well, he had asked for it.

On the island of Pantellaria – and later on, when we returned to the mainland at Sousse, and, again, when we moved down as a Battalion to

Tripoli, much of our off-duty conversations, when the jerrican of wine was circulating late at night, came to be about religion. I suppose that it was inevitable. Many of us had been on close terms with sudden death, and knew well enough that there would be another random cull from amongst us before long; and the newcomers, who had not yet experienced battle, knew it too. One night – probably during the previous campaign, now I try to recollect it – Gough had held an outdoor service; and, to his surprise as well as ours, had found that his congregation included most of the Battalion. When the campaign ended, he had requisitioned a little Arab hut, and we had helped him make it into a tiny Church. 'There are no atheists in the front line', we told each other, sagely.

I must admit, here, that I am telescoping several of these conversations into one; and I may be wrong about the speakers. One or two made points which I have remembered ever since: in fact, I *have* remembered it all, after all these years, and do not think that I have invented anything. It does not matter where the conversation – or conversations – took place; only that they did.

To us, the war looked like going on for ever; and, always at the 'sharp end', none of us could rate our chances of survival as being very high. Alas, many were proved right. We were trying, once again, to work out the odds; and – its more interesting corollary – why God chose to end some lives at this stage, others later. Perhaps the thinking was puerile, but I still thought it mattered.

I repeated what I had once said to Gough, this time with a little more confidence, perhaps: my theory that God takes back souls who have gone as far in this life as they are likely to.

'Crazy!' Peter said, loudly. 'You make God appear like a sort of stockbroker, trying to sell shares at the top of the market.'

'I've heard this from you before,' Gough said, gently, 'and I still think you're wrong. Length of days isn't important. We are given life, and death – the *length* of a life is not so vital, when you come to think of it. If you die in your twenties, then you will never have old age to worry about. You will always be remembered by your family and your friends as a young man. But if you live on into old age, there may be people around, *wishing* that you would die.'

'But do you think that we are fated to be killed, soon?'

'No. I've never been too happy about the idea of bullets with a man's name on them. Predestination is a sad, bad creed. If the only alternative is free-will, then you must remember that neither the freedom, nor the will, is always your own.'

'I haven't a clue what you're talking about.'

'Well,' Gough said, 'neither have I, really. I was only thinking aloud. Obviously, you aren't exactly *willing* a bullet to come and hit you. But some nasty little German is willing it, all right. And vice versa: when you are shooting at Germans, you are trying to kill *them*, aren't you? Most of the evils which men suffer come from the ill will of others. But then, there's natural disaster, too: earthquakes, eruptions, tidal waves . . . Think about the weather in England, too. Half the people are praying for a fine day, and the other half are praying for rain. God can't satisfy everybody. Not all disaster comes from sin.'

'I've always thought,' Hugh said diffidently, 'that we have to allow for an element of chance, in the progress of our affairs. This business of getting killed, for instance. I can quite see that it seems unfair, in a way, to be killed when you are fairly young. But you've got to die sometime. If you are unlucky enough to get in the way of a bullet, then that's just too bad. But God knows – and you know, too – that you aren't going to live for ever. Why not sooner rather than later?

'As for me' he continued, 'I suppose that I'm quite looking forward to it. All God's promises come true. We have been promised eternal life – whatever that means – and I can't see why everybody spends all their life on earth trying to put it off.'

'It's all very well for you,' Michael grumbled, 'but I have my doubts here, about my reception on the other side. Also, when this damn war comes to an end, I hope to be able to contribute a little more to the welfare of mankind than I have, so far. I may even be in a position to do something useful.'

So the discussion went on. The idea of doing something useful for mankind, after the war was over, pleased everyone; and we may have gone on to mention our own personal hopes. I forget what they were now, but when the war did end, several of the survivors looked toward the Ministry. However, I was still sure that, for me, this was no more than a pipe-dream. I felt that I was destined for the slaughter-house, and had been anticipating it for years.

Was it at this stage that I surprised myself – and anyone else who was present – by embarking on a story? I was by no means sure where it would end. I had never done this before. Was it a sign of my increasing confidence, or was it only the wine?

'Did I ever tell you,' I began, knowing very well that I never had, 'about the men who brought up the bits and pieces to make a new steamer on one of the great lakes of Africa? I may have been told that it was Lake Rudolf, but I can't imagine why anyone wanted a steamer, there. Let's say that it was Lake Albert, for I believe that you can reach it from the Nile.

'The story is that it took them all they could manage to get the bits to the edge of the lake at all. Planks were not too difficult, I suppose, but the heavy stuff, like the boiler, had been forged in England and was brought out to Egypt by steamer. Then, it had to be floated up the Nile, for about two thousand miles. The chap who told me about this said that this boiler was enormous. When it wasn't aboard a lighter it had to be manhandled for hundreds of miles over the desert and through the jungle; and it took about a thousand people to haul it along, let alone the wretched characters who had to clear the way in front of them. It was deathly hot, the jungle was nearly impenetrable, there were savage tribes to contend with, there were wild beasts, and tse-tse flies, and mosquitoes. But, in the end, they got the kit to the lakeside, and a Scottish engineer bullied everyone into assembling the steamer, and riveting one plate to the next. It was a pretty formidable achievement. It was a paddle-wheel steamer, by the way. There was this single, gigantic paddle-wheel, over the stern. No one had ever seen anything like it, and everyone was incredibly impressed. The two Europeans who had supervised the building went on board, and they decided to give the ship a maiden voyage across the lake, to impress the natives, what?

'The two Europeans were leaning over the stern, smoking their cigars, watching this immense paddle-wheel thing stirring the mud in the reeds by the shore. What they didn't realize was that they were stirring up a sort of hippopotamus lavatory.

'These hippos had been going to that spot for thousands of years. They are creatures of habit, apparently. Well, the paddle-wheel of this steamer must have stirred it all up for the very first time. What's it called? Methane gas, isn't it? When these two men dropped their cigars over the side, there was an absolutely first-class bang, and the whole of the back of the ship fell to pieces. So they became a tasty snack for the crocodiles.'

Everyone stopped talking. Gough was looking at me a little strangely, I thought. He had never heard me saying anything like this before.

'Why tell us this?' he asked. 'It's an interesting story, and some people may find it amusing. But I suppose you think it has some bearing on what we have been talking about?'

'I think that what I'm trying to say is that, if God had a hand in the death of those two men, he went about it in a very curious way.'

'I thought that must be it.'

'But isn't it true of us here, as well? Here we all are, born and educated at vast expense, sent into the army, given rigorous training for a couple of years, and sent out here to defend our nearest and dearest against a wicked enemy. Isn't it all a bit of a trick? The people on the other side have had a lot of training, too. Then we start shooting, and somebody gets killed. It all seems so *complicated.* Why does God go through all this rigmarole, just to get people killed? There isn't anything they can do to change it.'

I sensed a certain amount of hostility, here. They were not amused at the thought that God was somehow just playing with their lives. But I was foolish enough to continue.

'Sometimes,' I observed, 'I am tempted to think that God wakes up every morning, collects a few archangels around him, and says: 'I say, fellows, who's for the chop today? I could do with a few juicy victims.'

This brought the discussion sharply to an end; and I was sorry, for it had been my fault. The others went. Gough said:

'Sometimes I despair of you, Chris. You have a gift. You can wreck a discussion more quickly than anyone else I know.'

'I know that I shouldn't have said all that,' I agreed disconsolately, 'but I'm still puzzled. Don't other people try to work out the odds, then try to find reasons?'

'What about the others? All the new boys were looking for comfort, not doubt. I'll have to start on them again.'

'Oh, help. I wasn't really thinking about them. I was just trying to air my own doubts.'

'Think of other people, for a change.'

'Actually,' I said, after a pause, 'I think I do believe in God, though I can't begin to see his plans. I can't help feeling that I ought to make some gesture, with my life, if ever I get out of this. Do you think that God has some special plan for me? Perhaps I should go into the Church, or something.'

'You're getting very close to offering bargains to God,' Gough warned me. 'Don't. It doesn't work that way, and you'll only get hurt. *Don't* say to him, "Let me live, and I'll dedicate my life to you" – that sort of thing. God will tell you if he wants you. It may not be what you want, or even what you *think* you want.'

'All the same, I'd like to express my gratitude in some practical way,' I said stubbornly. 'Aren't we born for a purpose?'

Gough (or was it Peter, later?) said: 'You remind me of the pansy, who said, "Oh, my *dear,* Jesus has been absolutely *sweet* to me!" You're inclined at times to think that you and God have some kind of intimate relationship, which is much deeper than yours – or his – with anyone else.

'Yes, of course, we are born for a purpose,' he continued later, more thoughtfully. 'But God must be used to us failing to fulfil his purpose, don't you think? Think of the number of times we ignore him, and go our own way! Multiply this by the number of people in the world, all

159

SOMETHING ABOUT A SOLDIER

through the ages, all out for their own ends; and you can't then *begin* to think that he has entrusted you, and you alone, with some vital role in getting the whole of mankind into the Kingdom. Maybe God loves you very much – he does, you know – but don't kid yourself that he *relies* on you, will you? The staggering thing is that he still thinks that it is all worth it. If you have a jeep, say, with all four tyres just about to blow, with a leak in the petrol tank, an electrical system which continually brings you to a shuddering halt, with burnt-out plugs, which uses more oil than petrol, and which is liable to collapse in a heap on the ground at any moment, you would turn it in and get another. Why doesn't God just pack it in? As he is beyond space and time, I suppose he can see the end from the beginning.

'God is more powerful than Colonel Terence, you know. He doesn't think like him. He hasn't given you an order to do something, which you have promptly disobeyed, and put the whole battle-plan at risk as a result. (Gough was right about my hero-worship of Colonel Terence, who could do no wrong, in my eyes.) My impression is that he tends to face you with a conflict of alternatives, and that he doesn't help you in the least to decide which to take. One alternative may be right, and another wrong; but you don't *know* till you have chosen – and possibly not even then. He then picks up the pieces. Amazing, isn't it? Anyway, you are not to *worry*. Consider the lilies of the field. All will be well.'

With this, then, I had to be content. I wished that I could have Gough's faith, and Peter's peace of mind. I wished for much more, too. I was lamentably short on the virtues.

In the distance, the terrestrial battles passed us by; but they were not far away. One morning, at the end of June, we awoke to see a vast fleet of ships steaming past us, and heard the mutter of distant guns. Sicily was being invaded.

So the first landing was being effected before our eyes on the continent of Europe. (But was this true? We ourselves were already in Europe, we realized. Though Sicily was thought of as Europe – at last! – Pantellaria was too, in fact.) Now, though, we were no longer in the front line: our heroic defence of the island no longer made the news. Put another way, it suggested that our days of leisure were coming to an end.

Our corner of the Mediterranean was now crowded with ships. Not all of them seemed to know what they were doing: one landing-craft, it was said gleefully, landed its troops on Malta by mistake, when its skipper read his compass upside down. Another story was that all the top brass of the airborne division, now being used in anger for the first time, were dropped a mile out to sea. Why did we think that so funny?

160

The day came for us to clamber into another landing craft, and to return to Sousse. We were to 're-group' for our next role; though where this was to take us, and in what capacity, was a mystery known only to the High Command.

Alas, we soon heard the sad news that we were ceasing to be a motor brigade. We would be infantry, once again.

Well, we had expected this. We ourselves were to blame, to some extent, for we had voiced our own misgivings, recently about the role of a motor brigade in war. Anyway, the Brigade itself remained: the Sixth Grenadiers, the Second Scots and the Third Coldstream, under the command of Brigadier Julian Gascoyne. But it ceased to be independent. It joined with two other brigades, the 167th and the 169th, to make up the 56th Division, part of X Corps. To our dismay, we then discovered that this Corps was to form part of the American Fifth Army, under General Mark Clark.

So it may be that I can now boast about being an American soldier for a while; but, to be truthful, junior officers could not really tell the difference. It may have meant more to our divisional commanders and their staffs – sparks seem to have flown there, occasionally – but all we had now were new, faceless organizations to grumble about.

Back in the Battalion, the faces were changing. Most of the old regulars, who had been serving in Palestine before the war began, had returned to England by now; and with them had gone many of the senior officers – Desmond Holmes, David Kennard, and Guy Knight, the company commanders. Only David Forbes remained, as second-in-command of the Battalion. Large new drafts had come in. It was possible to re-form No. 1 Company, lost at Mareth, and to get it up to strength. It was to be commanded by Bill Gore-Langton, once the Adjutant at Pirbright – and I imagine that he was given John Harley as his second-in-command, to provide a modicum of continuity. In No. 4 Company, Guy Knight was replaced by Roger Beck. Number 2 Company lost its exclusive anti-tank role, and became a 'rifle' company like the rest. Michael Brodrick, the youngest of them all, was promoted to command it: I was overjoyed.

Then to my own delight, I was returned to No. 3 Company. Our new Company Commander was Mervyn Griffith-Jones, the previous Adjutant (I had mixed feelings about this, at first, for my chronic loathing of all adjutants had once extended to him as well: like all of them, he seemed to have no warmth at all.) His drawl and unapproachability, I soon discovered, had been a mask which had gone with his office; and we were soon to be friends. For a short time, I even became his second-in-command; but, when the next campaign began, a more senior officer,

Ken Sweeting, was moved over, and I went happily back to my old platoon again. Reg Brewer was still the Platoon Sergeant, and most of the other familiar faces were not only there, but pleased to have me back.

Although the reorganization had begun at Sousse, it continued when the Battalion moved to Tripoli at the beginning of August. This was to be our point of departure for the invasion of Europe. All the ports along the North coast of Africa had their troop concentrations, their training areas, and their fleets of landing craft to take them across the Mediterranean when the time came. It was a busy time for us. It must have been a logistical nightmare for the staffs responsible for organizing this immense armada.

All this had begun when we were still at Sousse; but when the Battalion moved to Tripoli I was, once again, left behind for a spell. I found myself in a field hospital for a few days, with a constriction of the throat which I was told was pharyngitis: quite painful while it lasted, but the swelling soon went down. I picked up a lift from Bobby Chaworth-Musters (John's younger brother) who was fairly new to the Battalion, and was taking down a consignment of Bren gun carriers. Once again, I was able to act as a guide to the Horseshoe Battle, already enshrined in Regimental lore. Goodness, it was bleak! There was no relief from the burning, gritty sand; and, to judge from the occasional distant explosions in the night, most of the wicked minefield was still there, underground. Camels, wild animals, even the occasional Arab for all I knew, were still at enormous risk.

We found the Battalion in an olive grove just outside Tripoli. It was not an altogether pleasant spot. After dark, our Tilley lamps seemed to attract the scorpions from under the stones, large, black ones whose sting could be lethal, and it took some agility to avoid them as we went across the mess-tent to replenish our mugs with water or wine. It was wise to shake our shoes when we put them on.

Michael – rather typically – was keen that we should all be fully prepared for our new role: on foot, and presumably on some Mediterranean shore. This meant not only marching, but carrying everything we might need on our backs.

Mervyn did not think that this applied personally to him. But he sent me, with some of our men, on a route march with Michael. Golly, it was hot! We were all in 'Christmas tree' order, carrying all our arms, and enough ammunition for our Brens to keep them shooting for weeks. Each man also had to carry a gas-mask, a gas cape, a groundsheet, a full water-bottle, a knapsack with all personal gear inside, and a steel helmet to top it all. We marched fifteen miles that day, in temperatures in the neighbourhood of 120 degrees; and I can still remember the sizzle of our sweat as it fell on the melting tarmac. No one died! But it took several days to get over it.

Later, we had a full-scale dress rehearsal, in which we embarked in a landing craft, then landed at dawn near Zuara, some fifty miles to the West. This was less energetic, but more chaotic. Everyone learned something new about the sea; and the sailors learned something about putting soldiers ashore.

Sea-borne landings against a determined enemy are far from easy, as we were all to learn. We were now introduced to the many categories of landing-craft, most of them built in America and brought across the Atlantic in ever-increasing numbers.

The smallest were the LCAs. (Landing craft, assault.) These were the 'herring boxes without topses', which carried the first troops ashore from as close to the beach as the supporting ships could safely sail. Their only safety was in numbers: if one was sunk, that was too bad; but the others continued on their way. They were flat-bottomed craft, of course, and had a let-down ramp at the bow.

Next came the LCI. (Landing craft, infantry). These were also flat-bottomed, drawing only a foot or two at the bow, but with a powerful engine, and a naval crew to navigate it for long distances, to the beach-head and back to base. Each one carried about a hundred soldiers, in extreme discomfort – we were to cross the Mediterranean in one, when the time came – and at the bow were two sliding ramps, ostensibly to land us dry-shod when the bow hit the sand. The provident skipper was meant to throw overboard a 'kedge' about a cable's length before touching – a very heavy anchor and cable at the stern, worked by powerful capstan – so that, if he had not run his ship too far up the beach, he could winch it back again when he had said goodbye to his passengers. He generally remembered to do this. If his passengers hesitated, though, they might easily find themselves back in North Africa.

Next came the LCT. (Landing craft, tanks.) These were about the same size – say a couple of hundred tons – but the shape was very different. Each would carry four tanks, or trucks, reversed in to a 'hold' through the gap created by a hinged ramp at the stem, hauled up when the ship went to sea to create a 'weatherproof' bow. My impression is that they were not too safe in rough weather.

An LCT went as far up the beach as an LCI, and had the same great kedge out aft. On landing, the vehicles roared off across the ramp – woe betide the truck that stalled! This could mean sea water in the carburettor, unless a special air intake had been fitted for the operation – the heaviest vehicle emerging last. The very loss of weight probably meant that the LCT would float away without a pull on the kedge. It would be advisable for the crew to hoist the ramp again, though, before putting out to sea.

There were many other 'specialist' ships, of course; but the list would be lop-sided without the inclusion of the LST (Landing ship, tanks). These would take anything up to thirty vehicles, depending on size and weight; and on two 'floors', with a lift from one to the other. At the bow, there were two 'doors', not one, opening sideways; not down. The weight of the ship – let alone the weight of the vehicles it carried – generally meant that the bow hit the beach some feet below the water-line; so all vehicles must be prepared for a swim, air-intakes aloft. It was said that tank crews were not happy about this arrangement, for it was always possible that they would not only be ducked, but drowned: I do not know the statistics, but I can see their point. We had all too little time for trial of all these craft; but more than enough for error.

So it was with considerable interest that we all took part in our practice landing at Zuara. It seems that reconnaissance had been a little rushed, this time as well, for we hit an uncharted sandbank about a hundred yards from our beach. The ramps went down with a splash; and we ran madly overboard, but into deep water. Fortunately, no one was drowned; but we hoped that, next time, when we did this in earnest, some intrepid volunteer would investigate beforehand, to be sure that our beach was fairly steep-to.

So our preparations went on. Other units were doing the same things at their embarkation points, up and down the coast, but we were given no idea of the scale of it all. Nor, for that matter, were we given any idea of where we were going. August surrendered to September.

As the pace of preparation quickened, we found ourselves, day by day, working more closely together as a unit. It was a heady experience. For the first time since I had joined the army, I knew without thinking consciously about it that I had become a part of an efficient military machine.

Though I could not put my finger on how he did it, yet I knew that the credit for this must go to Colonel Terence. He had had a difficult inheritance. He cannot have found it easy to assume command of the heroic 'remnant' which had fought its way out of the shambles of Tobruk. Only about 190 officers and men had remained in the Battalion: veterans these, a legend in the Middle East, and fully aware of it, they must have felt that they, and only they, were capable of passing on the secrets of warfare in the desert. They had covered themselves in glory and their chests with medals. They were an elite.

Colonel Terence had had to treat them with some diplomacy, at first; and he had had to graft the new intakes on to them, without allowing undue hero-worship amongst the new officers and men, or undue scorn amongst the veterans. He had led them into action in Tunisia; but, in his first big battle, the worst had happened, once again. He lost the major part of his command at Mareth; and, for the rest of the Tunisian campaign, the Battalion was virtually unable to take an effective part.

He was not to blame, of course. He, and the rest of the Brigade, had been misled by faulty intelligence, and had come up against a whole German division, the best in the *Afrika Korps*. But this had damned him. He was unlucky: this is failure enough, in a fighting battalion. We even gained the impression – false, perhaps – that he was not a favourite with his own Brigadier.

But everything was different, now. With the old desert veterans back in Britain, Colonel Terence could claim at least as much experience of battle as his officers. True, two of his company commanders – Mervyn and Michael – had fought before Alamein, but the vast majority had experience of, at most, one campaign. The other company commanders he had virtually chosen himself.

And the desert days were over. We were no longer a motor battalion, but infantry; and no one had the advantage of him, any longer. No one knew what we were to expect, anyway, for none of us knew where we were going. He could guess about the next campaign as well as any of us (and all of us, alas, were wrong.)

He loved to act the bluff, brainless blimp. 'The black races begin at Victoria Station,' he would declare. He would say dreadful things about Gough Quinn, poor man – not, I suspect, that it worried Gough very much. But, for all his idiosyncrasies, he towered above us; and I became his devoted admirer.

I suppose that war has to be like this. Battalions, regiments, armies are built up till they became a hyper-efficient, confident entity. Then they are thrown into a battle. If they suffer heavy casualties, then they lose this hard-won identity; and the survivors can only begin again at the beginning, slowly to build up a new corporate consciousness – ready for the next massacre. But this is what war means.

No wonder I hated it all! It seemed so pointless, so wantonly destructive – and it must be remembered that, during a war, no one ever knows, as historians do, when, or how, or even if it will end.

I now began to console myself, for the first time, with the thought that, when I died, I was going to die with my friends. I was one of them now. I might even be useful.

PART III
SALERNO

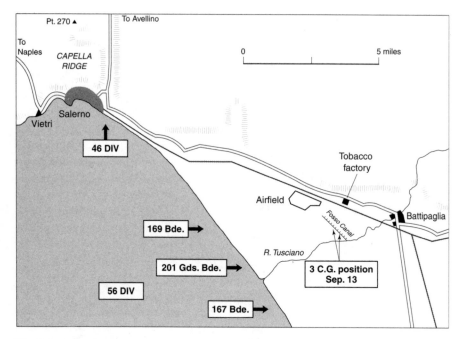

The Salerno landing areas.

20

INVASION

Now it was time to go back to war. We knew that the next campaign was going to be different to the one before: bigger, more decisive, dirtier, and one in which we would have the complication of fighting amongst a civilian population. As for myself, I was still sure that the next theatre of war would be the 'corner of a foreign field' in which my bones would rest. Too bad: I had been incredibly fortunate to live so long. The bones of many brother-officers lay bleaching in the desert; and in some ways, I remember envying them.

But, still on this earth, we had no idea where we were going, what was to be the next theatre of war. Perhaps, I thought, everyone knew except myself.

Sicily had fallen to us, by now. Logically, our next landing should be on the Italian mainland; but, in the tent which did duty as an officers' mess, treading carefully between the scorpions to refill our mugs with wine from the communal jerrican, we pointed out to one another the long, mountainous leg of Italy and the slog of fighting our way up it till we reached the plains of Lombardy. No chance of manoeuvre here! Monty would have no opportunity to repeat his 'left hooks' around the flank into the wilderness, and we would be forced to attack head-on.

But, we wondered, had the High Command dreamed up a better plan? Given sea power, could we not land, perhaps, at the top of the leg – or, for that matter, in some other country altogether – the Balkans? The French Riviera? For some mad reason I had put my money on Turkey, ignoring its neutrality, and the self-evident fact that it was the most distant corner of the Mediterranean. The others argued for even less likely landing-places.

We ignored one calculation, though. The High Command set much store on air power – we amateurs imagined that an aeroplane could stay in the air for as long as its pilot wanted – and this, I imagine, was to prove the determining factor. On 2 September, the Eighth Army invaded the mainland of Italy by the shortest sea-route available: a couple of miles across the straits of Messina to Reggio. It met little resistance.

Troops landing on the beaches at Salerno, 9 September, 1943.

A general view of the landings at Salerno in 1943.

It could be argued that the Germans simply did not think that this would be worth our while. They were right, in a way; but they were wrong, though, if they thought that this would be our *only* attempt. Maybe the Eighth Army did look upon this landing as its contribution to the invasion of Europe; but this was only one of the two armies which took part. The American Fifth Army was far larger; and it was entrusted with the major landing, on the beaches along the Gulf of Salerno, over a hundred miles up the western coastline.

Nearly half of the Fifth Army was made up of British troops; and to a couple of British divisions, the 46th and the 56th, was given the hardest section – the left, or Northern half of the long beach, up to the city of Salerno itself. These troops were 'battle-hardened', more experienced than the Americans at that time. My impression is that our generals did not anticipate any major difficulty, for they had a secret which none of us knew, as yet: the impending surrender of the Italian army, timed for the evening of 8 September, just as our many separate fleets were closing with the coast.

The Germans had heard about this, however. It seemed to us, when we eventually landed, that they were waiting on the beach. I have never been told how; but it could not have been difficult for any senior German liaison officer to guess – even to be told, off the record – that the demoralized Italians were at the point of surrender. Anyway, the German authorities acted quickly.

Our Battalion moved down to its 'assembly area' close in to the city and nearer the sea – I seem to remember a racecourse track – out of contact with civilians (who could be spies.) But our imprisonment was not absolute, for I remember a couple of excursions.

The first was to be the funeral of Hugh Venables. A day or two before we moved, he had been rushed into hospital; and before I had even realized that he was no longer with his company, he was dead, I think of meningitis.

Several of us went to the funeral, in some graveyard which may or may not have been available for British expatriates. His was the first 'formal' funeral I had ever attended, and I found it inexpressibly horrible – so different from the other rushed burials, shallow in the desert sand, in the aftermath of a battle but, because we were once again in a hurry, in a macabre way, also improvised. There was no coffin. There was the misery of loss, but also the foreboding that Hugh was only the first of us to die in the coming campaign. His body, wrapped in an army blanket, was tipped off a stretcher and fell into the grave with a thud which I can still hear.

So Hugh has gone before us, I thought sadly to myself. It seemed as though my theory, that God took his most beloved early to himself, was justified, for no one of us was nearer than he. This did not console me much, it is true, for his friendship had meant more to me than I knew; but, all the same, I felt – deep down, somewhere – that he had entered into the joy of his Lord, and was happy for ever, dancing with the Cherubim.

After the Last Post that night – that haunting evocation so familiar to us all, for it had sounded over Hugh's grave just as it sounded now over the assembly area, calling all to leave their cares to God and sleep – Michael took me outside the arena for a late night stroll. We sauntered down to the quay, where we were to embark on to our landing craft the following day.

Michael was a major now, a company commander – quite an achievement for a man who was certainly not more than two years older than I. (He must have joined the Supplementary Reserve when he was due to go up to Oxford, only to be called up before he got there.) It seems that I was still a subaltern, at that moment, but a few days later, my captaincy came through: not that it mattered.

Rather typically, Michael had hauled me out to tell me something about the duties of a company second-in-command. Well, *he* should know: he had been one throughout the previous campaign, as I had every reason to know. I should remember the gist of it, but have to confess that it escapes me. (One thought only has occurred since: why tell *me*, and not his own new second-in-command?)

Then, unexpectedly, he began to talk about himself and his family. (Strange, that we talked so little, between ourselves, in the Mess and elsewhere, about our homes: perhaps the military small talk, the recent reminiscences, the immediate problems, and the anxiety about what was likely to happen next, were enough.)

He told me that his father was dead. He had been Earl of Middleton, a member of A.J. Balfour's government, responsible for Ireland, and then Secretary of State for War. The title had gone to his half-brother. I must meet his own mother, Michael said: he was sure that I should like her. She had been born a Stanley, close kin to the Earls of Derby. (Help! I had not realized that I had been consorting with such blue blood.)

The difficulty, Michael said, was that his family – both sides, I presume – hoped that he would enter politics when the war ended. He had all the right connections. On the other hand, he was wedded to the army; and could think of no career other than this. (Nor could any of us, just then. The war looked like lasting for ever.) And Michael was a soldier through and through.

But I was not shocked that he and his family should consider a political career for him. The word 'meritocracy' had not yet been coined, and I imagine that we still believed in heredity! What did surprise me was that he should mention this to me, of all people. I could hardly have been less qualified to make an intelligent comment. But I was quite flattered: I hope I was able to assure him that he should do just as well in politics as he had in the army.

On the quay, we leant in the darkness over a pile of crates. In the companionable silence, I felt very close to Michael, aware of the next adventure that we would be meeting together. Suddenly, he said:

'Well, what about you, and your future? I don't see you as a future Prime Minister, quite frankly. Your gifts are with other human beings. But people like yourself should aim at the top, you know. Do you want to be the Archbishop of Canterbury?'

'Don't be an ass.'

'Well, maybe that's not quite right. But you have gifts, you know. You seem to have a genuine interest in other people, for instance. Why should *I* suddenly start telling you about my own family, my ambitions? You just stand there, and everyone begins to talk. I've often noticed it.'

'So what?'

'Well, it's quite rare. And the other side of the coin is that you are absolutely determined not to tell other people about yourself. Perhaps the two go together.'

'You must be kidding.'

'No. No kidding. I really want to know. You aren't going back into that compound till I found out more about you.'

'Well, I'll try,' I said. 'I had absolutely no idea that you, or anyone else, would want to know. Perhaps I've been wrong about this; but really, until I came to this Battalion, I was always scared stiff of my brother-officers – and dead frightened, too, that I shouldn't be able to match up to them. I remember saying to Peter that I once saw a crate on the troopship, with the label "Not Wanted on Voyage!", which described my state of mind exactly. I thought that it might be written, like some sort of birthmark, between my shoulder-blades, where I couldn't see it, but where everyone else would read it whenever they looked at me from behind.'

'So *that's* why you're all so bottled up. We must do something about this. Go on, though.'

'I've always considered that I'm privileged, to be with people like you. I haven't any particular claims to greatness: no towering intellect, no confidence, no connections, no nothing. My one aim in life is not to let you all down. But when these damned Germans start shooting at me, I shall probably run away again.'

'Don't be ridiculous. Everyone thinks the world of you. Why, when

173

you got out of the bag, everyone says that you cleared the whole right flank of the army as it advanced. Colonel Terence got a bouquet from the Divisional Commander, for "having such a resourceful young officer under his command."'

'Absolute balls. I was terrified out of my wits. It wasn't like that, anyway.'

'Well,' Michael said, 'you're Colonel Terence's blue-eyed boy at the moment. There'll be plenty of opportunity for getting medals and glory, in the next campaign.'

'I just don't see it. I'm not even sure I want it. I am as sure as anyone can be that I shall be written off in the first few days. No need to think about the future. It's years since I've even expected to have one. There's no point in being ambitious. I just want to stay alive a little longer – and, frankly, I'm not even sure about *that.* Better get it over with as soon as possible, I sometimes say. I felt really quite envious when we were at Hugh's funeral. He won't have to go through all these agonies, any more.'

'Was he a great buddy of yours? I didn't quite realize.'

'Yes, I think he was. Isn't there a Latin word, *caritas,* which means 'caring'? I wish these Christians would use it instead of the word 'love.' I'd *like* to be able to be able to say that I loved Hugh, but it would be misunderstood. I'd like to say that I love Peter, and – yes – that I love you. But you would be horrified.'

Michael said, 'It's probably rather dangerous to get worked up about the meaning of friendship, just as we are getting ready to fight another war. Somebody is bound to get hurt.'

'Well, you can't have it both ways. Or at least *I* can't. It seems important to me to care for people, personally, even if they are just about to push up daisies: "passing the love of women," as David said about Jonathan. Of course, when a great friend dies, it's going to hurt like hell; but that's no excuse for not loving him as long as he's alive. This kind of loving is the only consolation I can find in this dreadful war, and I'm not going to give it up. Sooner or later, we're all for the chop, anyway.'

'Of course,' said Michael, 'we're all going to die. But it needn't be tomorrow: it may not be for another fifty years. If we all throw in the sponge, and refuse to plan ahead, for our own lives and for the future of the country, then we're going to lose the war for a start, and life – if we still have it, of course – won't be worth living anyway. Let's *assume* that we're going to get away with it. Come on! We're going to be the vanguard into Europe. What was it that Henry the Fifth said to his soldiers before the battle of Agincourt? We are going to be famous, and our names will be in the history books, whether we live or die. Aren't you glad to be one of us?'

I thought about this, as we continued to pace the quayside, in the dark. It was true: I *did* feel glad, to be with Michael, and with all the others. This matter of life and death, suddenly, seemed to become less important. My fears would never go away, of course, but at last I seemed more able to absorb them, now.

'So when the fighting stops, you go into politics, you think? You should have a lot to give, there.'

'Maybe. And what about you?'

'Well,' I said, slowly, 'I certainly shan't stay in the army. I have never felt at home in it. I think I should resent the idea of spending my whole life trying to prevent what I am trained to do from happening. It would seem rather a waste of effort.'

We began to walk back to the compound. After a while, I said: 'Wasn't somebody saying, not long ago, that if he survived he would dedicate the rest of his life to religion, as a sort of thanksgiving? I suppose I'm wondering if I should do something like that.'

'It seems a bit of a waste.'

'Yes, I wonder about that, too. Perhaps, if I do survive, I'll be able to find out if there's anything in it, or not. For the moment anyway, the question doesn't arise. But I'm not making any *promises* to God about all this, by the way. I shouldn't like him to think that I'm begging for my life.'

'Complicated, isn't it?'

'Well, yes, I suppose it is. But it isn't urgent.'

On the following day – it must have been 4 September – we all went aboard our LCI. Michael's company was complete; but I also fitted in, with a contingent from No. 3. I could never have imagined the discomfort: all we could do was to sit, with the gear we carried on our backs, on 'hard-arse' benches, for about five days and nights. My valise, bedroll, even a change of underwear would come later, in one of the company vehicles, in an LCT – which, I thought, doubled the chances of something going wrong.

A vicious little storm blew up as we cleared Cap Bon and crossed the narrows. Many of the men were sick. I wondered what they would be feeling like when we landed – wherever that would be – and hoped that the Germans would be looking the other way. Rounding the western cape of Sicily, we sailed into calmer water and felt a little better. We came to rest at Termini, a town on the northern coast, and had a swim, from one landing craft to another.

We moved off on 7 September. So it was to be the 'leg' of Italy: the long, sandy bay below Salerno, about a hundred miles to the North, well ahead of the Eighth Army, still moving up the toe.

175

Our LCI was commanded by a Lieutenant in the RNVR who had been one of my brother Richard's teachers at his prep school. My impression was that it would have been better for him to have carried on teaching; but to transport us in convoy was no great tax on his navigational powers, for the sea around us was studded with ships. We were less likely to get lost than to cannon into a neighbour. (But why did I always look so unkindly on these officers of the 'Wavy Navy'? They were doing an essential job.)

Off went our latter-day Vikings across the Southern Tyrrhenian Sea. All was calm, here: if we could not sleep properly at night, we could at least doze throughout the day, for there was nothing to do. We passed the Lipari Islands during the night, and could see the glow of Stromboli; then went slowly, slowly, on to our rendezvous. By late afternoon of 8 September, those of us who were on the lookout became aware of the hazy outline of an island, steep and mountainous – Capri? – then, emerging out of the mists further East, what was to gain definition as the Sorrento peninsula.

I thought about this. Was it possible that we were too early? If we could see the Italian mainland, then surely it would mean that the Italians would be able to see us?

And suddenly I knew. I still remember the brilliant flash, as the setting sun caught the first bomb falling from the sky. It hit the water a few hundred yards away, the first of hundreds to fall around us that night. Our destroyers moved in to provide anti-aircraft protection; and for the next twelve hours there was uproar all round. Looking back on it now, I suspect that I was exaggerating the danger; but, at the time, I could not see how the enemy bombers could miss. Soon, the whole gulf was illuminated with flares. Each flare would burn for about a couple of minutes; so the flare which dropped a couple of minutes upwind of us was interesting, to say the least, for before time was up, the plane which had dropped it would dive in underneath, and drop its stick of bombs on the ship it could see below it. Ours?

Our ship was certainly seen, and bombed; but it was a small, and difficult, target, I expect.

I nearly wrote that this was the worst night of my life; but, alas, there were many more to come. There was no question of sleeping. I prowled about the deck as the bombs screamed down around us. For a craven few minutes I even tried to hide right at the stern of the landing craft, behind the kedge capstan, guessing that it would be safer on deck than down below, and safer, with this enormous gadget to protect me, than anywhere else on the ship. But shame drew me out. I had to show an example to the other bewildered guardsmen, several of whom were already becoming shaky. The naval ratings at least had the consolation of firing into the air with their Oerlikon guns (though they could not see the German aeroplanes beyond the flares) or doing whatever sailors do to keep their ship from sinking. But we could do nothing but wait for the bang. By now, the ship was motionless: the leading assault craft were going in, and we were waiting, in what I guessed was a queue, for daylight, and our turn to get ashore.

Dawn came at last. We found that we were only a few miles offshore, with the mountains behind Salerno to the North of us, and a long, low coastline ahead, with distant peaks behind it, silhouetted by the brightening sky. 'Not many of us will forget the sight,' I wrote in *No Dishonourable Name.* 'I remember so well the red sun rising over the mountains beyond Eboli, turning the grey water round us to a limpid green, touching the peaks behind Amalfi and Capri, making the dull war-paint of the ships glisten as they all edged in towards the shore . . . The sea around was covered with ships: small, fast launches bouncing to and fro for no real reason, landing craft awaiting their turn to rush the golden beach which lay like a pencil across our front, destroyers belching their shells into the brown; and behind, the giant cruisers, monitors and battleships which were shooting us in.'

And then it was our turn. The ship's engines rang 'ahead' and we seemed to form up in parallel lines as we steamed in toward the beach. I looked at the line to starboard, half a mile away, and gulped as I saw a landing craft, vertical in the water, screw and rudder pointing at the sky. 'Deep water here, then,' I thought to myself. Was it? At least it meant that we were unlikely to hit an offshore sandbank. It meant dry feet – for us.

It was not for a few moments that it struck me that this LCI might be taking many of my own friends to the bottom. (All was well! I never discovered who the victims were.) Then it struck me, forcibly, that the same fate might be in store for our own ship. The noise around us was too shattering for any thoughts to linger (who brought back that famous story of the pansy at Dunkirk, complaining afterwards, 'Oh my dear, the *noise* . . . and the *people!*' It had been one of our favourite lines, whenever we had a party.) As we closed with the shore, we had to seek out a stretch of beach without too many other craft drawn up, bows-on. The skipper on the bridge was shouting to his crew, in the bows to get ready with the ramps, in the stern to cast overboard the great kedge which would pull the ship off when we had landed, and through the voice-pipe to the engine-room to stop. We queued up, ready to disembark. Sliding in between another LCI on one side, and a great LST on the other, a naval rating of the beach party frantically signalling us in, we came shuddering to a halt. The ramps went down with a crash. A few hesitant shuffles down the twin ramps, and we were in Italy.

The legend is that I was carrying a bottle of gin in each hand. Perhaps I was. In all the noise and confusion it was hard to know where we were and what we were supposed to be doing.

I clearly remember the terrifying scream of a couple of fighter aircraft, zooming low over us as we landed.

Every gun in the fleet opened up, and the noise was impossible to cope with. One of the aeroplanes seemed to be hit, and I seem to remember a plume of smoke issuing from it.

'**MESSERSCHMITTS**!' Some officer yelled.

'Mustangs?' shouted another, less confidently.

I am inclined to believe that they were Germans: surely no British pilot would be stupid enough to fly low over a line of allied ships, drawn up along a beach at the moment of disembarkation? But these were crazy moments. I went flat on to my face. Both bottles of gin were shattered. *Not* a good landing.

It took a minute or two to come to terms with the situation.

I found then that we were marching in two parallel lines up a beach of soft sand, marked like a Pirelli girl's bottom with the imprint of tank-tracks and tyres. There were stacks of equipment left unguarded and unorganized. The bluejackets who were controlling the actual landings seemed to know what they were doing, though, and the infantry was finding its way off the beach and into the sand-hills beyond. There were a few prisoners, both German and Italian, most of them clustered together under the sand-hills in the hope of dodging their own fire. I was impressed. It seemed that we were ashore, and in some force already. We were dry (thank goodness, we seemed to have landed on a steeply shelving beach) and no one seemed to be shooting directly at us, at least for the moment. The LCI which had brought us in had kedged itself off, and I have no doubt that its crew were driving it away from the danger zone as fast as the craft would go. I was sorry not to have said goodbye to the skipper, but, at the moment of landing, we had both had our own preoccupations. He was out of it, now, I thought, a little ruefully. From this point, it was up to the soldiers to do what they were paid for.

We continued on our way, edging to the left along various paths, found a lateral road, and came to rest in an apple orchard, half a mile in from the beach. 'Just like England!' my Corporal Palmer remarked. Well, at least it was green.

21

ON THE BEACH

The Gulf of Salerno is bounded on the north by the high mountains of the Sorrento peninsula. They rise almost vertically out of the sea, and must reach a height of nearly 4,000 feet: difficult country! (A few Commandos had landed there during the previous night, presumably to take the few towns, Vietri, Amalfi; and Positano, which perch on the southern flank of this formidable face, and guard the passes which penetrate northward through to the plain of Naples.) The mountain chain continues eastward behind the city of Salerno (which itself guards yet another pass through to the north;) but here, the line of the coast bends south-eastward, to allow access from the sea to a widening wedge of flat country, extremely fertile, well irrigated by the rivers which flow down from the central spine of the Appenines, parcelled out into ditches or canals. The beach must be fifteen or twenty miles long, an almost straight line from north-west to south-east.

We could see for ourselves why this had been chosen for our invasion beachhead. There were no offshore obstacles; there were no cliffs to inhibit access to the hinterland; and there was flat country on which the invaders could set up their base. But it had two disadvantages. The first was that the entire plain was overlooked: we were always conscious of beady eyes in the northern hills, watching our every movement through binoculars, ready to counter-attack if there were a chance of splitting the invading force into two. The second disadvantage was that there were hardly any other stretches of the Italian coastline which could compare with this. Surely the Germans were *expecting* us to land here?

Sometime during the previous night, the news of the Italian surrender had come in. It had cheered us, of course. I seem to remember that we had been expecting it, though, more or less; and we were by no means sure that it meant an unopposed landing in the morning. Even so, our generals must have been astonished at the warmth of our reception. Stories circulated about treachery.

Anyway, this was to be our battlefield. We were more or less in the middle, with the 46th Division to our left, beaching almost on the out-skirts of Salerno City; and our division, the 56th, on the right of the British front. Two American divisions were landing further down the beach to the south-east, towards Agropoli and Paestum. Other divisions, both British and American, were due to come in behind us when we had cleared the beachhead.

So the Fifth Army landed, on 9 September 1943. The Americans ran into difficulties almost immediately, I am told. At that stage of the war, we had little respect for the American army, which had not covered itself with glory in Tunisia; but we had little respect for any army but our own, and did not appreciate that the Americans only needed experience. Anyway, our own two divisions fared little better than they did on this occasion: our 46th Division failed to get into Salerno, and our 56th met immediate opposition further down the bay. It had been intended that we should capture a small airfield, some three miles in from the beach, on the first day, so that our fighters could make use of it; but alas, we could not dislodge the German defenders. We probably prevented the *Luftwaffe* from using it; but it must have been ten days before we could use it ourselves. Beyond this airfield, the main road ran east-south-eastward to Battipaglia, and thence to the 'foot' of Italy. But we could not reach that, either.

I still have my doubts about the wisdom of invading Italy at all. I realize, of course, that there was something to be said for continuing the momentum of our advance, now that Sicily was taken. I can also appreci-ate the political factor. The Russians had been bearing the brunt of the land war for two years, had suffered losses which must have been astro-nomical, and could not see why their Western Allies were holding back. Roosevelt and Churchill may have felt that an immediate gesture was needed, even if this would inhibit the build-up of essential supplies to North-West Europe and the Pacific.

But the 'soft under-belly of Europe', the Mediterranean coastline facing us, was not soft at all.

I have come to know the Mediterranean coast of Europe a little better since the war; and I have yet to find country over which it is easy for an army to advance. This 'leg' of Italy must be about the least promising. It is long and narrow, to begin with. Its central spine is a range of moun-tains, up to eight thousand feet high; and high ridges run off it, sideways to left and right, often to the sea on either side. There is a series, then, of splendid defensive positions, none of which can be outflanked. Any small German force could (and did) contain a far larger force of the allies, and would be able to cause heavy casualties, at little loss. It had been difficult enough for us, the invaders, even to land.

But we were ashore, anyway. We had not been the first, of course: the assault craft had gone in before dawn, and had cleared the beaches, not without a struggle, and by mid-morning the leading troops of our division were engaged about a mile in from the beach. The 201st Guards Brigade was still in reserve, the 3rd Coldstream was the reserve battalion of the Brigade, with No. 3, I was relieved to find, the reserve company of the Battalion. At least, we now had time to sit and eat from the forty-eight hour ration packs which fitted snugly into our mess-tins, topping up our bully-and-biscuit with some of the delicious apples we found on the trees beside us (too many, alas: our digestive systems were not attuned to unlimited fruit.)

There was too much noise for comfort. The Spandaus were ripping away in the distance, and occasional German shells landed in the trees nearby. The little information which seeped through to us indicated that, so far, our leading troops had failed to secure the day's objectives, the airfield more or less in front of us, a tobacco factory beyond it to the right, and the main road from Salerno, through the village of Battipaglia a couple of miles further on. It was hard to know if this were a serious matter.

By evening, we ourselves were moved forward another mile. In the distance I could see the abandoned airfield: we seemed to be getting ready to advance, tomorrow, up the right-hand side of it, with the tobacco factory as an objective.

Another brigade, the 169th, made up of three battalions of the Queen's Regiment, were to continue their advance along the northern perimeter. But ahead of us (though we did not know it) were the veterans of the 16th Panzer Division recently back from Stalingrad, getting ready to burst through our little bubble and to cast us back into the sea. For the night, though, all was quiet. Mervyn had put each of the platoons on three sides of a plantation of tobacco, a couple of acres of it, every plant about ten feet tall: with hindsight, perhaps rather a mistake, for the platoons were out of touch with one another, and there could be little point in merely defending tobacco. The inevitable happened: I was woken in the small hours and told that Germans were infiltrating into it.

This could be serious. I sent runners out to warn the platoons to left and right, and found Raymond Nares, one of the platoon commanders. We listened.

'What do you make of it?' I whispered.

'There's someone in the tobacco.' (Pretty obvious, really.)

'Do you think they're Germans?'

'I've no idea.'

'Well, let's go and have a look,' I said rather crossly, not from courage, but because I simply could not believe that any Germans would be silly enough to lose themselves in that noisy jungle, and I was tired.

We found them eventually. They were pigs. In the general chaos of the landing, either the troops, or even the farmer himself, had let them out of their bondage. I wonder how many survived the next few days? Loose pigs would be treasure trove to troops out for loot.

At about noon next day, the Grenadiers moved forward along the side of the airfield, whilst the Scots Guards moved right-handed toward the tobacco factory.

Both battalions had casualties. Our brigade was no longer in reserve, it was clear; and it was now in the forefront of the advance – and this only twenty-four hours after landing. Were any reserves landing on the beaches behind us? I had my doubts.

It seemed possible that our battalion might be called in, too, to execute some kind of 'pincer' movement, out beyond the main road, and round to meet with the Grenadiers in Battipaglia. Michael Brodrick went forward in a carrier to reconnoitre.

The carrier received a direct hit from an enemy mortar, and Michael was killed almost instantaneously.

(A few months before, in Tunisia, I should have been utterly shattered by this death. Now, more hardened perhaps, there did not seem time for me to mourn. It looked as though we would all be dead, too, within hours. We must all sell our lives as expensively as we could. Odd though, I thought: the death of Hugh Venables had moved me far more, though he had not been as close a friend as Michael. Back in Tripoli. I suppose that I had not been able to build up my protective armour of indifference to the sudden death of friends; but now, on the battlefield, it seemed almost inevitable. Michael had, in a way, lived for this moment. He would have had no regrets.)

The Scots Guards continued onwards, between the airfield and the tobacco factory, just short of the main road; and our battalion moved along to their right, to face the tobacco factory, only a few hundred yards away. The Grenadiers, still hoping for their breakthrough into Battipaglia, kept up their pressure on the extreme right of the Brigade. The third brigade of the division, mostly made up of Royal Fusilier battalions, superbly supported by the Royal Scots Greys in their Sherman tanks, slotted in to the right of them again. Then came a small river, the Tusciano, with the American sector to the south of it.

No, there were no reserves, now. All our infantry formations were fully committed. What if our thin red line should break?

The next day was worse. (At least, I *think* it must have been the next, but I remember Peter telling me that in my first account of the landing, which he read in *No Dishonourable Name* I had the tally wrong; but it is 11 September in the official history of the regiment.)

The Grenadiers continued to press toward Battipaglia, taking two Coldstream companies along with them, and building for themselves a dangerous salient. The Scots Guards put in a heavy attack on the tobacco factory that night, but it did not succeed. In the centre of the beachhead, then, we were dangerously exposed.

Our Brigadier, Julian Gascoigne, visited us that night, whilst the Scots were putting in their attack. The noise was indescribable: we were less than a quarter of a mile away from the action, in the yard of a fruit farm, the full crates of tomatoes providing a bogus feeling of protection. The Germans decided to give us a fright, by lobbing down a 'stonk' just beside us. The Brigadier was in his soft hat, smoking a cigar as he chatted to us; but when the shells screamed down on us, he was the first into the slit trench we had dug for our headquarters, and wearing the steel helmet of one of our signal corporals who had taken it off to put on his headphones. I wonder what happened to the cigar.

I was a few yards away at the time, and took shelter behind the tomato crates. I should have known better. A shell landed on the other side and tipped about a thousand crates and a million tomatoes over me. I have been suspicious about tomatoes, ever since.

Not a good day, all things considered. The Brigadier went back to think about it. We stayed where we were, and thought, too. It seemed, to me at least, that our invasion was running out of steam; and I did not fancy the thought of another Dunkirk.

Then, on the following afternoon (or have I got this wrong? With the sky about to fall around us, I was losing count of time) the Germans counter-attacked around Battipaglia.

I never really found out what went wrong. It seemed that the Grenadiers – and the Fusiliers beside them – were suddenly attacked in great force; and for a couple of hours or so there was a gap in the Grenadier line which, if they had known, the Germans could have penetrated, all the way through to the beach.

I had been taking a couple of wounded men back to Battalion Head-quarters, less than a mile behind us. But, crossing a small road, I was nearly run down by one of our three-tonners, travelling at the speed of sound, men leaning out of it and yelling 'To the beaches!' I parked my vehicle in the middle of the road, to prevent any more vehicles from following the first, and saw Billy Straker-Smith, who had just become Adjutant, running towards me.

'Get back to Mervyn!' He shouted. 'The Germans have just broken through the Grenadiers, up near Battipaglia, and you will have to counter-attack, at once.'

I raced back to our company headquarters, puzzled and panicky. I found Mervyn drawling interminably into the field telephone. He refused to be interrupted.

'Mervyn,' I spluttered, when he put down his telephone and looked quizzically at me, 'Billy says that the Grenadiers have run away, and we must be ready for an immediate counter-attack'.

Mervyn cleared his throat, and said nothing at all for about a minute. Then he said:

'Nonsense.' Another silence. Then, after a while:

'Everything is quite all right, now. It seems that a couple of companies panicked for a moment; but the Grenadiers counter-attacked with the other two, and restored order. As there's nothing for us to do here, I'm turning in for a doss.'

He did, too. I was left in charge.

It must have been about that time that the High Command came to the conclusion that we must not push our luck any further. The order came to consolidate.

So we consolidated. The Grenadiers must have pulled back a little from their exposed positions on the edge of Battipaglia, to slot in between the Coldstream to their left and 167 Brigade to their right. We stayed in our farmyard, sampling the fruit, and digging in along the line of the 'Fosso Canal' – which served as an excellent anti-tank ditch – with the Scots Guards to our left, still threatening the tobacco factory. Further along to the north-west, on one side of the main road or the other, the battalions of the Queen's Regiment which made up 169 Brigade dug themselves in gratefully. The feeling of relief was almost palpable. We all began to feel that, short of an unforeseen catastrophe, we might just be able to hold this front after all.

Behind us, we were told, reinforcements were landing on the beaches. Our old 'muckers' of the 7th Armoured Division were said to be landing; our own 'B' Echelon was disembarked, and we even collected some re-inforcements, to replace the casualties we had suffered in the Battalion, so far.

We had had quite a pasting. Michael was dead. Bill Gore-Langton, commanding No. 1 Company, had lost an arm, as had Peter Daubeny. John Harley and Teddy Skinner had been killed, soon to be followed by Johnny Longueville; and other officers kept getting in the way of flying metal. Christopher Loyd, I seem to remember, was hit in the bottom; and

I went to find Peter Wyld in the Casualty Clearing Station, one day, delighted with a flesh wound in the thigh, and only longing to be back with his mortar platoon again. There were gaps amongst the other ranks, too.

So we became a little more confident. We had to assume that the beachhead would hold. Other units – the Americans in particular – still felt unsure of themselves; and there was a good deal of dirty fighting in the suburbs of Salerno. But we, protected by the Fosso Canal, and well dug in, ought to be able to keep any German counter-attacks at bay.

We were now on the defensive. This, at least, meant stopping in one place; but we were not resting.

When we had first landed on the beaches, there had been loose talk of getting to Naples within a couple of days – and my impression is that the High Command had, to some extent, banked on this. For instance, we had all been issued with little metal tubes, pill-boxes, containing a new magic drug called Mepacrine. Mosquitoes, we were told, were quite a pest in the area in which we were going to land, and we must take these pills lest they were malarial. However, there were only enough pills to last us for a few days: after that, we were assured, either we would be out of any malarial belt, or we would be getting fresh stocks through the ports. If we unscrewed the other end of the tube we would find a mosquito-repellent cream.

The experts were certainly right about the mosquitoes: they had bred in their millions in the stagnant water, and were now waiting for us on the beaches. After their usual diet of Italian peasants, our pink bodies were a gift from heaven, and we were all mercilessly bitten. We came to the conclusion that they found the mosquito-repellent cream even more delicious. It was hard to tell whether the Mepacrine had any effect on us, the victims, for we ran through our allocation in a matter of days. The biting intensified.

Meanwhile, the Germans were constantly attacking. Days passed. They knew that we were building up stocks on the beachhead, and they also knew that we were still holding on by our eyebrows. It was essential to push us back into the sea before the Eighth Army, rushing northward from the 'toe' of Italy without a great deal of opposition and due to reach us within the week, joined forces, and would thus enable us to retreat overland, if we must.

Around the city of Salerno itself, and in the passes through the mountain barrier to the north, separate engagements came one after another. It seemed that the 46th Division was just managing to keep open the narrow corridor between the city and the beaches along the gulf. South of us, the Americans held. In the middle, facing Battipaglia, we heard the

185

continual rumble of vehicles by day, preparing for assaults which were generally launched at night.

There were two small road-bridges over the Fosso Canal in the Coldstream sector, one (ours) between the fruit-farm and the tobacco factory, and the other four hundred yards to the right. Though No. 3 Company had plenty to do, yet the main German attacks were launched on the right, where No. 1 Company had more than one scare. The most serious, perhaps, was a head-on attack on their bridge by armoured half-track vehicles, crammed with troops. Sergeant Jackson, who commanded an anti-tank gun, missed the first two at point-blank range (when questioned about this, his excuse was that he thought they might be two of ours!) but he then destroyed the next pair. As we had now closed the door, as it were, someone decided that the two which had penetrated might as well be left to their own devices: it would be a good laugh if they found Battalion Headquarters! In the meantime the Gunners were called on to provide defensive fire; and a lethal 'stonk' from the 65th Field Regiment, RA, landed on the unfortunate German infantry, waiting to exploit a break-through.

Two nights later the Germans tried again, inflicting casualties but failing to penetrate with their half-tracks. The German troops disappeared into the dense tobacco plantations, and had to be rounded up. Dick Ker, who had just taken over the company, filled himself with glory, that night, I was told.

Ken Sweeting, whom he had replaced, came to join us in No. 3 Company as second-in-command to Mervyn, so my few days of high responsibility came to an end. I was not too disappointed: I could go back to my old platoon, No. 9, and all the old familiar faces, Reg Brewer and the section commanders, Glover, Batty and McKay – and, I was pleased to see, Corporal Lovelace, who seemed to be everywhere at once. 'We were a happy crowd,' I wrote a couple of years later.

Number 3 Company was attacked a day or two later. I was in bed, of all places, ordered to rest, as I had a streaming cold and a slight temperature. I slept through the worst of the attack, only a couple of hundred yards away; but I was tipped out of it by a salvo of our own shells, many of which fell among us. This was not altogether surprising, for the defensive fire 'targets' were very close to our own front line, and the gunners – they did marvels – were themselves too close to ensure the correct trajectory for their shells.

By 16 September we were feeling confident; and on 18 September we were told that the Eighth Army had reached us at last.

Our beachhead was now secure – only nine days, but, looking back two years later, I was sure that it had been longer – and we could now consider how we were to get through the mountains beyond.

The Germans had retreated. There was a ludicrous moment, possibly in the morning of 17 September, but more likely on the 18th, when the Scots Guards battalion on our left was ordered to capture the tobacco factory. We were asked to provide support on their flank as they went in; and my platoon was ordered forward. I took a couple of men up to the outside wall of the compound, beyond the Fosso Canal, treading delicately, as this had been our battleground for nearly a week. It was strangely quiet, now. I found the body of a German soldier lying on the road, and wondered uneasily if this were a booby-trap; so Sergeant Glover, Willie Mitchell and I left him on one side, as we crept stealthily round the perimeter.

Since no one was shooting at us, we began to hope that the rumour was true, that all the Germans had withdrawn. A small section of the wall had been broken down, and, greatly daring, I peeped inside. There was not a soul in sight.

We took up positions of nonchalant idleness, and waited for the first of the Scots Guards to arrive. It was good to watch them advancing as carefully as we had done ten minutes earlier; even better to shout a greeting and to tell them that all the Germans had gone. The battle of the beaches was over.

Christopher photographed at some time between 1944–45.

22

INTO THE HILLS

It appeared, then, that we had won another battle. Did we altogether appreciate its significance? One of our old enemies, Italy, had collapsed, and we had established a secure foothold on the mainland of Europe: surely a relief to our statesmen and even to the critical Russian leaders. But would this help us to win the war?

We could already see the first of the barriers which we must tackle next, the first line of mountains. There were Germans on its slopes now, spraying us with occasional bursts of shellfire.

I collected the impression that my companions, too, saw difficulties ahead – or did they take each day blithely, as it came? My admiration for them knew no bounds. I felt privileged to be with them. Perhaps their calm, their superiority, came from their very refusal to acknowledge difficulty and danger until they met it.

The assurance that I had at last been 'accepted' gave me a new confidence. There was no longer any question of being relegated to 'B' Echelon. One fear, then, had been neutralized. Although it was impossible to forget that I was liable to be killed at any moment – we were all gladiators in some vast, global arena, where the spectators would show no mercy – yet somehow, the thought that I should at least die with my friends was such a comfort that private terrors began, at long last, to subside. I was no longer alone.

It must have been during the evening of 18 September that we finally left our farmyard, with some regrets. It had had its uses. From the upper floor we had been able to peer through the trees at the walls of the tobacco factory, and we had been relatively confident that we could defend it.

(Incidentally, the fruit had been excellent. Though the tomatoes were overripe, the apples had been delicious; and some of us were particularly attracted to a fig tree, trained against a wall which faced the Germans. The game was to crawl across a balcony, then reach over the coping and grab the soft, black fruit before the German sniper in the factory could loose off a round. The figs would taste all the sweeter.)

Peacefully now, we marched the company sedately past the tobacco factory to the main road, and across it into the fields beyond. Not only the crops were overripe. The foul stench of putrefaction assailed us through the night; and it was a relief to find, in the morning, that most of it came from the bodies of cattle, not men. There must have been a good deal of shelling, out there, during the previous week; or possibly the cattle had strayed on to a minefield. All the same, we had a reasonable night's sleep: I logged out for about four hours without a break. We collected some shelling, in the morning, though.

During the day, we pulled out our maps, for we were to move on, into the hills.

It seemed that the main road out of Salerno hugged the coast, westward, for a few miles; then bent sharply north at Vietri to penetrate the widest gorge, through to the next 'plain', with the city of Naples at its northern end. (I write 'plain' in inverted commas, because it looked far from flat, and it had Mount Vesuvius in the middle of it.) This pass, north of Vietri, had a village along it, somewhere, named Cava (I never went there; but I understand that there was some bitter fighting in that area, and I do not think that the whole length of the pass had yet been cleared.) It must have been obvious that the main weight of our advance would be along that route.

However, east of this, an even steeper valley took a secondary road almost exactly due north from the city of Salerno itself, towards Avellino. (I never reached this, either.) Another advance along this route was planned.

To our Brigade was awarded the honour of advancing up this secondary valley, where the road would take us toward Avellino. If no more, it would keep the Germans guessing; but if the main road proved impassable, then it was up to us to open up an alternative route to the north.

So that night (but *which* night? I assume 19 September) trucks came to take us into Salerno. We set off before dark, along the main road; but it was pitch-dark when we approached the city, and we must have 'debussed' somewhere in the middle of it. I found it an eerie place. No one seemed to be about (was there a curfew?) and we had almost come to expect the rip of Spandau fire from German patrols. Someone must have reconnoitred our route, for it was not long before the loom of the darkened city was below us, and we were stumbling, swearing, up a steep track into the clouds.

Morning found us on the shoulder of a mountain, about a thousand feet above the city, looking down on its roofs and its deserted streets. The line of the quays indicated a large port, without a ship to be seen in it, as yet.

189

But beyond it, the panorama of the gulf was something I shall always remember. It was peppered with our ships – I remember being reminded not of pepper but of nutmeg grated on blue junket – and I began to understand the magnitude of a modern invasion. All craft were on the move, all about their business, whatever it was (or, conceivably, keeping on the move only to flummox the U-boat captains as they risked their boats among this mass armada) all grey, all purpose-built for their myriad specialist functions, all there to provide us with their support. I was inexpressibly moved: never, I thought, would I see the like of this again.

We were very near the top of what we called 'The Pimple', the highest mountain immediately over Salerno. It was shaped like the Matterhorn. There was only room for one platoon – not mine, on this first day – on the forward cliff of the mountain, looking up the Avellino valley to the north. We tried to make sense of the mass of information passed on to us by the officers of the Durham Light Infantry, very pleased, it seemed, to be on their way down, but possibly, I thought, to a less pleasant spot.

John Hamilton and his platoon were awarded the place of honour on the first day, on the northern precipice overlooking the enemy in the valley below. A second platoon, under Raymond Nares, was guarding the slope which led down to the right and connected with No. 2 Company (they also claimed possession of a 'Pimple', which confused us all) whilst the third platoon, mine, was in reserve. To begin with, it was all very gentlemanly. Mervyn put the Company Headquarters into a small concrete hut: not an inspired choice, as it turned out, for it seemed that the Germans could see it, and all the activity which it generated.

During the day, Gunner Forward Observation Officer (FOO) clambered up the track to pay his respects. He was 'spotting' for a battleship, he told us. Had we any suitable targets for a salvo or two of sixteen-inch shells? Mervyn told me to cope with him. I rang up John Hamilton.

'Well,' said John, cautiously, 'I can't really say that we are in immediate danger of being overrun. Any Germans who want to come up here will be utterly out of breath when they arrive.'

'But are there any troop concentrations, in the valley?'

'I can see quite a lot on the main road. Will that do?'

'Try pricking off a largish group, and a vehicle or two, near some obvious feature which we can identify on the map.'

Eventually John was able to find us a target. The FOO was delighted. He got his attendant signaller to make contact with his battleship – *Rodney*, I think – and within a few minutes some enormous shell screamed over our heads.

'Spot on!' John shouted down the telephone. 'I'll bet those Germans had a fright. Can we try another lot?' It seemed a rather expensive way to frighten Germans, I thought; but, all the same, we tried again, once or twice. It made a change.

Raymond's platoon was in the forward position next day. This meant that my platoon was plugging some of the gap between us and the other 'Pimple'. (To be honest, I remember looking down not on a pimple but a hospital, occupied, I thought, by our No. 4 Company. Perhaps Michael Howard's pimple was further away.)

We seem to have equipped ourselves with a machine-gun, mounted on a tripod; and, during the day, Corporal Blackham was firing it at parties of Germans in the distance. They retaliated. By mid-afternoon they registered a battery of guns on us, and soon we were having casualties.

We found ourselves in considerable trouble, for one of the wounded, Corporal Mountford, was below us, and, if we were to rescue him, we would have to expose a large stretcher-party, to carry him up the precipitous slope to Company Headquarters, then down the other side. Sergeant Glover dashed downhill to him, and somehow managed to pull him out. By this time, shells were landing all round us, a stretcher-party received a direct hit, and it looked as though Company Headquarters was going to receive one, too, at any moment. We found poor Sergeant Newman with a nasty hole in his thigh, Guardsman Flynn with his foot almost blown off, and Corporal Mountford with a hole right through his neck. But he was still able to speak, a little incoherently, and he was not bleeding overmuch.

We were running out of stretchers by now, and soldiers to carry them down the mountain. In the meantime, we were helping to evacuate Company Headquarters, to lay new telephone cable, to keep an eye on everyone, if only to count heads after the shells had crashed down around us, and, for that matter, to defend our line, and to relay targets for own guns back from the forward platoon. I was amazed at Mervyn's coolness. In the heat of battle, he continued to drawl his instructions; and, when my wrist gave out through putting undue weight upon it – the men on the stretchers seemed unbearably heavy – he took my place. All my old prejudices against him vanished, that day: it was hard, dangerous work, but his example steadied us all under relentless German fire, till the shades lengthened and the evening came, to bring us back to relative peace.

My calculation, then, for what it is worth, is that we took up our company position on the top of this horrible hill during the night of 19/20 September. (Our regimental history seems to confirm it.) The 20th was fairly quiet. The 21st was the day I have just described, from my own point of view at least; and on the 22nd it was my turn to take my soldiers around to the front of the hill.

I found it a worse day than the one before. It must have been bad for the rest of the Company, too, but at least they had learned by now to keep their heads down, and Company Headquarters had dug itself in at a fair distance from that death-trap of a hut.

Our problem was simpler. We occupied some slit trenches, dug before our time, presumably by the Durhams, and occupied now for over a week. The Germans knew exactly where we were: it was the obvious spot for an observation post; and they knew well enough that they *were* observed, for our gunners were continually shooting at them. The Germans, therefore, did all they could to blow us off the peak. As far as I know, they did not attempt an attack. They could keep us in the bottom of our slit-trenches with long-range machine-gun fire, and then blast us out with gunfire.

We had to hope, then, that their machine-guns were not accurate at this very long range (and I do not think that anyone was hit with a bullet) and that the shells would go over our heads, then down into the city of Salerno. Wretched Salerno! At least, most of the population would have time to dodge them. A shell had its own way of announcing its arrival. First of all came the explosion as the gun fired (many of us claimed that we could tell from this if the shell were coming directly at us) and then, a few seconds later, the moan of the shell in the air. If this grew to a shriek, then the shell was coming very close indeed; and, by now, most of us could tell, surprisingly accurately, if it were an 'over' or an 'under'. It was claimed that the shell which was to land on our heads could never be heard at all, but this titbit of mythology was impossible to prove.

As the salvo approached, then, there were several layers of concern: would one of the shells hit us, or would they all merely deafen us? I was becoming paranoic about noise, ever since my eardrums had been blown in at Mareth; and this was torture. More often than not, one shell of each salvo *would* land, very close, and the only thing to do was to burrow lower into the slit-trench. Another, usually of the same salvo, would miss the peak altogether. This game, this constant repetition of uncertainty, was to last all day. No one prayed more earnestly for darkness than I.

Then there was the recent history of the slit-trench to bear in mind. I imagined that all previous occupants had suffered the same miseries; and all previous occupants had, naturally enough, stayed anchored in this slit-trench all day. The smell of human waste was now becoming unpleasant, to say the least. The sun was hot, there could be no rest, and the morale of the troops was as low as my own. The only, minor consolation was that there was absolutely nothing I could do about it. But evening came at last.

'Gough Quinn came up to see you,' Mervyn began when I came in the Company Headquarters.

'How kind of him!' I exclaimed. 'I'm glad you stopped him from coming round the corner.'

'I didn't. I'm afraid he's dead. It was a direct hit.'

Oh, *hell.* Another friend written off: Hugh, Michael, and now Gough. It looked as though the death-cart was closing in on all of us now. I only hoped that Peter was still alive.

'Slightly better here, today, on this side of the hill.' Mervyn tried to change the subject. 'One of John's men was wounded, but he wasn't too bad. He was able to walk down the hill, with a bit of help. Can't remember his name. John will be coming in here, in a few minutes.'

I may have written about these two days the wrong way round, for in the Regimental History it is written that No. 3 Company came under the heaviest shellfire on 22 September, not the 21st. At all events, it was on the night of the 22nd that No. 2 Company put in its attack on the other 'Pimple'. Have I lost a day somewhere? My memory, far from reliable here, I admit, is that we became aware of a considerable relaxation of pressure during the 23rd, for we were able to watch the Scots Guards, and beyond them the other brigades of the 56th Division, trying to force a route up the eastern flank of the Avellino valley. Though distant, the noise was as bad as ever. The Germans had brought up a new weapon, the *Nebelwerfer*, which fired off six mortar bombs at once. Each bomb was fitted with some kind of banshee whistle: it must have terrified the lives out of any troops who had the misfortune to be underneath. The forest caught fire. The valley filled with smoke.

Our Grenadier Battalion tried to push up the floor of the valley, and found it heavy going. It may have been on that day, the 23rd but more likely on the day following, that they took the Capella Ridge, a wooded spur descending into the Avellino valley from the main mountain chain to the west. Thus, they leapfrogged past our various 'pimples' which overlooked both the valley and the sea. Our task of defending Salerno itself and – more important perhaps – the main road along the coast to Vietri, then into the mountains beyond, was now over. After dark on 24 September we stumbled back down the steep path and into Salerno again, utterly weary.

No one imagined that our war was over, yet. From above it all, we had been able to see that the Germans were not going to let us move up the Avellino valley without trying to stop us. We would have to fight all the way.

23

HILL 270

There was no rest for us that night. We came down from our mountain when dark fell; and were busy disentangling ourselves, somewhere in the city, till well after midnight. Then we were off, on foot this time.

It was a dreary slog, up the Avellino road towards the north, punctuated by a series of stops, none of them explained. No one knew what was happening anyway. Whenever we stopped, we collapsed; and struggled to our feet again when we were told to move on.

The valley was – still is, I imagine – very steep and deep. I may be exaggerating the height of the surrounding mountains at 4,000 feet; and its walls were not vertical, of course. Every mile or two, a spring, rising in the mountain wall to east or west, had carved itself out a subsidiary valley to bring a small stream down to the main river, which ran south to the city, then the sea. On the map, it looked rather like a fish's backbone. In the depths, crossing and recrossing our road, wound the railway-line from Salerno to Avellino. Each east-west side-valley would be separated from the next by a spur, out from the main chain of the mountains, eroded down to less than a thousand feet – this varied, of course – with, more often than not, a small village tucked away and off the beaten track, heavily wooded at that height. The trees – I remember the cypresses and poplars, of course, but there were probably chestnuts and walnuts and a host of others up these side-valleys, protecting the vines – were very beautiful to us invaders from the sandy desert; and it would have been a pleasure to sit in one of those quiet villages, in the shade, drinking the local wine, half asleep. I was thinking about sleep most of the time, not surprisingly. It was a commodity in very short supply.

The first spur on the western side must have been the 'Pimple', then. I do not remember looking back at it, perhaps because it no longer meant anything to me, perhaps because it was still dark.

The second spur was the Capella Ridge. (I did not know this at the time, and have only recently read its name in the Regimental History.)

It is, it seems, 600 feet high: rather lower than the next one. Point 270, presumably indicating a height in metres. Capella was densely wooded to the crest, possibly with ilex, growing out of juniper, bay and broom, not unlike the *maquis* which covers the hills of Provence and Corsica, and can be almost impenetrable. Up the flank of the great mountain to the left, vegetation became more sparse until, near the crest, the bare rock showed.

We wended our slow way up a mule-track from the road, on the lee side of Capella. By this time the sun was up. Mervyn called his platoon commanders to the crest, and we looked across the dip in front of us at the next crest, Point 270. This, I slowly realized, was becoming a formal 'O-group' – not as common as we had been led to expect during our training days for, more often than not, we had been coping with emergencies which followed one another without giving us time to draw breath. However, this time, we had leisure. We had a distant view of our objective, and we even had maps. What I did *not* have was a pencil! It was not long before I lost the map as well.

'Well, now,' Mervyn said, 'the situation is as follows, more or less. Our Brigade's task is to advance up this valley. So far, the Grenadiers, who took this hill two nights ago, I think, have probed on, and last night they took that hill in front of us which, you can see, is marked 270. It was quite lightly held, they say. But there weren't many of the Grenadiers, either; and when the Germans brought up some reinforcements during the night, the Grenadier outposts had to withdraw. They are re-grouping around us on this ridge, and it's our turn to take over, and go on to the

Mervyn Griffith-Jones, Christopher's Company Commander in Italy.

next one. Then, I expect that the Grenadiers will leap-frog through us; and so on, all the way to Avellino.

'The Kiddies (Scots Guards) are advancing up the other side of the main valley. Everyone seems to think that the bulk of the opposition will be on our side, not theirs, which is a cheering thought for us all. But, all the same, this Avellino road is a piece of cake compared with the main road, through Cava.

'Well, we have to tackle Hill 270, starting from here at noon.

'Now, the Grens have been up there already. They are rather kicking themselves for not digging in there last night, because they only withdrew when a few Germans turned up and caught them with their trousers down, so to speak. There shouldn't be much difficulty in pushing the Germans off it again – or have I heard that said before? I think we'd better expect something fairly serious . . . But you can never tell in this thick country . . . Mind you, it's as difficult for them to see us as for us to see them. They don't know what's going to hit them; and if there *are* lots of them, then they're new to it.'

(I am paraphrasing this, at least to some extent, but I think that I have the gist of it right, for it was easy to remember.) Mervyn continued:

'On their way back, the Grens found that they didn't have to go all the way down to that little village in the valley, and then up here again. They've sent out a recce patrol this morning to check, and the news is that, if we start down this track ahead of us, then turn left when we see a guide, we will be able to contour round to the left, under the main mountain wall, along a track which keeps us all under cover, till we get to that little farmhouse underneath the left-hand side of Hill 270. Can you see it?'

We saw. It looked reasonable; but it also seemed that, when we had passed these buildings, we might have to start running.

'Number 1 Company will go first', Mervyn continued, 'So you won't get lost. When they get to that farm, they belt along under the hill, at the same height, more or less. Then the theory is that each man in the company does a sharp left turn, so that everyone goes up to the top in line abreast.'

'I hope they remember their drill,' I remarked a little facetiously. I hoped that the planners of this operation knew what they were doing.

'It doesn't matter much if they don't, exactly.' Mervyn was not fussed. 'Number 1 takes the right of the hill, and we go up to the left of them. As we have less far to go, we ought to keep in line with them, more or less. Your platoon, Raymond, on the right, please – it will be your job to latch on to the left-hand platoon of No. 1 Company. John (Hamilton) will be on the left, and Chris will be in reserve to you both. If I were you, Chris,

I'd go up the hill behind Raymond, on the right. Stick to the bushes. John's route looks a bit more exposed.'

There were some more instructions. We were still carrying all our gear, for instance; and Mervyn promised to find a dump, on the way, where we could shed our gas-capes, and other impedimenta not immediately necessary; and he said that he hoped to set up a new Company Headquarters in the area of the farm. It all seemed quite neat. I thought; but the hill looked steep. Oh, well.

I brought my own section commanders up to the crest, among the trees, and gave out orders formally, as Mervyn had done. It was a glorious morning, I remember, and it was hard to envisage our enemies formed up on the hill opposite. In between us, down in this little side-valley, the village slumbered, only the bell in the campanile sounding the hours to noon. I had a shave. We all brewed up a drink of tea, below the crest, and wondered what was going to hit us. There had been too much talk about 'artillery support' to make me altogether complacent. If our guns tried close support, shooting us in, as it were, then the shells would either go over the top of the hill altogether or, if they were 'shorts', would land among us. But I kept my misgivings to myself. I was a worrier, I knew.

So, at noon, we set off, over the crest of the Capella Ridge, and down the steep track through the woods, quietly. We found the sunken side-track which was to carry us round under the mountain, and plodded along that. Birds were singing in the trees.

It was too good to last. As we were walking through the woods, and getting close to the farmhouse under the hill, the rip of Spandau fire jerked us all out of our dreams.

As No. 1 Company broke cover, and emerged into the more open ground around the farm, the Germans opened up with every weapon they had. We followed. The row grew more intense. There must have been a dozen Spandaus firing at once, now: 'a team of giants ripping up a tarpaulin' had become standard verbiage. It was impossible to distinguish individual shots. They concentrated first of all on the farm area, on the men of No. 1 Company as they dodged through it on their way to the trees; then on the platoons of No. 3 Company: us. This was no place to wait around. It was soon all too evident that the farm was a registered target for German mortars, as well.

Raymond led his men into the trees. John Hamilton found that he was leading his platoon up a series of open terraces, recently harvested and almost totally without cover, with streams of bullets pouring down all round him: all utterly lethal, I thought, as I led the third platoon into the relative safety of the trees.

But the unbearable noise, the streams of bullets, and the bang of mortars and grenades, rolled down the steep slope from above, were almost as continuous here. This was no German 'outpost'. The High Command had got it wrong again, and we were all doomed. There was no way through this. The only sensible course of action was to turn our backs to this torrent of fire and run, like rabbits, down the steep hill and into cover. Some did.

As before, I seemed able to divide my reactions into two. The first was one of uncontrollable terror, with flight the only course out of a situation which was more than the human animal could stand.

The second reaction enabled me to observe. Perhaps this is an unusual human phenomenon: there was nothing particularly brave about it, I must make clear at once. Perhaps, then, it is worth trying to note down some of these observations, which I still so vividly remember.

Superimposed on the terror, first of all, was the predictable Bulteel gloom.

This was the expected finale, then: a steep, wooded Italian hill, the last human view that I should enjoy. I waited for the agonizing impact of bullet, blast or shell-splinter which would begin my death-agonies. I could only hope and pray that these would not be prolonged. There was one commonly-held theory, that the 'hit' – if it were final – would be too overwhelming for the pain to take charge. But there was contradictory evidence, too. I had seen men in uncontrollable pain, pain so terrible that death only brought relief. Perhaps it depended on whereabouts in the body the impact came. I did not know. There was all that silly stuff about the 'joy of battle'; of men losing themselves in some berserker rage, taking it to death with them. Alas, that would not be my fate! I was altogether too aware of what was happening, and would keep this awareness until the final release.

I was also well aware of the beauty of what was to be my final resting-place. The trees enveloped me, but the blue sky shone through them; and I could scramble through the bushes of broom and juniper, pulling myself up the steep slope with my arms, and, every now and then, finding an exposed root or low branch for extra leverage. Lucky I had two arms to pull with, I thought . . . then I suddenly remembered that, once again, I had forgotten to carry a weapon! I had a pistol in my holster, but had not even thought to load it that morning. No wonder my men were finding the ascent more difficult than I. They could only use one arm to help themselves.

I noticed, next, that autumn must have come. Leaves were falling off the small trees around me. They must be deciduous trees, then. I had not seen any since I had left England.

Well, there was nothing unusual about this, at first glance. But then I realized that these were evergreens, ilex and the like, and that they should not be falling in the latter weeks of September for they were not supposed to fall at all. It did not take another second to realize that German bullets were knocking them off the trees.

The leaves were falling in a shower all round us: it seemed that there was almost as much metal around us as air. My God, I thought, I couldn't possibly live through this. It was too much.

But then came the compensating thought. I remembered our charge at Mareth, where the Germans had been firing at me, point-blank, maybe with the same intensity. If they had failed to hit me then, possibly they would fire over my head now. I could see the same streams of tracer bullets – one in three, one in six, one in ten, whatever it was; and now I looked more carefully.

Yes, it was true: they were doing the same thing again.

The first bullet or two must have been aimed at us, myself and the guardsmen beside me. These were the dangerous ones; but, every time, the 'track' of the bullets would rise as the muzzles of the Spandaus rose. These Germans did not seem to realize that the recoil from one round lifted the spout, or lowered the shoulder-piece, till every shot after the third one went into the upper air. The more the gun fired, the less accurate it would be.

This did not mean that it was safe to stand around, of course. Everything depended on the Germans failing to notice that their bursts of fire were inaccurate after a shot or two. It was up to us to keep them nervous. They must not see that, at close quarters, they ought to be picking us off one by one, with single shots, not spraying us like this. And it was better that they should spray us with their Spandaus than roll grenades down on top of us. We charged on.

I also remember that I was wondering all the time why I was charging at all. Was it for my king and country? Was it for freedom? Was it for my family, my neighbours, for the women and children with whom I had been brought up? Was it for personal glory? No, no to all of these, a thousand times no.

It came to me in a blinding flash: I was fighting with my men, my comrades. I was charging with my regiment. To hesitate now would be treason. The Coldstream Guards were going to get to the top of this hill; and I was with them. I could not let the Regiment down.

All this, and much more, in a hundred feet of climbing! My mind was working faster than my feet.

This hill was incredibly steep. Sometimes, a convenient bush would allow a handhold, and the few exposed roots helped a little. Against this, there were loose stones to trip over, rather than turf, and we were overloaded, as usual, with all the gear soldiers take into battle, increased by additional belts of ammunition and Bren gun magazines; all top-heavy.

Some human bodies came hurtling down the hill at us, and our Bren gunners shot from the hip. It was only when they landed at our feet, dead, that we saw that they were British soldiers.

Now we saw the German slit trenches above us: and Germans in their coal-scuttle helmets blazing down on us.

'**Charge**!' I screamed. (How many young officers give this order twice, and live?)

'Oh, *do* be careful, Sir!' Sergeant Glover shouted, over to the right. I giggled: it was all so ludicrous. I had my two redoubtable Bren gunners, Haigh and Evans, one on each side of me, carving out a corridor of lead to protect me; but I had to be sure that they kept more or less level, for I was very sure that I did not want to get ahead of them. All the same, it was important to get up to the German slit-trenches as soon as we could. Raymond Nares must have lost most of his platoon by now, for he was with me, wounded in both arms but still able to wave an empty revolver. As we closed, he rushed on ahead, and jumped into a German slit-trench, using his weapon as a club. We were there! There were Germans surrendering beside me.

No time to deal with them, I thought. The important thing was to get to the summit as soon as possible.

We could see the skyline, not fifty yards ahead. The angle eased, the trees gave way to shrubs, then grass, then bare rock; and we were there, at the top. Puffed, astonished – and *alive*! – I wondered what I was supposed to do next.

This was no time for self-congratulation: we all realized this at once. 'Information about the enemy . . .' came first; but there did not seem to be any. Surely we had not killed them all? There was every indication that they had withdrawn over the crest; and that, suitably reinforced, they would be back in a matter of minutes to push us back down that precipitous hill again.

I looked forward, and down, my heart sinking. The crest was bare rock, a knife-edge, but, a few yards away, both behind and before us, the bushes were low, but thick. Germans could crawl up within ten yards of us, throw their hand-grenades and loose off their Schmeissers, before they charged in with the bayonet. Would we be better off *below* the crest, then? If we went back a little, then we would lose height, and surrender the moral advantage; but if we moved forward we would bury our noses in the bushes, and would have no field of fire at all. Best to stay on the crest, then; but would our little entrenching tools have any impact at all on the bare rock? There was only one way to find out.

'Information: own troops . . .' There did not seem to be many of them, either. Raymond's platoon had been almost wiped out, and there was no sign of John Hamilton at all: there was every chance that his entire platoon had been annihilated on those murderous terraces. I counted fifteen of our men. From a company of over a hundred we had few left, then. What had happened to No. 1 Company? I *must* make contact, if there were anyone left to make contact with.

'Section Commanders!' I yelled. 'Dig in. Get the men to dig anywhere they can make a hole. I'll run along the crest to find No. 1 Company. I shan't be a minute.'

In a hundred yards, I found one. It was Lionel Buxton, lying, desperately wounded, hardly conscious. I gave him a drink from my water-bottle, then had to run on.

Then came two more young officers, both dead. There must have been a massacre, here; but where were the bodies of the men they had been leading? Both were complete strangers . . . Was I going mad? Nothing made any sense at all.

Then, to my enormous relief, I found the No. 1 Company Sergeant-Major, Misty Wright. Slow of speech, and walking slowly, here was a man relaxed and under control.

'Hallo, Sir!' He shouted over the continuing din. 'Glad you're all right. I was coming along to see you.'

'Good to see you, too, Sergeant-Major. I was beginning to think you'd all had it. You've lost some blokes, I see.'

'Aye, it was rough. I can't find my officers, even.'

'I've found three of them. Mr Buxton's over there, on the crest, but very bad, I'm afraid. And there are two other young officers, both dead. I don't even know their names.'

'That'll be the two lads that just joined, I suppose. You haven't seen Captain Ker, then?'

Just at that moment, Mervyn arrived, panting, puce in the face. I looked at him, astonished: had he really come up, alone, through that inferno? He could not have known if he would find us, or Germans, at the top.

'Oh, well *done*, you lot! We've made it!' He was thrilled.

'Mervyn, there's a bit of a shambles, really. I've only got fifteen men left. Here's Sergeant-Major Wright. How many left in No. 1 Company, Misty?'

'About twenty, Sir. There's a couple of sergeants still upright, but we don't seem to have any officers left. Have you seen Captain Ker, Sir?'

'Dick? Badly hit in both legs, I think. I was hoping to find Lionel. Have you seen him?'

'Well, yes. But he's very bad, too. And the two platoon commanders are dead.'

'What about No. 3 Company?'

'Raymond's there, but he's wounded. No sign of John Hamilton yet, or any of his platoon.'

'Well, they can't all be dead. But we are desperately short, of course. Let's see if John has got up to the top yet.'

The three of us went quickly back to find my men, on the crest. It dipped a little at this point to form a shallow saddle between the ridge of Hill 270 and the main bulk of the mountain to the left. The men were digging in as best they could, just on the forward side of the crest; and one or two were hacking at bushes, to improve their field of fire a little.

'But, you know,' Mervyn said, considering, 'this is the obvious spot for a counter-attack; and even if they don't want to charge, they can throw hand-grenades at you out of the bushes, without being seen. You haven't considered the reverse slope, have you?'

'Yes. And the actual crest, too. But we can't dig in the bare rock at the top; and we really can't afford to let *them* get to the top, then lob grenades down on top of us.'

'Yes, I see what you mean. Quite a problem. What about your lot, Sergeant-Major?'

'Same with us, Sir. But I thought I might go down the other side, when I've got a moment, and see if I can get one of my sergeants right forward with a Bren, so that he can warn us if anyone's coming. I'll tell him to keep well to the right, out of your line of fire. He may even be able to see right across, in front of us.'

'What we need,' Mervyn said, 'is more soldiers. Quickly. Hold on for a few more minutes, you two: I don't imagine that the Germans are ready for an immediate counter-attack, as they're bound to be demoralized, and they don't know much about us, either. Merge the two companies together, somehow; and prepare a space for another full company, say, in between you.'

Off went Mervyn down the hill, actually running. I had never seen *that* before. We must be in a mess, I thought; and I grinned at Misty. But officers do not make jokes about brother-officers in front of other ranks . . . Just at that moment, John Hamilton arrived, hot and even more dishevelled than Mervyn had been.

'Hallo, John!' I exclaimed. 'I was getting worried about you. Are you all right? Where's your platoon?'

'Here it is!' John said, with a theatrical gesture. 'Only the two of us left.

It was murder on those terraces, I can tell you. And then, after all that, we were pinned down by a sniper up on our left. We had to take cover.'

It was wonderful to have John there. On the strength of this, I got Raymond to take down a party of walking wounded, and some German prisoners. Misty went off to find the survivors of No. 1 Company; and within a few minutes (or was it hours?) one of the platoons of No. 2 Company staggered up to us on the crest. Once again, I did not know the name of the platoon commander, another new arrival, hot, dusty, but surprisingly unflustered. I think he was Hank Tom. He was very appreciative.

'What a hill!' He began. 'We only just made it, without any Germans in the way. You must have had hell.'

'We've lost a lot of soldiers,' I said. How many are there of you lot?'

'I think the whole of No. 2 Company is here. On the hill, anyway. Where do we go?'

'Who's in charge?'

'Alan Davidson is Company Commander. But I think that Michael Howard is the senior officer on the Hill.'

'I'll come and find him in a minute. But I think I'd better merge No. 1 Company with No. 3 first, as we haven't many officers. So we'll stay together, here on the left, while No. 2 can fit in on the right of the hill. I'll tell Michael. Hurry. There'll be a counter-attack at any minute.' I was obsessed about this. The Germans must still be trying to sort themselves out, for we had a breather. However, they did counter-attack.

But by this time, I had connected up with Michael Howard, with another platoon: and the men of No. 1 Company had sandwiched themselves in, between us and No. 2. We had done something to improve our positions. The counter-attack was a tentative affair, not fully pressed home. There was more Spandau fire, and some grenades were lobbed at us from the bushes nearby; but we could blast away back at them, and I do not think that any of them gained the crest.

We were short of everything, though, and I still thought that we were in danger. Bren gun magazines were particularly short, and I sent some men off, back down the hill, to pick up 'empties' which the gunners had discarded. But the real lack was of water. We were all desperately thirsty.

Then came another shock. I was standing on the crest, near the saddle, when one of the guardsmen, Rutland (who had been in my platoon in the Sixth Battalion) suddenly doubled up and collapsed.

'Bastard got me in the stomach,' he whispered. 'Take care, Sir. It's your black beret he's after.'

Of course, I should have been wearing my steel helmet, but I seem to have lost it, somehow. Without that, and without a loaded pistol either,

I was hardly doing myself justice as a soldier! For the moment, I dodged behind a tree: this must have been a sniper, now installed up the mountainside beside us.

We dragged Rutland under cover; but he died a few hours later; and the same sniper hit Standley, yet another man from the old Sixth Battalion. But I think he survived.

For the rest of that dreadful day, we were plagued by this sniper on the mountain slope beside us. As this saddle, at the top of the 'terraces' which John had climbed, was sparsely vegetated, we decided on discretion rather than valour, and stayed among the bushes just beyond the crest, hoping that we would not be charged from close quarters (Germans, we were told, did not like bayonets.)

But this meant that we had to get used to German mortar fire. Generally, we felt safe enough in our slit-trenches from everything except direct hits; but I had to keep moving, to keep in touch with my new command, and to deal with the wounded, as well as I could. To me, the sniper-fire was more of a menace than the mortars, for the black beret I was wearing was a give-away. (It was all I had: the blistering summer had been too much for my khaki service cap. I even wondered if it would be proper to appropriate a steel helmet from one of the dead men lying around. But it seemed a kind of desecration, somehow. We are all superstitious, and I felt, too, that if it had failed to save one life, there was a good chance that it might fail to save another.)

David Forbes, the second-in-command of the Battalion, appeared during the late afternoon; and I showed him our positions. He was very complimentary.

'Did you realize,' he said, 'that everyone on the ridge behind us had a grand-stand view of a set-piece attack by a battalion? It doesn't often happen. The Grenadiers were shaken to the core, and they have been full of compliments.

'By the way,' he continued, 'have you heard that Colonel Terence was hit?'

'Serious?'

'Not too bad, I think. But you can never tell. I've taken over, on a temporary basis, then. Can you pass it on?'

'That was nice of him.' John said, as the royal party moved off, to look at No. 2 Company's position, I imagine. 'David really knows what he is talking about. I wonder if he actually saw us as we were climbing up the hill?'

'If he saw anyone, he saw you,' I said. 'I simply don't understand how you made it. It was open country all the way; and those little terraces must have been lethal.'

HILL 270

'They *were*, for most of my platoon. Do you know what I was thinking of, at the time? I wasn't really concentrating on the bullets, and all the other muck they were throwing at us. I was thinking of the view we had of the hill before we even started. It seemed to me that it looked just like a baby brontosaurus, with its tail down in the valley, and suckling its mother brontosaurus. You know, it *did* look alive, somehow. The spine seemed to be wriggling, all this bare crest, which looks like armour. Then there was the mother mountain, lying on its side, and the head of the baby deep in one of its teats. I thought I was dreaming. In fact, I even wondered if I were dead, for a moment.'

'Well, don't do any nuzzling yourself, or you will be. I wish we could get rid of that bloody sniper.'

I seem to remember Simon Codrington coming up, with orders to stalk and demolish this sniper, but I cannot remember how he fared. Perhaps we were coping now with a second counter-attack, which came in at last light; but I cannot remember much of that, either. We called for defensive fire from the Gunners: not a bad idea in theory, but very difficult for them, as their shells, if they were to hit the enemy, were almost certain to clip the summit of our hill first. Our men, thinking that they were in the middle of another 'stonk', could only swear. They had had enough to put up with, already. As dark fell, I found Misty Wright.

'Can't they leave us alone?' He complained. 'Trouble is, I'm going bomb-happy. If it's OK with you, Sir, I'll wait till this little lot is gone, then I'll find the deepest slit-trench the Germans dug for us, and have a bit of a kip.'

When the counter-attack had petered out (I am not sure that it was meant to be serious) and when dark had fallen, Misty Wright quietly disappeared; and John and I had a gossip about the events of the day.

'Well, it seems that we have won something,' John said. 'But I wonder if it was all worth it? It's all very well, David Forbes telling us that we have shortened the war by a week; but how does he *know*? I've lost all my soldiers, except one. You've lost a lot of yours. Number 1 Company has been nearly written off, once again, and you and I are left, at the top of a hill, about a mile nearer to Berlin, and knowing perfectly well that there are about a thousand more hills like this to climb, with Germans at the top of them throwing things at us. And *then* we have to get over the Alps! Anyway, we're going up a side-valley. Everyone else will drive up the main road, if it's been cleared. It seems that an awful lot of effort has gone in to all this, with precious little to show for it.'

This was the post-battle reaction, which all too often sets in when the tension subsides. I thought that I had better try a little encouragement.

'Maybe. But you never know. Some Germans may think that this has been the last straw. We're out to "break their resistance," whatever that means, not just to kill them all.'

'What about us, though?'

'Well, what about us? Everyone seems to think that we've won a victory. It's supposed to do something for morale, you know.'

'Yes; and did you hear what the men are saying about Sergeant-Major Wright? I don't know if it's true. Did you see it?'

'No. What?'

'Well, they're saying that he winkled out three German Spandaus on his own. He got up the hill behind them, and charged them with his rifle and bayonet.'

'He's just told me that he's bomb-happy, and that he's going to find himself the deepest slit-trench in Italy.'

'I think he was pulling your leg.'

(Misty was awarded an immediate Distinguished Conduct Medal. But the story is that, when the King read the citation, he asked for it to be 'up-graded' into a Victoria Cross.)

During the night, a few stragglers returned into my platoon. When the attack had been going in, the bushes and trees had caught fire behind us, and a strong wind had carried the blaze up the hill. The dead had been burnt where they lay; but the slope was littered with wounded, German and British, and they had to be moved quickly to a safer place. My 'Headquarters Section' just behind me – this, of course, included the Platoon Sergeant, Reg Brewer, and my servant, Willie Mitchell – had been diverted to this dangerous but essential work, and were only now free to report back.

We had to hold on for another whole day, the 26 September. The noise had subsided by this time. I expect that the Germans had retreated – they were in danger of being cut off – but we left them to it, thinking that we had done our share, and that it was someone else's turn to push forward. The word came up that the Scots Guards were due to replace us at any moment. It would be they who would continue the advance, then.

They arrived after dark. This was just as well, for we could not wait to get away. We collected the remains of our gear, and set off down as – for the first time in months – the rain began to fall. We must have been a sorry sight: lucky that no drill sergeant (or anyone else, for that matter) could see us! Most of us were slightly wounded (I had had to pull a piece of shell-splinter out of the flesh of my calf, for instance, but it was not particularly painful) we stumbled off down the hill, without regrets.

24

DOWNHILL

Own, down, down. When we had welcomed the Scots Guardsmen, and shown them the layout of our positions as well as we
could, then we gathered our remnant together, and stumbled off
down the precipitous hill in inky darkness.

We had to contour round from the farm buildings, as we had left a
cache for our spare equipment beside the path, just beyond it; and what
we needed now, more than anything, were our gas-capes. These may or
may not have been useful against poison gas, but we looked to them to
keep dry. The rain was coming down as though it meant business. It did:
it went on raining, then snowing, right through the winter, I believe.

That march was a nightmare. The path seemed endless, and we were
tired beyond belief. It seemed to me that there had been an earthquake
since we had last walked along it for, now, it was a continuous obstacle-
course of enormous boulders, each one of which could be negotiated only
by feel. When we reached the road, at last, down in the bottom of the
valley, we collapsed for a rest in the pouring rain. The men could not
smoke: it was raining too hard, and we were forbidden to show lights. So
the 26 September came to a miserable end; and we marched – staggered
rather – into the next terrible day, into the outskirts of Salerno. It seemed,
though, that someone must have known where we were going, for we
found ourselves under a roof, at last.

I suppose that there were blankets, for most of us stripped off and slept
like dead men. I was shivering, uncontrollably. In one way or another I
felt terribly ill. Was this the reaction after the battle, I wondered?

Light came. Men stirred. I found that I *was* terribly ill.

Though I remember nothing of all this, I imagine that Reg Brewer sent
for David Forgan, the Medical Officer; for later on that day I became
aware that I had been taken to a general hospital. This, in itself, is worth
a comment: by that time, with the troops still battering their way through
the mountain chain (they may have emerged that day on to the Naples
plain) a general hospital had been established somewhere close to

Salerno, complete with beds, wards, doctors and nurses. Were the shells still landing around them?

I became conscious sometime that day (or the next?) and found Peter at my bedside. He must have told me that I had malaria; and that very many of the guardsmen had it, too. Though he, and others later, were to claim that I had not taken my Mepacrine, in fact I had – until my own stock ran out: the mosquitoes around Battipaglia must have been a vicious pack, for they spared no one. Here was another reason for the Battalion to take a temporary rest. Fortunately, most of the victims seem to have recovered fairly quickly.

Michael Howard was also in the hospital, though, for the severe cases had been taken in. However (did Peter tell me this?) there was no space there for long-term medical cases: all the sick, and the badly wounded for that matter, were shipped back quickly to the general hospitals in Algeria.

I next found myself at sea. It may have been the next day, though time ceased to have any meaning to this patient, during his rare lucid moments. My temperature was soaring. I seem to remember that some-one told me it had reached 108, though this is surely impossible? My head felt as though it had been split in half with an axe.

The poor old *Leinster* used to be the Channel Packet from Holyhead to Dublin, I believe. No more: the Germans got her on her next trip across from Salerno to Philippeville, on the north-eastern coast of Algeria. At least, this is what I was told, later. Hospital ships, incidentally, sailed unescorted. (They were painted white, with prominent red crosses, and were lit up at night.)

Lying in my bunk in the *Leinster*, quite near death I think, I went through a curious spiritual experience, the memory of which is as clear today as it was then. Perhaps this has been my underlying reason for writing these reminiscences at all.

A nurse brought me a bottle of fizzy lemonade, poured it into a mug and held it for me to sip. It was delicious. Cold drinks were not as common in those days as they are today; but there were refrigerators on these ships; and the drink was out of this world. In fact, I thought that I *was* out of this world: the pain vanished, the sweat stopped running, and I must have tumbled almost immediately into peaceful, cool, refreshing sleep.

And I had a dream. I dreamed of Cornwall, and of peace, and sun-shine, and the shade of trees, and the leaves fully out in late May. I could not quite place the spot, but it was one of the steep valleys I knew and loved . . . Helford, perhaps? (I nearly wrote down the Luxulyan Valley, perhaps my favourite, except that at the bottom of this hill there was a wide river, deep enough to float the sailing-ship I saw ghosting past me on its way in from the sea.) All was calm and serene; the trees green, the water blue under a blue sky, the birds singing, the air moist and good.

I had never been more happy. Here was a country where war was unknown. The grass was lush, the wild flowers in bloom. There could be no thirst here. I found a shady grotto, where the big rocks were covered with moss; and from the roof of the grotto dripped single drops of water: ting, ting, ting. I cupped my hands to take some and took it to my mouth. For some unaccountable reason, the *number* of drops I had taken seemed important to me, and I understood that this might stand for the number of years that I was to be allotted in this earthly paradise.

Ever since, I have wondered how many drops I took. From that moment, though, I ceased to worry over the threat of violent, early death; though I appreciated at the time that it would have been wrong for me to have taken an accurate count. Naturally, I wanted to stay on this wooded hillside; but some insistent voice told me that it was no more than a dream. Soon I must return, to fight my way out of this silly, degrading illness.

And so, with sad reluctance, yet perhaps with some new awareness that life had purpose after all, I came back to semi-reality; to the almost un-endurable headache, the sweat, the bodily weakness, the delirium stabbed with sudden flashes of fuller consciousness. The hospital ship ploughed on, undisturbed as yet by bombs and torpedoes; and in my rare spells of semi-sanity I thought about my dream, longing to return to it.

What had it been? Why had it been sent? Who had sent it? I had little doubt from the beginning that it had been sent from God; but the 'why' of it was more difficult to conjecture. Did this mean that God had given me a vision of the beauty of this world, so that I should ever be mindful of his will that I should remain in it?

I was not to be gathered up, then, into the everlasting arms. A pity, in a way: I had been so nearly there. I had been ready, even anxious, to shuffle off the mortal coil, and to join the favoured ones who had gone before.

If I were to stay on, then, what was I to do about it?

The first duty was to shake off this crippling illness. It was not going to be easy: it would need time and unbending determination. Though God seemed to want me to stay alive, this did not mean that I could merely let him get on with it! (It seems that at last I was becoming just a little more sophisticated in my theology.) So now, instead of abandoning myself to the easy option of dying I must struggle on, doing the best I could, putting up with everything the doctors and nurses were going to throw at me. (This forecast proved correct: they did.)

After that, I must see what God had next in mind for me: one thing at a time. There must be a *reason* for this manifestation, surely? God would tell me, when the time came, what my next move would be. This first move was quite enough to be getting on with for the present: the malaria was not going to disappear in a day.

Enough for now. Back, into delirium once again.

Back again, later on, hours or days later, I began to debate within myself the source and authenticity of this dream. It was all very well to tell myself that God had been giving me a clear message. Alas, it was not: many other people would tell me that it was phoney; and sooner or later I should be having doubts of my own.

Frankly, this was not the sort of message one would expect to find from God. It was just as likely to have been sent from Satan. Why not? He was always there, seeking whom he might devour; and, in my present state of craziness, I must be easy prey.

Perhaps it had even been a 'natural' phenomenon. Delirium must surely give way, sooner or later, to more rational thinking, even to more rational dreaming. Perhaps this very presence of a nurse at my bedside, with a cooling drink, had brought me back from madness? I was quite prepared to admit that this temporary respite had, in some inexplicable way, changed the course of my illness, and that the resulting spell of sleep had strengthened me to face the next onslaught of the fever. Some subconscious will had stirred. The human animal has vast reserves of determination; and the urge to live, the instinct of self-preservation, might have been brought into play at this time of crisis. But was that all?

It seemed, though, an unusual manifestation of the human will to survive. So I thought, as lucidity ebbed and flowed, in the hours, days, weeks and months which followed. I am still uncertain. To put the conundrum at its simplest, can I claim that I owe my continuing life on earth to the outgoing power of the Holy Spirit of God, or to a bottle of fizzy lemonade?

The *Leinster* brought its dilapidated cargo into the port of Philippeville; and sailed off, to be sunk. A convoy of ambulances took us off to another general hospital, sited on a hillside above the port. Its wards were Nissen huts: twenty to thirty beds in each.

I was in the next bed to Michael Howard (or was I? It was difficult to know who I was myself, sometimes.) I vaguely recall a sudden rumbling and shaking, and being told that it was an earthquake! But I may be imagining it, either the statement or the earthquake, for that matter. What I do recall – on another occasion of course – is the Sister taking my temperature, and running off to show it to the doctor, who was on his rounds at the time. He gave her a rocket, for panicking. I wonder what the reading was.

Michael must have got better because, sooner or later, he went back to the Battalion in Italy. I was not improving. By mid-November I had jaundice and dysentery as well; and the doctor drew a diagram of my spleen, for me to take on to the next general hospital in Algiers. I did not know what a spleen was, what it did or what it looked like, but it fascinated him. The malaria was interesting, too, he told me. There were two types, he said, 'benign tertiary' and 'malignant tertiary' malaria, and I had them both at once. There was mention of anaemia, too. My red blood corpuscles were disappearing fast, he said, and he was recommending a blood transfusion. Anyway, I had better go on to Algiers for a second opinion.

There was a hospital train, which took the seriously ill and wounded on to Algiers; and I was wheeled on to it, perhaps early in December. I remember sitting up on my stretcher on the station platform in the sunshine, eating dates; then, still on the stretcher, in blue army pyjamas, being carried in to a converted cattle-truck with brackets from floor to roof, three stretchers hooked on to each pair of brackets, one above the other, all of us with an army blanket apiece. Away he went, up a long valley, till we reached the town of Constantine. It was dark now, much colder.

This has been my only visit to Constantine, and I do not want to go back. It is – or was – the main town of eastern Algeria, high on the *Bled* or central table-land, and on what I imagine was the main railway-line from Tunis through to Algiers. It was here that the French-speaking medical staff left us to our own devices: either they left the train altogether, or they spent the night in the equivalent of an officers' mess further down the train. I never saw them again. We were left on our stretchers, with a single blanket each, and no clothing but our pyjamas, in our bare cattle-trucks, helpless.

Soon, snow began to fall, and found its way through the louvres of the cattle-trucks on to the stretchers below. The dysentery cases had been allotted the lowest stretchers of each three-decker, so that they could find their own way to the lavatory: a hole in the floor of the truck, where wind and snow would whistle up on to the squatting patients. Having relieved themselves, they would crawl back to their stretchers, only checking for corpses, who no longer needed blankets. Who wrote about triangular wheels? All these patients were, in one way or another, seriously ill when the nightmare journey began. Not very many can have survived that night.

So the darkness, and the blizzard, slowly gave way to daylight and driving rain, as we came down off the highlands. No food . . . No visits . . . A black hole. We had slipped through the mesh of care.

Even when we arrived in Algiers, and were carried out of our prison, after nearly twenty-four hours, we were left on our stretchers on the station platform, in the rain, the blankets sodden and the cold almost unbearable, till the ambulances finally came, to take the living away.

Then there were more months in a general hospital near Algiers. I was to become a guinea-pig. The doctors thought that my case was an interesting one, but they were puzzled, I think.

When I had a bout of malaria I was issued with thirty grains of quinine a day. When this seemed not to do me any good, they tried thirty grains of mepacrine instead: even worse, I thought, as my skin went yellow, and no one was sure if this was the result of the mepacrine, or jaundice; but, whatever it was, it did not bring me much cheer. In the meantime, the anaemia was getting worse. The sister would come round every morning with a blunt needle, which she would ram into my finger-end; but, as there was no blood circulating to the extremities, she would ram another finger – I would moan, or even scream, when I saw her coming. Eventually, the doctor, who had been present at one of these entertainments, suggested that she might try extracting blood from ear lobe: much easier. He decided not to remove my spleen, after all. I suppose that my condition was improving, at last.

In February, it was decided that I was fit enough to return to England.

There was a bed in the *Llandovery Castle,* now a hospital ship; and I was even able – with a stick – to get to the saloon for meals. The last sight I had of Africa was the waterfront of Algiers, beautiful beyond belief in the afternoon sun. Gibraltar was even more lovely. But there was a sea running as we rounded Cape St Vincent; and I surrounded myself with glory by being sick in the doctor's lap. He just would not move fast enough! Perhaps he felt a little sick, himself.

The ship broke down, somewhere off Ushant, and we were adrift for a day, smack in the path of the U-boats as they reported back to Brest and Lorient. Did they respect our red cross and all our illuminations, or had they merely run out of torpedoes? We could only hope for the best.

We got going again, eventually, and sailed for England.

In watery daylight, we steamed slowly up the southern coast of Ireland. I was feeling stronger, for I could stand on deck and lean against the rail, thinking that the Emerald Isle was not as green as I had expected. We were fairly near the shore. I guessed that the Royal Navy had not been allowed to lay mines in Irish territorial waters, but that hospital ships were allowed right of passage.

We berthed at Avonmouth, about a year and a half after we had embarked there. It had not changed much, I thought. Had I?

During the dreary, convalescent months which followed, I had an opportunity to reflect on my adventures; and I cannot say that my findings were particularly startling.

True, the war outlook was beginning to improve now. The Russian army had raced westward over the steppes, and their great country had been freed from the invaders: the war was now in Poland, and in what we were to label later as satellite countries. Before long, they would be over the German border. The seas were safer. The Americans were beginning to reconquer the islands of the central Pacific; and, almost every night it seemed, a thousand bombers raided the industrial heart of Germany. In England, immense dumps of material were under guard in every wood and warehouse, the Southern Counties swarmed with American soldiers, the harbours and estuaries were crowded with ships: 'Operation Overlord' was due at any time.

In contrast to all this massive activity, our exploits in North Africa, and even in Italy, hardly seemed to matter. Had they been worth while at all?

True, the Germans had stuck their necks out in North Africa, had overextended themselves; and we had been able to chop them back. But the scale was infinitesimal, in comparison with the global war now being waged. Perhaps the British people had exaggerated the significance of the part their own troops had played.

Had Monty and his Eighth Army been just a little too cocky?

On any global calculation, their successes had been minor. But not all campaigns need be grand; and I think it could – perhaps still can – be said that the victories of the Eighth Army in the Western Desert and in Tunisia had a greater significance *at the time* for the weary, discouraged people of Britain than any successes achieved later in the war. They had proved that the British army was, man to man, as good as the German. They had also proved that, with the assistance of Russia and the United States of America, the war could be won, in time. During those eighteen months, the tide had turned. There was a great deal yet to be done, of course, but the British and American forces, which crossed the English Channel and landed on the beaches of Normandy in June, 1944, were led by experienced generals, and followed by disciplined, battle-hardened troops, confident that they would be able successfully to tackle and defeat the enemy. Their confidence was justified in the event

It is also worth stressing that wars are fought by people. There is no

The man rather than the soldier – Christopher at the time of his engagement to Jennifer Previte.

greater glory in fighting a global battle – say the Normandy beachhead, or Stalingrad, or the Somme, or Waterloo – than there is in fighting a skirmish between a couple of opposing platoons in the middle of the Sahara. Men win, lose, are gallant or run away, are decorated or are killed, no matter how great the battle. I often used to feel that I would be more at ease on a desert patrol than in a set-piece battle with thousands around me. Probably, we all felt that. In retrospect, then, I am not ashamed to have missed the big battles. The small battles were quite bloody enough for me.

But did I feel that I had justified *myself*? This worried me at the time; and it still does, a little, though it is rather late in the day to do anything about it.

When I returned to England, I would think, in my bad moments, that the entire expedition had been an utter waste of time. I had been taken half-way round the world, trained and then retrained, only to take a very minor part in a very small campaign; then I had been ill and had had to come home again. None of it sounded very memorable.

My excursion must have cost the country thousands of pounds. I found it difficult to believe that the money had been well spent; and that the lives of all those who took me there and back again had been justifiably risked. True, I had shouted at my soldiers and had told them to charge the enemy, which they did. But they did not know that I myself never fired a shot in anger. They had done what soldiers are presumably paid to do. I had only been a passenger.

I had seen many countries and their peoples in this short period, and had grown a little older and wiser for the experience. But this is not primarily what wars are for. On this, and on other counts, I considered, it would have been more profitable for me to have stayed at home. I was not much of a soldier. My friends had had to carry me all the way.

These were the thoughts of my gloomier moments. Sometimes, though, I reckoned that I had been privileged to observe a triumph. To some extent, perhaps, I had earned the right to be looked upon with some envy by those whose turn had not yet come. I had led my soldiers, not with distinction, but competently on the whole, and had not – quite! – let them down. By good luck, and possibly with a touch of good management, I had not let many of them die. Perhaps in a war, where everything is horrible and crazy, this was as good as I could expect. In a war, *somebody* has just to wait about to be shot at. It is not particularly heroic, of course; but, then, I had never expected to be much of a hero.

And perhaps it is not altogether surprising that, now I have reached retirement age, I have come to live on the south coast of Cornwall.

EPILOGUE

Ten years later, Peter Wyld came to visit me at Cerne Abbas. We had been seeing a good deal of each other, at irregular intervals; but I remember this visit particularly clearly.

He had lost a leg in the fighting around Monte Camino; but he had recovered well enough to become the Assistant Regimental Adjutant when he was issued with his artificial leg at Roehampton. By this time, I too was on my feet. By the summer of 1944, I was back at Pirbright, helping to train our recruits, and boasting to the newly-commissioned officers about the rigours of war.

When the war ended in 1945, Peter was rapidly demobilized, and went up to Oxford. But I had to take my turn, was shunted into a staff job in the South of France for another year, and was not allowed to leave the army till the summer of 1946. We overlapped at Oxford for a very short time. Peter, though, finding it increasingly difficult to adapt to the academic life, soon went down, and went to work as a publisher. He was still unsettled. It was not long before he went to the theological college at Cuddesdon, was ordained, and began his ministry as a curate in Stafford.

I took my first degree at Oxford in December 1948, and stayed on to begin on a B. Litt. course. But my grant ran out. By Summer 1949, I had to find myself a job; and I was lucky to be offered a history teaching post at Wellington, my old school. I entered the teaching profession with some misgivings but found, rather to my surprise, that I enjoyed it.

But, I wondered, had I been led safely through the war for this? Was God keeping me for some higher purpose? If he had a vocation for me, then sooner or later he would surely give me a hint.

I thought that I had found it when I joined the Society of St Francis, as a novice, in September 1954. In one splendid, profligate gesture, I had stripped myself of my worldly ambitions and, symbolically, thrown myself naked before Christ in his sanctuary.

I had put in two or three months when Peter came; and was just beginning to appreciate that this single gesture did not solve all problems for the rest of my life. Had I misread the signals? The going was extremely hard, to say the least; and I was once again, by my own volition this time, in a totally alien environment.

216

'What do you make of your vow of obedience?' Peter asked, with the vestige of a grin. (A novice only takes the one vow, of obedience. The vows of poverty and chastity come later.)

'Well,' I said, 'Obedience has never been a strong point with me. You ought to know that, by now. Poverty and chastity look like being a walk-over, at least for the moment. But I wonder why we have to learn obedience first? My guess is that the bosses just want to rub it in good and hard, quick.'

'Who *are* the 'bosses'? Who are you supposed to obey – just anyone who is higher in the pecking order than you? Is there a seniority list, like the army?'

'No, it doesn't seem to be like that, exactly. Of course, if I am told to dig potatoes, say, then the brother who has been put in charge of the potato-digging squad tells me what to do. But, in the end, it seems that the ultimate obedience is due to Father Algy (the Father Guardian) and the Holy Spirit.'

'Golly, what a pair!'

'The trouble is that the two don't always seem to see eye to eye. Father Algy is a wonderful man, I know; but sometimes he seems to go off the rails a bit, and all too often he isn't even here. What does a novice do when he is told to do something he can *see* is utterly wrong? Am I entitled to put in a contrary request to the Holy Spirit, or is that just what I *mustn't* do? I get quite fussed about it, sometimes.'

Later . . . 'Chris, are you absolutely *sure* that this is the right thing for you? I don't want to be rude; and I certainly don't want to exert any undue influence on you. But I can't see you making a go of it, to be honest.'

'Why not?'

'You're far too stubborn and impetuous to make any sort of monk. Why didn't you ask around, before you jumped off the rails like this?'

'Who was there to ask? It seemed to me that my life was my own responsibility. It would have been wrong to ask anyone else to make the decision for me: it was a matter between me and God. I just wanted to do what he told me. He sent me here, more or less; or at least I thought he did. Why shouldn't he?'

'Ah, you *thought*, did you? Do you still think so, now that you're here? You look utterly miserable to me.'

'I couldn't help thinking that God was calling me to some special service, so to speak. Then *this* came along. It seemed to me that I ought to give it a go.'

'I guessed it. You thought that you had lost out on some game of Russian roulette. No, not that. What do I mean? You thought that, during the war, you had made some kind of bargain with God; and that, as you owed him your life, you were in honour bound to give it back to him. You do get yourself into a mess sometimes, don't you?'

I was beginning to get cross with Peter. But I had to admit that it had cost me more than I expected to jump in at the deep end, like this: I was getting more and more uneasy. But the thought of jumping out again was worse. Peter continued, remorselessly: 'Wasn't someone saying, in the desert somewhere, that people shouldn't try to make *bargains* with God? He won't have it. Okay, you didn't actually have a bet with him, or make a bargain about your future, but it seems to me that you came pretty close to it. You seemed to be treating God as a sort of tetchy, demanding, bargain-making boss, a sort of spiritual Colonel Terence. But even Colonel Terence didn't think like that; and the workings of God are in a different category altogether. It's a mistake to be anthropomorphic about God, I'm sure.

'And, for goodness' sake, don't imagine that God thinks you are indispensable, in some way. His plan for the redemption of mankind doesn't depend entirely on you. Wasn't somebody saying, in the desert, that he must be pretty used to the prospect of being let down continually by little people like you and me. To think – even to dream – that God looks upon you as his own pet, and his sole agent in the world for the saving of souls, is a form of arrogance bordering on blasphemy.'

'I *didn't* think that. I certainly don't think so, now. Look, I'm not finding it easy here, I admit; but – well – I ought to face a challenge every now and then. Shouldn't we all? I don't see how I can find out what God wants for me unless I go out and look.'

'What happens next?'

'Didn't Winnie-the-Pooh say that "having got so far, it seems a pity to waste it"? Things will sort themselves out soon. Either I shall get more used to obedience; or I shall be given a chance to show a little initiative myself; or I shall be given work which I can understand, and even do, properly. I just don't know. This is for others to work out for me.'

'How is your health holding up?'

This was a difficult one. 'I'm still getting malaria every so often, of course. Now, it seems that I must have a hernia operation. I'm just not used to this heavy manual work. I'm finding it a bit difficult to sleep, at present.'

'Well,' said Peter, rather heavily I thought, 'I suppose that we will all have to stand by, and collect the pieces, in case it all goes sour on you. These people here don't seem to care.'

As Peter predicted, it did all go sour on me. Father Algy died. His successor had very different ideas, of course, and I cannot say that I found it any easier to communicate with him. After a few months, I was sent on to the enclosed monastery at Glasshampton, in Worcestershire, where I found the life rather more congenial.

There, I came under the novice master, Father David; and loved him on sight. It was he who had the courage – or the spiritual insight – to tell me that I must put my pride back into my pocket and return into the world. I have never ceased to be grateful to him.

But it left a void. There seemed no alternative but to go back into teaching, for I had been happy as a schoolmaster. When Wilfred House offered me another post at Wellington – albeit a slightly junior one – there was little point in quibbling, for I had no money at all. I had to suffer, once again, the almost total lack of confidence I had experienced when I first joined the army. It took some time to get re-established; and to be able to face the colleagues who, two years before, had bidden me an emotional farewell.

Did they want me any longer? Did anyone want me any longer? More seriously, did *God* want me any longer? He did not seem to want me in his sanctuary, anyway.

So indeed, what next?

THE TIMES OBITUARY

Christopher Bulteel, MC, Headmaster of Ardingly College, 1962–80, died on October 11 aged 78. He was born on July 29, 1921.

In a varied and fulfilled life, Christopher Bulteel participated in the Salerno landings, became for a time a member of the Society of St Francis at Cerne Abbas, was a distinguished history teacher at Wellington College, headmaster of one of the principal Woodard schools for 19 years, and in retirement, the first director of the GAP Activities Project, a national organisation of benefit to school-leavers all over the country.

His true vocation was as a schoolmaster, for Bulteel inspired a great sense of loyalty in his pupils and implanted in them a love of learning.

Christopher Harris Bulteel was born at Charlestown, St Austell, Cornwall. His Cornish roots remained important to him, and he grew up with a love of the sea and sailing. In retirement he kept a small cottage at Mevagissey.

He was educated at Wellington College, from where he was due to go up to Merton College, Oxford, when war broke out, but instead he joined the Coldstream Guards, his father's old regiment. As a captain, he saw action in some of the fiercest fighting in North Africa and Italy.

On the afternoon of September 25, 1943, at Salerno, he led his platoon in a frontal attack upon the precipitous side of a hill, defended by enemy machine-gun posts. Though his platoon was taking heavy casualties, he gathered his remaining men together and they made their way between the enemy posts, assaulting them from the flanks and rear, so managing to take what had appeared to be an impregnable position. For this action he was awarded the Military Cross, the citation stating that "throughout the battle his leadership was fearless and unfaltering, his own personal bravery beyond all praise." Shortly afterwards Bulteel contracted malaria, the debilitating after-effects of which returned intermittently for much of his life.

On demobilisation in 1946 he returned to take his degree at Merton. In 1949 he became an usher (master) at his old school. Like many

Christopher at Ardingly College.

boarding schools at the time, Wellington was still in a time-warp of prewar values, and the atmosphere was pretty philistine. Bulteel became a quiet but pervasive influence for civilisation, showing his pupils the values of the gentler and contemplative side of life. That he was in no way short of the manly virtues himself added to his effectiveness. He was prominent in reviving Wellington's Walworth Mission near the Elephant and Castle in London.

In 1954 he left Wellington to become a novitiate of the Anglican Franciscan Order at Cerne Abbas. His departure was regretted at Wellington, but the parting was a brief one. He returned in May 1956; his spiritual beliefs had been strengthened, but the physical demands and ascetic life of the order had exacerbated his uncertain health.

At this time he participated in the work of the Abbeyfield Society in Bermondsey, helping and housing old people. He was its chairman for

Christopher, shown third from the left, at prep school.

seven years, during which time its ownership of houses multiplied a hundredfold. At Abbeyfield he met Jennifer Previte, whom he married in 1958.

Bulteel remained at Wellington until 1961, for the last two years as head of the history department. He then went as Headmaster to Ardingly College, one of the Woodard Schools, founded by Canon Woodard in the mid 19th century to counter what he saw as the evil of "education without religion".

Bulteel's predecessor at Ardingly was the formidable George Snow, who had become Bishop of Whitby. Bulteel commented that following in the wake of such an extrovert was like "trying to catch up with a Boeing on its way down the runway".

Although Bulteel was Ardingly's first lay head, he was ideally suited to the pastoral side of the Woodard ethos. He was faced with a myriad problems, including finance, political hostility and the changing ethos of society. After Snow's reign, which had seen capital expenditure on essential improvements to facilities, the Bulteel years were ones of consolidation as he worked to clear the debt.

But he was a quiet innovator, too. Although not entirely convinced by the benefits of coeducation, he introduced girls into the school's sixth form, after a *crie de coeur* from parents following the closure of a convent school at East Grinstead. Archaeology and business studies entered the curriculum in a similarly low-key manner. The art school and the school farm flourished, and with George Robb, the former Tottenham Hotspur and England player in charge of football, success on the games field was achieved against much larger schools.

Bulteel retired from Ardingly in 1980 but remained active as director of the GAP Activities Project at Reading. Thereafter he and his wife lived at Malmesbury, though they spent several months at Mevagissey each year.

Christopher Bulteel is survived by his wife Jennifer, and by a son and two daughters.

INDEX

The index is arranged alphabetically on a word-by-word basis, except for those subheadings under Captain Christopher Harris Bulteel MC, which are arranged chronologically. Page numbers in *italics* refer to illustrations.

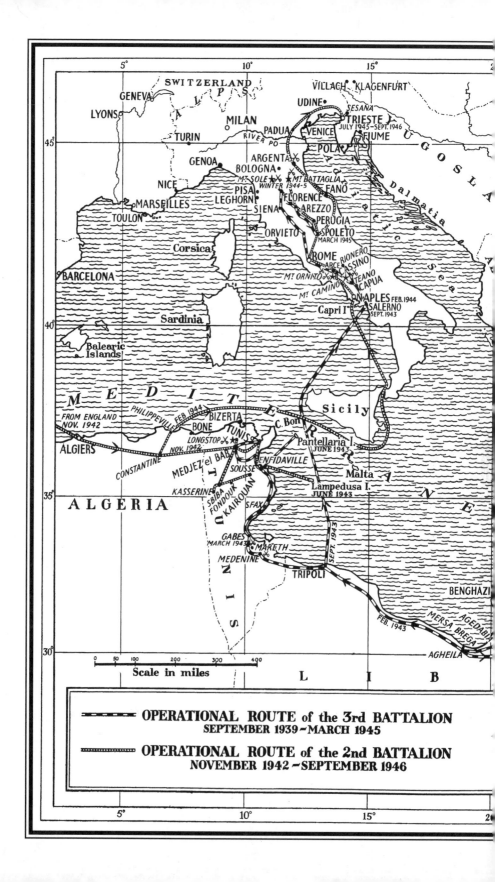

OPERATIONAL ROUTE of the 3rd BATTALION
SEPTEMBER 1939~MARCH 1945

OPERATIONAL ROUTE of the 2nd BATTALION
NOVEMBER 1942~SEPTEMBER 1946